Instructor's Manual
for
Economics of Development
Fourth Edition

INSTRUCTOR'S MANUAL
for
Economics of Development
Fourth Edition

Malcolm Gillis
Dwight H. Perkins
Michael Roemer
Donald R. Snodgrass

by
Bruce R. Bolnick
Northeastern University

W · W · NORTON & COMPANY · NEW YORK · LONDON

ISBN 0-393-96853-7

W. W. Norton & Company, Inc., 500 Fifth Avenue, New York, N.Y. 10110
   http:\\web.wwnorton.com
W. W. Norton & Company, Ltd., 10 Coptic Street, London WC1A 1PU

1 2 3 4 5 6 7 8 9 0

Contents

Part II
Answers to the *Study Guide*
***and Workbook* Exercises**

Introduction

The Contents

A course in the economics of development can cover a lot of ground, ranging from peasant agriculture to international finance. In between, it touches on virtually every branch of economics: micro and macro, labor, industrial organization, public finance, money and banking, human capital, growth, trade, environment, and so on. This *Instructor's Manual* is intended to help steer you through the maze of topics covered by the *Economics of Development*.

For each chapter of the textbook, this manual provides an annotated outline, accompanied by notes on changes from the previous edition of the textbook, and teaching suggestions (Class Notes). This overview is followed by a bank of multiple-choice questions and paired identifications that can be used for quizzes or exams.

The manual also provides an outline of the applications and exercises in the *Study Guide and Workbook*. This outline makes it easier to focus the course by letting students know which applications and exercises (i.e., which topics) they are to study. The exercises are designed to help students understand and master the analytical and technical material from the textbook. As noted in the *Study Guide* preface, no one learns to play the oboe by reading an oboe book and listening to lectures. One must practice. The exercises provide the practice sessions to help students absorb the economics of development. For more information, see the section entitled "To the Lecturer" in the Preface to the *Study Guide*.

Roughly the last half of the *Instructor's Manual* contains answers to all the *Study Guide* exercises. This arrangement gives you the option of assigning exercises as homework problems. In return for this flexibility, however, you will have to arrange to make answers available to your students. If you do not assign exercises as homework, the easiest way to do this is to place a copy of this section of the *Instructor's Manual* on reserve at your library. If you do choose to use the exercises as homework, then you can place a copy of the answers on reserve sequentially, to fit the scheduling of the homework.

Suggestions for Student Assignments

If you want to assign extra projects (required or optional) to get students involved beyond the textbook material, here are some suggestions:

1. Traditional assignments: Term papers, book reports (now often disguised as "critiques"), and take-home essays and are still high on the list of options. For longer papers it is helpful to insist on a two-page outline early in the process.

2. Mini-research papers: These are five- to seven-page papers based on a modest research effort (perhaps three to four related articles, or the equivalent), unlike a major term paper. You can provide a list of topics or have the students browse through the library and select suitable topics. One advantage of restricting their choice is that it is much easier to generate an active classroom discussion when a number of students have examined a common issue.

3. Data scavenger hunts: One valuable output from a course on the economics of development should be that students learn how to find international data using standard reference sources (see list below). To stimulate the process, spend an hour in the library pulling *very explicit* data items out of United Nations, International Monetary Fund, or World Bank reference books. Give the list to the students, along with a bibliography of reference resources. Ask them to track down the numbers and hand them in, along with precise reference citations and commentaries.

4. Hypothesis testing: This is a more thematic version of the data hunt. Provide several simple hypotheses about economic development for students to analyze empirically, for example, the hypothesis that countries with higher rates of population growth have lower rates of economic growth. Let students gather the relevant data for a few dozen countries and test the validity of the hypothesis. They can do this using scatter plots, simple tabulations, or more-advanced statistical analyses, according to their capabilities. Many interesting hypotheses can be examined using data from the *World Development Report* alone, but there is value to framing questions which get students to use a wider variety of data sources. One warning: real-world data often misbehave!

5. Literature reviews: This assignment gives students a taste of academic research in the field of development economics. It is also an exercise in reading thoughtfully, carefully, and critically. (Every author has a point of view to express.) Ask students to browse through recent issues of several economic development journals (a list is provided below), pick an article relating to the course on a subject that is of interest to them, and write a commentary or evaluation—not just a summary.

6. Analysis of development performance: Have the students prepare a methodology for judging a country's economic development performance empirically. What characteristics and indicators should be examined? What are the markers for good performance? Then have them apply this framework in a five-page analysis of development performance for a country of their choice, using readily available data. Alternatively, you can ask for a comparison between two countries. Either way, you might

screen the choices to ensure that the countries are ones for which adequate data are available.

7. A journal or scrapbook: Assign students to keep track of current events relating to developing countries, using newspapers and weekly news magazines with good international coverage. (Make that nondisaster news, given the proclivity of the press to focus on crises.) Major newspapers and magazines with good international coverage are available in most libraries. Have students keep a "journal" of notes on what they read, along with comments reflecting their own thoughts or reactions. At the end of the term students submit the journals plus a wrap-up essay on what they learned about development economics from keeping abreast of current events.

8. Group projects: Groups of students can tackle more ambitious projects. For example, have them write a country study identifying and evaluating the development strategy, government budget priorities, trends in industry and finance, progress against poverty, and so forth.

References

The single most useful reference source and supplementary text is the World Bank's annual *World Development Report*. Each year's edition provides a thorough and insightful analysis of a major topic in economic development[1], an appraisal of the recent trends and prospects for the world's developing countries, and over thirty tables of data on socioeconomic indicators for well over a hundred countries. Even if you don't have the students buy this inexpensive book, you should get a copy for yourself. You will find it to be extraordinarily helpful, providing facts at your fingertips to illustrate or reinforce points made in lecture, to answer students' questions, and to match preconceptions (yours or theirs) against realities. For information on obtaining a copy, contact the

---

[1] For example, the *World Development Report* highlighted:

Population and development, in 1984
International capital flows to developing countries, in 1985
Agricultural policies, in 1986
Industrialization and trade strategies, in 1987
Public finance in development, in 1988
Financial systems, in 1989
Poverty, in 1990
"The challenge of development," in 1991
Development and the environment, in 1992
Investing in health, in 1993
Infrastructure for development, in 1994
Labor markets, in 1995

Publications Office of the World Bank, 1818 H Street, N.W., Washington, D.C., 20433, or Oxford University Press.

Presumably taking a cue from the success of the *World Development Report*, the United Nations Development Program began in 1990 to publish a similar annual report, with a different angle on economic development. The *Human Development Report* emphasizes indicators of progress on the issues of poverty and welfare. Like the *World Development Report*, this book is published by Oxford University Press.

In addition to the two reports just mentioned, you may find the following references helpful.

1. International data sources: Most of these reference periodicals may be found in your library.

   Commodity Research Bureau, *Commodity Yearbook*
   Congressional Information Service, Inc, *Index to International Statistics*
   UN, *Statistical Yearbook*
   UN, *Yearbook of National Accounts Statistics*
   UN, *Yearbook of Industrial Statistics*
   UN, *Demographic Yearbook*
   UN, *Yearbook of Energy Statistics*
   UN, *Yearbook of International Trade Statistics*
   UNESCO, *Statistical Yearbook*
   IMF, *International Financial Statistics*
   IMF, *Direction of Trade Statistics*
   IMF, *Government Finance Statistics*
   FAO, *Monthly Bulletin of Statistics*
   World Bank, *World Tables*
   World Bank, *World Debt Tables*
   World Health Organization, *World Health Statistics Report*

   Other statistical periodicals are published by organizations such as UNICEF, UNCTAD, regional development banks, UN regional commissions (such as UNECLA), and the ILO.

2. Major economic development journals (partial list).

   Economic Development and Cultural Change
   Journal of Development Studies
   Journal of Development Economics
   World Development
   Journal of Developing Countries
   Journal of Developing Areas
   World Bank Economic Review
   World Bank Research Observer

Also see the *Journal of Economic Literature* index of economics articles and selected abstracts, under classification numbers 110 and 120.

One more journal meriting special attention for an undergraduate course is a joint publication by the World Bank and the IMF, with articles that are short, readable, and highly topical:

Finance and Development

3. General reference works on the economics of development.

    John Eatwell et al. (eds.), *The New Palgrave: Economic Development* (New York: Norton, 1989).

    Hollis B. Chenery and T. N. Srivanasan (eds.), *Handbook of Development Economics* (Amsterdam: North-Holland, 1989).

These reference books include advanced material, but large sections are accessible to good undergraduates.

4. The Internet. This rapidly evolving system already (in mid-1995) offers access to an enormous amount of useful information. For example, you can call up the CIA World Factbook,[2] the Penn World Tables data set of macroeconomic statistics using purchasing power parity methodology,[3] the latest world population statistics from the United Nations,[4] position papers on many aspects of development from the United States Agency for International Development,[5] or complete summaries of World Bank research papers on Africa.[6] This handful of citations just scratches the surface.

---

[2] URL: gopher://nwoca7.nwoca.ohio.gov/11gopher_root%3a%5b_reference._CIA%5d

[3] URL: gopher://nber.harvard.edu:70/00/.nber.info

[4] URL: gopher://gopher.undp.org:70/00/ungophers/popin/global/purpose

[5] URL: gopher://gaia.info.usaid.gov:70/11/welcome

[6] URL: gopher://ftp.worldbank.org:70/00/Welcome

PART I

**Teaching *Economics of Development:*
Annotated Chapter Outlines,
Question Banks, and Summaries
of *Study Guide* Applications**

CHAPTER 1 **Introduction**

Chapter Outline

I. The textbook opens with the story of Rachmina Abdullah, a young Malay woman who left her family village to work in a Japanese electronics factory in the city of Penang. Rachmina's story vividly illustrates the profound economic and social changes underway in developing countries, affecting billions of poor people throughout the world. Starting from this personalized example, the textbook aims to help students understand the economic forces underlying these historic changes in the world economy and how economic policies influence the process for better or for worse.

II. The first step is to introduce terminology distinguishing different stages of development. Some basic terms include: developing versus developed countries; less developed countries (LDCs); low-income, lower-middle-income, upper-middle-income and high-income countries; industrial or OECD countries; transitional (postsocialist) economies; newly industrializing countries; third world; and North versus South.

III. Economic development is not synonymous with economic growth. Beyond rising income per capita, development also entails basic structural changes and wide participation of the people of each country. A key ingredient in what Simon Kuznets called the epoch of modern economic growth is the application of science to achieve increased production.

IV. The label "developing country" covers a diverse group of economies spanning a wide continuum of conditions. Income per capita remains the most useful single indicator of development, though it is far from ideal. One limitation is that international comparisons require conversion of national statistics into common currency units, usually U.S. dollars. The conventional conversion method, using exchange rates, is seriously flawed. A more accurate method uses purchasing power parity (PPP) calculations. This method shows that income differences between rich and poor countries are less acute than one finds in statistics based on exchange rates.

V. Important regularities characterize the process of development. Examples include increased industrialization and urbanization, higher energy consumption per capita, and improvements in literacy and life expectancy. Nevertheless, there is considerable variance from country to country.

VI. Most LDCs have achieved steady growth over the past three decades. Some, such as China, Indonesia, Malaysia, Korea and Thailand, have grown remarkably fast. Others, mostly in Africa, have experienced declining incomes since 1965. Virtually all LDCs have made great progress in education and health care.

VII. The textbook views development as a complex process that can best be understood by combining economic theory, empirical analysis, and consideration of the institutional context. The authors view economic development first and foremost as a process involving *people*. Other themes include the role of government, the mobilization and allocation of capital, the role of international trade, and sectoral development. These themes compose the outline for the book.

In the New Edition. All the statistics have been updated, generally to 1992 (based on the *World Development Report 1994*). The major innovation is prompt introduction of PPP measures of per capita income. Unlike the *World Development Report*, the four-part income classification used in the data tables is based on PPP comparisons: the low-income range includes countries with up to $2,000 income per capita (in 1992 PPP$); the lower-middle-income range up to $5,000; and the upper-middle-income range up to $10,000.

Class Notes. Chapter 1 contains easy material, so you can move through it quickly. The PPP conversion method is the only technicality. You may wish to review some elementary points like the definition of GDP and GNP, and how to compute per capita income. (If you are using the *Study Guide*, point out to students that the first chapter provides a brief review of basic principles of economics.) It is important to call attention to a few fundamental points about economic development:

> Economic development is broader than economic growth, in that it also entails fundamental structural changes and broad-based participation.

> LDCs form a diverse group in virtually every respect. Provide a selection of statistical examples to support the point. Even so, there are regularities to the development process, including general patterns of structural change and socioeconomic progress.

> In many respects, including literacy, infant mortality, and life expectancy, as well as industrialization and urbanization, virtually all developing countries have achieved remarkable progress.

To generate discussion, invite students to think about and verbalize how day-to-day living conditions for various types of households and workers differ between rich and poor countries. Amenities and aspirations that students take for granted are unavailable to most citizens in developing countries. Also encourage students to look carefully at data tables in the text and to ponder the meaning of the numbers. Gaining an awareness of the empirical record is part of the course.

Finally, point out that LDCs compose most of the world's population. The economics of development is not a sideshow in the study of the human condition, but a central, dramatic theme. On this score, be aware that many students have weak geography backgrounds. To check their knowledge of the world, ask what they know about Malaysia. Then insist on the importance of looking up basic facts about countries discussed in the text or in class. It is very helpful to introduce students right away to the data set provided by the World Bank in its annual *World Development Report*. An equally valuable data source is the annual *Human Development Report* from the United Nations Development Programme.

Question Bank

Multiple-Choice Questions

1. If a country achieves a rapid increase in per capita income by discovering new oil reserves, it is experiencing

 * a. growth but not development.
   b. development but not growth.
   c. both growth and development.
   d. neither growth nor development.

2. Which of the following empirical statements about low-income countries is not a valid generalization about changes since 1965?

   a. Infant mortality rates have fallen substantially.
 * b. Rapid population growth has more than offset GNP growth.
   c. Manufacturing has increased as a share of total output.
   d. Primary-school enrollment rates have risen sharply.

3. By the World Bank's classification system, Malaysia, Mexico, and Brazil are

   a. low-income countries.
 * b. upper-middle-income countries.
   c. industrial economies.
   d. backward economies.

4. According to Simon Kuznets, the key characteristic of the epoch of modern economic growth is

   a. expansion of heavy industry.
   b. a rapid decline in population growth rates.
   c. high rates of saving and investment.
 * d. the application of science to problems of economic production.

5. While working in the Japanese electronics factory in Penang, Rachmina Abdullah

    a. earned the equivalent of $2.50 per hour.
    b. managed to save nearly $200 per month.
*   c. set aside from $5 to $20 per month to send home to her family.
    d. grew accustomed to spending most of her wages on clothes and cosmetics.

6. With reference to low-income countries in the early 1990s, the answer is 73 percent. What is the question?

*   a. What share of the population lived in rural areas?
    b. What was the annual growth of value-added in manufacturing?
    c. What was the adult illiteracy rate?
    d. What was the secondary-school enrollment rate?

7. For a country where income per capita is growing by 2 percent per year, how many years will it take for average incomes to double?

*   a. 35 years
    b. 96 years
    c. 14 years
    d. 180 years

8. Which indicator is *inversely* related (meaning that it falls as per capita income rises) to per capita income?

    a. The adult illiteracy rate
    b. The infant mortality rate
    c. The share of the population living in rural areas
*   d. All the above

9. In 1992, gross national product in Nepal equaled the equivalent of $21.9 billion (based on the PPP conversion method). The population was 19.9 million people. What was the average level of income per capita?

    a. $2,000
*   b. $1,100
    c. $1.1
    d. $436

10. Converted using the exchange rate, 1992 per capita income in Colombia was just _____ percent of that in the United States; the PPP conversion method shows that Colombia's income per capita was actually ____ percent of that in the United States.

  * a. 6; 25
     b. 50; 85
     c. 2; 4
     d. 0.5; 0.8

11. Which of the following indicators has a close positive correlation with GNP per capita?

   * a. Energy use per capita
     b. The share of services in national income
     c. Spending on necessities as a share of total consumption
     d. All the above

12. For low-income economies taken as a group, (including China and India), what happened to the average level of income per capita over the period 1965 to 1992?

     a. It fell 2.3 percent per annum.
  * b. It rose 3.6 percent per annum.
     c. It fell 0.1 percent per annum.
     d. It rose 7.5 percent per annum.

IDs and Paired-Concept Questions

These terms can be used individually as short-answer identification questions, or they can be used in pairs. In the latter case, ask students to explain (1) the meaning and significance of each of the two terms and (2) the relationship between them.

1. Economic growth, economic development
2. Modern economic growth, modernization
3. Low-income countries, middle-income countries
4. North, South
5. Newly industrializing economy, transitional economy
6. GDP, per capita income
7. World Bank, OECD

8. Industrialization, urbanization
9. PPP method of conversion, exchange-rate method of conversion
10. Infant mortality rate, primary-school enrollment rate

Study Guide Applications

Worked Example

The Worked Example shows how to discern regularities in the development process—and variations around the underlying patterns—by plotting international cross-section data. The example uses data on per capita GNP and infant mortality rates from textbook Tables 1–1 and 1–3.

Exercises

1. The first exercise gives students a turn to evaluate a development pattern applying the methodology from the Worked Example. The case in point is the relationship between per capita GNP and child mortality rates in 1992.

2. The exercise uses a numerical example based on Zambian data to show how distortions can be introduced into international comparisons of per capita income when exchange rates are used to convert from national currencies to dollars. The exercise also provides a simple example of PPP-based data conversion.

3. Exercise 3 reinforces the understanding of basic development patterns by asking students to match simple graphical relationships with major development characteristics mentioned in Chapter 1.

4. Given three specific examples, students are asked to write brief word portraits of differences in living and working conditions in LDCs versus industrial countries.

5. The exercise introduces the doubling time formula for examining the implications of different growth rates. The formula is based on compound exponential growth, which gives an approximate "rule of 70": doubling time = $70/R$, where R is the annual growth rate in percentage units.

CHAPTER 2   Starting Modern Economic Growth

Chapter Outline

I. Most of the textbook deals with processes that accompany economic development. The focus of Chapter 2 is on getting started. Do internal or external barriers retard the transition to modern economic growth for some countries? Why do some countries develop earlier than others? Why do some stagnate while others grow? The main point of the chapter is that there is no simple answer to such questions. Political and social factors are just as important as economic conditions in explaining the transition to modern economic growth.

II. Different countries have approached the task of development from highly diverse historical backgrounds. Preconditions have differed in many dimensions, including the effects of colonialism, cultural and political integration, commercial practices, education, and experience with self-government.

III. The diversity of historical experience reveals that substitutes exist for most alleged "prerequisites" for development. Poor countries today need not recreate conditions that existed in Britain or the United States before development can succeed.

IV. Although there is no simple list of prerequisites to assure development, one can identify various impediments to initiating or sustaining development. Internal impediments can include absence of self-rule, political instability, and political pressures reflecting the self-interest of entrenched constituencies.

V. International conditions can also present obstacles to development. The text first outlines the positive potential of international links, including comparative advantage, vent for surplus, and the "advantages of backwardness" described by Alexander Gerschenkron. Next, theories of imperialism are explained, ranging from the traditional Marxian view to various modern analyses of how international capitalism hinders development. The text accepts that international influences can have a profound effect on development and that the effect is sometimes negative. But surely the effect is not wholly or universally negative. Postwar experience refutes the radical thesis that development prospects will only improve if a country disengages from the international capitalist system.

In the New Edition. In all essential respects, Chapter 2 has not been changed from the previous edition of the textbook.

Class Notes. The classroom treatment of Chapter 2 can follow several tracks. If you prefer to devote teaching time to more analytical material, regard Chapter 2 as introductory reading that requires little more than a brief high-lighting of main themes in class. At the other end of the spectrum, there is considerable scope for supplementing the textbook material. According to your interest you could use Chapter 2—with or without outside readings—as a springboard for more thorough treatment of colonialism, imperialism, or the movement toward multiparty democracy to increase accountability in government. You can also devote a lecture to the economic history of Britain, the United States, and Japan, along with a discussion of how development conditions differ for LDCs in the postwar era. Another possibility is to present historical statistics on "the gap" between the rich nations and the poor nations, as well as different groups of developing countries.

In deference to time constraints, I tend to streamline lectures on this material, touching on only a few main issues in class. I feel that the concept of "gains from trade" and the influential theory of imperialism merit some emphasis. I also discuss political obstacles to development with reference to stagnating economies, which can be identified quickly from the latest *World Development Report*. An interesting assignment is to have students compile their own list of stagnating economies and to write a short paper on conditions in one such country.

Question Bank

Multiple-Choice Questions

1. The textbook identifies several historical conditions that facilitate the transition to modern economic growth. Which of the following is not one such conditions?

   a. A well-developed system of commerce, transportation, and finance
 * b. A diversity of language, culture, and ethnic identity
   c. A tradition of self-government
   d. A tradition of emphasis on education

2. Which country gave birth to modern economic growth, with its Industrial Revolution in the late eighteenth century?

   a. Japan
   b. Germany
 * c. England
   d. United States

3. Marx argued that an original accumulation of _____ is a precondition for modern economic growth, but Gerschenkron found that there are many _____ for such accumulation.

    a. capital, prerequisites
    b. power, substitutes
* c. capital, substitutes
    d. power, prerequisites

4. In numerous LDCs, government attempts to reduce costly and inefficient food subsidies have provoked riots by

    a. farmers.
* b. urban workers.
    c. the military.
    d. wealthy capitalists.

5. The textbook discusses the issue of currency devaluation as an example of

* a. how political factors can prevent a government from adopting a policy that would promote development.
    b. postcolonial economic imperialism.
    c. the conflict between social goals and economic development.
    d. the type problem created by lack of democracy.

6. One important counterexample to the theory of imperialism is the case of _____, which achieved rapid growth and falling inequality while increasing its integration into the international capitalist system.

* a. Taiwan
    b. Ethiopia
    c. Brazil
    d. no country

7. What name is given to the theory postulating that countries can gain by specializing in goods for which their relative costs are low, while importing goods for which their relative costs are high?

    a. The theory of vent for surplus
    b. The modern theory of imperialism
    c. The theory of laissez-faire capitalism
* d. The theory of comparative advantage

8. A distinguishing characteristic of Celso Furtado's theory of imperialism is its emphasis on

    a. the need of advanced capitalist countries for raw materials from LDCs.

* b. the link between income inequality and the demand for luxury products in the LDCs.

    c. the hostile exercise of military power by the advanced capitalist countries.

    d. how free trade destroys domestic industry in the LDCs.

9. Gerschenkron's proposition that there are "advantages of backwardness" is based on the observation that

* a. developing countries are in a position to learn from the experience of already-advanced countries.

    b. people in poor countries have very low expectations.

    c. it is easier for governments to control subversive information in countries with high illiteracy rates.

    d. all the above.

10. Many countries that gained independence after World War II found that the legacy of colonialism hindered their economic development. The list of hindrances included

    a. artificial political boundaries that covered diverse ethnic groups with little in common.

    b. inadequate access to higher education and training for nationals under the colonial administration.

    c. control of domestic commerce by foreign minority groups which had been brought in by the colonial power.

* d. all the above.

11. A common source of resistance to policies that promote economic growth is the fact that

    a. growth is not a desirable objective in many countries.

    b. countries must wait until the essential preconditions are established.

    c. many developing countries have no comparative advantage on which to base economic growth.

* d. growth-oriented policies often damage short-run interests of influential political constituencies.

12. The essence of a "big bang" approach to economic reform is

    a. letting economic conditions get so bad that reforms are welcomed as a relief.
    b. imposing high tax rates to finance government expenditures.
*   c. instituting the full range of structural and stabilization reforms over a short period of time.
    d. restoring growth through heavy military spending.

13. Argentina under Juan Peron is an example of

    a. successful structural adjustment imposed by a strong leader.
*   b. how populist policies can stifle growth and development.
    c. achieving rapid growth through vent-for-surplus exports.
    d. foreign imperialist interests draining economic surplus.

14. At the time of independence from colonial rule there were already hundreds of thousands of university graduates in _____, but hardly any at all in _____.

*   a. India, Zaire
    b. India, South Korea
    c. Zaire, South Korea
    d. South Korea, India

15. Most Latin American countries achieved independence

    a. shortly after World War II.
    b. in the 1960s.
    c. around the time of World War I.
*   d. in the early nineteenth century.

IDs and Paired-Concept Questions

These terms can be used individually as short-answer identification questions, or they can be used in pairs. In the latter case, ask students to explain (1) the meaning and significance of each of the two terms and (2) the relationship between them.

1. Prerequisites for development, Industrial Revolution
2. Advantages of backwardness, vent for surplus
3. Comparative advantage, imperialism

4. Colonialism, declining rate of profit
5. Internal obstacles, external obstacles
6. Takeoff, Peronism
7. Big-bang reforms, compradores
8. Political instability, self-government

Study Guide Applications

Worked Example

The Worked Example illustrates how problems rooted in the political economy can impede economic development. The mythical island nation of Kelapa has an economic structure that creates entrenched constituencies. These political interest groups oppose reforms that are needed to stimulate more rapid and more equitable development.

Exercises

1. Several hypothetical case studies get students thinking about how social and political conditions can foster obstacles to development.

2. Students are asked to identify and explain three disadvantages and three advantages of "backwardness," and then to examine the historical record to assess the balance.

3. A series of short-answer questions tests the student's grasp of the theory of imperialism, as outlined in the textbook.

4. A simple numerical problem illustrates comparative advantage and the potential gains from trade.

CHAPTER 3   Growth and Structural Change

Chapter Outline

I. Although economic development does not follow any single predetermined path, certain patterns and relationships generally characterize the process of growth and structural change. This chapter discusses the major empirical and theoretical tools that help us understand these common features of the development process.

II. The first step is to explain the concept and measurement of GNP and GDP. The text explains how international income comparisons depend on whether national currency values are converted to a common unit such as the dollar using exchange rates or purchasing power parity (PPP). The index number problem is also discussed in the context of choosing a base period for measuring real GNP.

III. Next comes the simple Harrod-Domar growth model ($g = s/k$). The book explains the incremental capital-output ratio (ICOR) using isoquant diagrams, with both a fixed-coefficient and a neoclassical production function. This leads to the neoclassical approach to growth accounting using the sources-of-growth model. For LDCs, capital formation and enhancements to total factor productivity (the residual in growth accounting) are both vital growth components.

IV. Moving from aggregate growth to structural change, the text explains Engel's law and then examines Chenery-style empirical analysis of cross-section patterns of development. This statistical analysis establishes average patterns of structural change for various categories of LDCs. Yet the trend lines should not be interpreted as norms for development performance.

V. A theoretical analysis of structural change comes next. The focus of attention is a detailed presentation of two-sector models of the relationship between industry and agriculture. The classical model of development, dating back to David Ricardo, is based on surplus labor and diminishing returns to agriculture. The book takes a simplified graphical approach to explain the well-known Fei-Ranis surplus-labor model, followed by a neoclassical two-sector model. These models generate contrasting implications. With surplus labor the supply curve of labor to industry is perfectly elastic initially, and labor can be withdrawn from agriculture without reducing food production. The neoclassical model denies these points. Both models, though, lead to the important conclusion that neglecting agricultural productivity impairs industrialization in the long run.

21

VI. The chapter closes with a discussion of patterns of development within the industrial sector. Hollis B. Chenery and Lance J. Taylor have distinguished early, middle, and late industries, but the utility of this classification has been undermined by technical change. Finally, the authors review the old theoretical debate about balanced versus unbalanced growth. This provides an introduction to Albert O. Hirschman's concept of linkage effects.

Boxed Examples. Case studies of China and Kenya are presented to illustrate how the presence or absence of rural surplus labor has influenced agricultural development strategies.

In the New Edition. Most of the changes in the Fourth Edition consist of revisions or updates of the statistics and examples, including changes in the numerical examples used in Tables 3–2 and 3–3 to illustrate methodological problems with GNP calculations. There is now a brief paragraph describing the new growth economics (at the end of the section on growth models), but the topic is not explored in any detail.

Class Notes. Plan to spend an ample amount of class time on core material from Chapter 3. Since the economics of development is as much a statistical subject as an analytical subject, the material on measuring GNP is just as important as the models. To underscore the importance of understanding the statistics, consider devoting a full lecture to textbook Tables 3–1, 3–2, and 3–3.

The Harrod-Domar (H-D) model is a cornerstone for subsequent material on planning, population policy, savings, foreign aid, efficiency, and technology choice. You can preview these themes while working through numerical applications of the model. Similarly, the book's discussion of the ICOR provides a vehicle for introducing isoquant analysis, which is used repeatedly in later chapters. The sources-of-growth equation nicely complements the H-D model by clarifying the role of physical capital relative to human capital and productivity.

Of the analytical tools, students will probably have most trouble grasping the two-sector models. If they have purchased the *Study Guide*, ask them to check out the Worked Example and Exercise 1. By devoting class time to this topic, you can help students master the models and also provide insight to later topics such as income distribution, population problems, labor markets, long-run effects of factor-price distortions, and the role of agriculture and industry. Weave these themes into your lecture on the models. Also, though not explicitly treated in the book at this point, open economy themes can be incorporated into your classroom discussion of these models.

Question Bank

Multiple-Choice Questions

1. A country's nominal GNP for a given year is defined as the total market value of

   a. labor plus capital plus technical change.
   * b. all final goods and services produced.
   c. all final plus intermediate goods and services produced.
   d. all final goods and services consumed.

2. In 1992, the population of Nepal was 20 million people and nominal GDP totaled 130,685 million rupees. The exchange rate averaged 42.7 Nepal rupees per US$1. Converting to dollars using the exchange rate, per capita GDP was

   a. $6,534.
   b. $3,060.
   * c. $153.
   d. $279.

3. Compared to the exchange-rate method, the purchasing power parity method of converting Nepal's per capita income to dollars gives a much higher result, because the exchange-rate method

   a. uses an earlier base year.
   * b. undervalues nontraded goods.
   c. excludes work performed by unpaid family labor.
   d. neglects the value of intermediate goods.

4. In Batterup the only product is baseballs. From 1990 to 1995 baseball prices doubled while nominal GDP rose from $2 million to $5 million. At constant 1990 prices, real GNP for 1995 was

   a. $5 million.
   b. $10 million.
   * c. $2.5 million.
   d. $4 million.

5. At constant 1985 lira, real GNP in Turkey rose from L27,797 billion in 1985 to L37,264 billion in 1990. The ICOR over this period of time averaged 3.9. What was the total value of the increment to the capital stock over this five-year period (also at constant 1985 prices)?

  * a. L36,921 billion
    b. L2,427 billion
    c. L9,555 billion
    d. L145,330 billion

6. Chenery and his research associates estimated average patterns of development for various types of countries using

    a. a neoclassical production function.
    b. the Fei-Ranis two-sector growth model.
  * c. international cross-section data.
    d. purchasing power parity comparisons of GNP.

7. Unlike isoquants for a fixed-coefficient production function, the isoquants for a neoclassical production function

    a. take labor as well as capital into account.
    b. are L-shaped.
    c. are capital-intensive rather than labor-intensive.
  * d. are smooth curves.

8. If the saving rate in Indonesia is 23 percent of GDP, which of the following combinations is consistent with the Harrod-Domar growth equation?

    a. ICOR = 15.4; GDP growth rate = 7.6 percent per annum.
  * b. ICOR = 4.0; GDP growth rate = 5.75 percent per annum.
    c. ICOR = 50.6; GDP growth rate = 2.2 percent per annum.
    d. ICOR = 1 percent; GDP growth rate = 22 percent per annum.

9. In Baldonia, the GNP growth rate is 6 percent per year and the capital stock is growing by 8 percent per year. Capital's share of national income is 30 percent. Using the sources-of-growth model, what fraction of observed GNP growth is attributable to capital accumulation?

    a. 30 percent
    b. 24 percent
    c. 75 percent
  * d. 40 percent

10. Suppose the savings rate for a low-income country is given. If production becomes less capital-intensive then the ICOR will _____ and the growth rate will _____.

    a. increase, increase
* b. decrease, increase
    c. decrease, decrease
    d. increase, decrease

11. In terms of the textbook's algebraic notation, a more capital-intensive production process is one with

* a. a higher value of K/Y.
    b. a higher value of s.
    c. a higher value of $\Delta K / \Delta Y$.
    d. a higher value of g.

12. The supply curve of labor to industry is horizontal if there is surplus labor in agriculture. This persists as long as

    a. the marginal product of labor (MPL) is less than the average product of labor in agriculture.
    b. the MPL in agriculture is less than the MPL in industry.
    c. the MPL is subject to diminishing returns in agriculture.
* d. the MPL in agriculture is zero.

13. Which implication of the Fei-Ranis model is not supported by the neoclassical two-sector model?

    a. Agricultural productivity should grow rapidly enough to prevent a rise in the relative price of basic foods.
* b. An increase in the population generates no increase in agricultural output.
    c. An artificially high wage in industry slows down the process of industrialization and structural change.
    d. Wage rates in agriculture in poor countries will rise more quickly when industrial investment is more labor-intensive.

14. The textbook study of Kenya illustrates a situation in which surplus labor in agriculture

    * a. emerged as a significant problem in the late 1970s.
    b. pressured planners to put great emphasis on agricultural policy ever since independence.
    c. has never been a problem because of an abundance of unused farmland.
    d. induced massive family planning efforts that reduced the population growth rate to 1.2 percent per year by 1990.

15. The turning point in the Fei-Ranis model is achieved when

    a. the price of food begins to rise relative to the price of industrial products.
    b. the isoquants in industry and agriculture become smooth, bowed curves.
    c. the aggregate growth rate becomes positive.
    * d. labor demand has increased enough to pull up real wages in both agriculture and industry.

16. The neoclassical two-sector model assumes that wages in agriculture are equal to

    a. the wage in industry plus a premium to compensate for the difficulty of farm work.
    b. an institutionally fixed subsistence wage.
    c. the average product of labor in agriculture.
    * d. the marginal product of labor.

17. Which of the following statements best reflects Hirschman's theory of unbalanced growth?

    a. A country should focus on industrial development because agriculture is not a dynamic sector.
    b. Industrialization requires a "big push."
    * c. Once certain industries develop, linkage effects will induce the development of other new industries.
    d. All the above.

18. What is the special significance of nontraded goods in relation to GNP measurement problems?

    a. Nontraded goods do not enter GNP because they are intermediate goods.
    b. Nontraded goods do not enter GNP because they are not sold in the market.
    c. There is no value-added in production of nontraded goods.
*   d. The exchange-rate method for international comparisons improperly values nontraded goods.

19. The central idea of Engel's law is that as family incomes rise,

    a. households face diminishing returns to labor.
    b. the working class becomes more revolutionary.
*   c. spending on food declines as a proportion of total consumption expenditure.
    d. industry becomes more capital-intensive.

20. Which of the following is a *backward* linkage effect from the automobile industry?

*   a. Stimulating steel production for use as an input in making autos.
    b. Generating higher incomes for workers employed in auto production
    c. Stimulating development of the transportation services industry
    d. All the above

IDs and Paired-Concept Questions

These terms can be used individually as short-answer identification questions, or they can be used in pairs. In the latter case, ask students to explain (1) the meaning and significance of each of the two terms and (2) the relationship between them.

1. Gross national product (GNP), gross domestic product (GDP)
2. Exchange rate conversion method, nontraded goods
3. ICOR, neoclassical production function
4. Harrod-Domar equation, L-shaped isoquants
5. g_K, a (from the sources-of-growth equation)

6. Engel's law, share of manufacturing in GDP
7. Marginal product of labor in agriculture, institutionally fixed wage
8. Terms of trade between agriculture and industry, surplus labor
9. Neoclassical two-sector model, labor-supply curve to industry
10. Cross-section data, average patterns of development
11. Balanced growth, big push
12. Imbalanced growth, backward linkages

Study Guide Applications

Worked Example

The Worked Example provides a step-by-step application of the Fei-Ranis model, emphasizing how lack of progress in agriculture can cause the intersectoral terms of trade to move against industry and thereby hinder industrial development.

Exercises

1. The students work through a variation on the Worked Example involving the effects of an increase in population in the Fei-Ranis model.

2. A numerical exercise (based on textbook Table 3–1) leads students through the exchange-rate method and the purchasing power parity method for converting India's GNP to U.S. dollars. The last part of the exercise covers the measurement of real GNP.

3. The exercise provides numerical applications of the Harrod-Domar growth equation.

4. This exercise gives students practice with isoquants, with emphasis on the difference between fixed-coefficient and neoclassical production functions.

5. Students solve numerical examples of sources-of-growth analysis and interpret the relationship.

6. This empirical exercise examines the "pattern" of how the manufacturing sector's share of GDP varies with per capita income, using 1992 data for 12 medium-sized LDCs.

CHAPTER 4   Development and Human Welfare

Chapter Outline

I. Chapter 4 probes the relationship between economic growth and the goal of improving human welfare. After World War II, economists tended to accept that the benefits of growth would trickle down to the poor. This complacent view was challenged by evidence of rising income inequality and a stubborn prevalence of poverty in many developing countries. Such evidence stimulated active concern with promoting more equitable growth. During the 1980s, poverty-oriented policies were pushed to the background by the need to cope with macroeconomic shocks. Since then, concern with poverty-oriented policy has revived, but not as an *alternative* to concern about growth. The evidence of the past half century shows that growth is necessary for alleviating widespread poverty.

II. The first step is to explain basic concepts and measures relating to human development, including the functional and size distributions of income, the Lorenz curve showing income shares, the Gini concentration ratio, the poverty line, social indicators of basic human needs, and overall indicators such as the Human Development Index (HDI). Tables provide up-to-date statistics for a wide range of countries. The discussion in the text emphasizes measurement problems, the distinction between relative and absolute poverty, and the difference between inequality and equity.

III. Is there a pattern to the changes in inequality and poverty that occur during economic development? With regard to inequality, Kuznets' inverted-U hypothesis still serves as a baseline. The hypothesis states that inequality first rises and then falls over the course of development. This hypothesis receives some support from cross-section data, but data for specific countries exhibit great differences. Thus, rising inequality is not an inevitable concomitant of development. Differences in inequality have been attributed to factors such as education, population growth, the structure of asset ownership, and control by entrenched elites. On balance, the determinants of income inequality are not well understood. Simulation studies have shown, however, that inequality and poverty are affected by policies, especially those which alter the internal terms of trade and those which affect rural-to-urban migration of labor.

IV. Looking at poverty, the empirical pattern is clear and simple: poverty is diminishing in countries that are growing rapidly, while in the absence of economic growth rising poverty is virtually unavoidable.

V. The theoretical analysis of inequality and poverty begins with an outline of the classical models of David Rechart and Marx, as well as a brief statement of the neoclassical theory of income distribution. The main vehicle for analysis is the Lewis-Fei-Ranis labor-surplus model. This model provides insight into why inequality may rise during the early stages of development. As long as the supply of labor is highly elastic, capital's share of income will rise and real wages will not improve much for the masses. Once the demand for labor begins to pull up real wages, however, these conditions reverse.

VI. The chapter explores four strategies for dealing with inequality and poverty: the traditional view, derived from the Lewis model, which can be summarized as grow first, then redistribute; the radical alternative, which is to redistribute first, then grow; the reformist strategy of redistribution with growth (RWG); and the basic human needs (BHN) strategy, which entails more direct assistance to the poor. The authors conclude that the most promising path to more equitable growth is to adopt policies that promote employment creation and to avoid policies that depress incomes in rural areas, where most of the poor live. Effective political commitment to egalitarian reforms is also essential—in the form of action, not just talk.

Boxed Examples. Four case studies of South Korea, Brazil, Sri Lanka, and India illustrate very different relationships between growth and inequality.

In the New Edition. The data tables and examples are revised and updated, with transitional economies integrated into the data set by income level (based on PPP estimates). The text now uses a simple hypothetical example to clarify the explanation of how Lorenz curves can cross and how different distributions can generate equal Gini ratios The topic of distribution-weighted growth is dropped altogether, while the human development index (HDI) is now accorded more prominence. Finally, the discussion of Kuznets' inverted-U hypothesis has been rewritten; among the changes, the regression test of the hypotheses (Equation 4–1) based on the newer data provides much weaker support than before. (The R^2 is .15, compared to .50 in the previous edition.)

Class Notes. The themes of human development and poverty recur in many of the later chapters, so it is vital that students master the fundamentals here. As much as one may wish to believe otherwise, students do get confused about the basic concepts and measures if they are not explained clearly in class. Along with clarifying technical details, I like to discuss the statistical and normative problems with measures of inequality, poverty, and human development. From taking this course, students should become wiser consumers of data and information. They should be aware of hidden pitfalls in many of the statistics that are widely touted in discussions of human welfare and development.

Also fundamental, but difficult, is the analysis of why inequality often increases and then declines during the course of development. I lean on the Lewis-Fei-Ranis model for part of the story, and also use examples illustrating how the inverted U can be a normal consequence of the fact that changes in the economy, such as reallocation of labor to more productive sectors or dissemination of innovations, affect some people before others. The analytical background provides a basis for previewing the equity dimension of many topics to be covered later, such as factor-price distortions, excess capital intensity, neglect of agriculture, and import-substitution policy.

The use of regression equations in the text introduces students to an important empirical tool. Discussion in class is probably needed to help students understand the tool. For data on welfare issues, your best source is the annual UNDP *Human Development Report*, published by Oxford University Press.

There are many supplementary topics to which you might devote class time. For example, you might delve more deeply into the political economy of income distribution. Or open students' eyes to problems of intrafamily income distribution and the subordinate role of women in many cultures. Or explain the Adelman-Robinson simulation model more fully. Or discuss how policies aimed at helping the poor (such as food-price controls) can produce adverse effects, particularly once general-equilibrium adjustments are taken into account.

Question Bank

Multiple-Choice Questions

1. Preoccupation with growth gave way to greater concern with equity during the 1960s when statistics showed decisively that in many developing countries

    a. only the rich benefited from high rates of growth.
    b. the poor were actually getting poorer.
  * c. large numbers of people were not benefiting and income inequality was rising.
    d. all the above.

2. If everyone in a country had the same level of income, then the value of the Gini concentration ratio would be

   a. 1.0.
 * b. 0.0.
   c. 0.5.
   d. infinity.

3. To draw a Lorenz curve showing the distribution of income by household, one should first rank all households according to

   a. household size.
   b. age of head of household.
   c. wage level.
 * d. income per capita.

4. In most low-income countries, what share of national income typically accrues to the richest 20 percent of the households?

 * a. 40 to 60 percent.
   b. 60 to 80 percent.
   c. 80 to 90 percent.
   d. 90 to 95 percent.

5. Lists of basic human needs differ, but most would include all the following *except*

 * a. access to television and radio broadcasts.
   b. minimally adequate nutrition.
   c. basic shelter.
   d. adequate clothing.

6. One study found that the Gini coefficient for Egypt (.403) was virtually the same as that for Australia (.404). From this information one can conclude that Egypt and Australia had virtually the same

   a. number of households in absolute poverty.
   b. percentage of households in absolute poverty.
   c. Human Development Index value.
 * d. none of the above.

7. The text cites all but one of the following as significant factors associated with less-than-normal inequality, relative to a country's per capita income. Which is the exception?

    a. Higher primary-school enrollment rate
* b. Higher food subsidies as a percentage of GNP
    c. Small-scale or communal farmers' dominating the agriculture sector
    d. Lower population growth rate

8. According to the textbook the single most important variable explaining intercountry differences in the extent of poverty is

    a. the literacy rate.
    b. the HDI.
* c. per capita income.
    d. population.

9. The boxed example of South Korea illustrates a case in which a high rate of income growth was accompanied by

    a. very high and increasing inequality.
    b. very high but declining inequality.
* c. low inequality and strong performance in alleviating poverty.
    d. low inequality but poor performance in alleviating poverty.

10. The textbook characterizes the radical model of development strategy by the phrase _____ first, then _____.

    a. revolution, jobs
    b. industry, consumer goods
* c. redistribute, grow
    d. basic human needs, capital goods

11. The Human Development Index (HDI) is a composite of three basic measures of human welfare. Which if the following is not a component of the HDI?

    a. Life expectancy
    b. GNP per capita
* c. Infant mortality rate
    d. Literacy rate

12. From the case studies in Chapter 4, which country experienced only moderate growth but made remarkable progress in dealing with manifestations of poverty?

    a. South Korea
    b. India
    c. Brazil
  * d. Sri Lanka

13. Which of the following policy instruments is most consistent with the redistribution with growth (RWG) strategy?

    a. Confiscation of property from the rich
    b. Investment in state-owned heavy industries
    c. High tariffs on imported goods to promote local production
  * d. Measures that reduce distortions to the prices of labor and capital to encourage more employment of unskilled labor

14. The textbook concludes that the two most promising reformist approaches to achieve more equitable growth relate to

    a. food subsidies and progressive tax rates.
    b. protection of domestic industry and establishing a minimum wage.
    c. infrastructure investment and nationalization of leading sectors.
  * d. incentives for productive employment creation and proper pricing of farm products.

15. On the basis of cross-section data analysis, which of the following statements is a valid empirical generalization?

    a. Income inequality is more severe in high-income countries than in low-income countries.
  * b. Absolute poverty declines with economic growth.
    c. In most LDCs the rich are getting richer while the poor are getting poorer.
    d. All the above.

16. What conclusion can be reached from the following data on income shares, from Table 4–1 in the textbook?

	Percent of income received by:	
	Lowest 40%	Highest 20%
Bangladesh	17.3	45.3
Indonesia	14.4	49.4

   a. Absolute poverty is more widespread in Bangladesh.
 * b. The size distribution of income is more unequal in Indonesia.
   c. Bangladesh has adopted a strategy of redistribution with growth.
   d. Bangladesh is growing faster than Indonesia.

17. The World Bank has estimated that by the year 2000 the number of poor people will decline to fewer than 100 million in _____, but will rise to more than 250 million in _____.

 * a. South Asia, sub-Saharan Africa
   b. Sub-Saharan Africa, South Asia
   c. East Asia (including China), Latin America
   d. Latin America, East Asia (including China)

18. Which of the following statements best captures the effects of economic growth on income distribution in Ricardo's classical two-sector model?

 * a. Landlords' incomes rise while capitalists' incomes fall.
   b. Real wages rise.
   c. Unskilled workers gain relative to landlords.
   d. Capitalists gain relative to both workers and landlords.

19. In the mainstream neoclassical theory, the payment accruing to each factor of production is determined by its

   a. comparable worth.
   b. bargaining power.
   c. political connections.
 * d. marginal productivity.

20. Kuznets' inverted-U hypothesis states that as economies develop,

     a. average household incomes first fall and later rise.
     b. industry's share of GNP first rises and later falls.
 * c. income inequality first rises and later falls.
     d. the population growth rate first rises and later falls.

IDs and Paired-Concept Questions

These terms can be used individually as short-answer identification questions, or they can be used in pairs. In the latter case, ask students to explain (1) the meaning and significance of each of the two terms and (2) the relationship between them.

1. Functional distribution, Lorenz curve
2. Global poverty line, poverty head count
3. Per capita GNP (PPP$), Human Development Index
4. Inverted-U hypothesis, Gini coefficient
5. RWG strategy; redistribute first, then grow
6. Asset ownership, size distribution of income
7. Reserve army of the unemployed, Lewis model
8. Rural poverty, prices of farm products
9. Structural adjustment, development with a human face
10. Trickle down, Lewis model

Study Guide Applications

Worked Example

The Worked Example demonstrates how to draw a Lorenz curve and how to calculate the corresponding Gini concentration ratio, using data on the distribution of income for Brazil.

Exercises

1. The problem asks students to duplicate calculations from the Worked Example using income-shares data for Hungary.

2. A simple set of hypothetical data on income shares is used to illustrate some of the problems encountered in measuring and interpreting income distribution statistics, including limitations of sample survey data, the definition of the recipient unit, the definition of the poverty line, and measurement problems related to life-cycle income patterns.

3. A hypothetical case study shows how the inverted-U pattern of income inequality can emerge in the normal course of development.

4. This problem examines the empirical relationship between economic development and human development, using the Human Development Index (HDI).

5. Students plot points from the regression equation relating inequality to per capita income (Equation 4–1 in the textbook) to learn how to interpret a regression equation and to confront the Kuznets hypothesis with actual data.

CHAPTER 5

Guiding Development: Markets versus Controls

Chapter Outline

I. Chapter 5 surveys the historic debate about the scope for market forces versus government controls in promoting economic development. The chapter reviews the strengths of the market mechanism, along with market failure problems stemming from monopolies, externalities, infant industries, underdeveloped institutions, and national goals such as equity. The pros and cons of central planning are outlined in parallel fashion with reference to the wave of reforms that swept through the socialist world around 1990.

II. The story of the "march toward markets" opens by explaining why most LDCs chose for decades to lace their mixed economies with strong controls. Experience demonstrated, however, that controls did not work well, and often generated counterproductive side effects such as wasteful rent-seeking and bribery. In contrast, market prices, competition, and outward orientation proved to be more effective mechanisms for generating growth and development.

III. While heavy-handed controls have fallen out of favor, creating markets is no simple matter. The text probes five elements needed as a foundation for well functioning markets. These are: (1) stabilizing macroeconomic conditions, (2) dismantling administrative controls, (3) ensuring effective competition, (4) letting relative prices reflect scarcity values, and (5) restructuring enterprises so managers are accountable for profitability and responsive to market signals. In the course of discussing these points, the text also explains the nature of stabilization and structural adjustment programs, and the issue of privatization and property rights.

IV. Chapter 5 ends with issues relating to the implementation of stabilization and structural adjustment programs. These include establishing credibility of the reforms and determining the timing and the magnitude of reforms. The options range from shock treatment, Poland-style, to a more gradual transition, as in China and Vietnam.

Boxed Examples. There are two boxed examples. The first explains Bolivia's successful stabilization program in 1985–86. The second provides a broad description of the stabilization and reform programs adopted in Indonesia during the period 1986 to 1990.

In the New Edition. Three substantive revisions are in the new edition. Perhaps the most important is a much more thorough treatment of the transition to markets in countries of the former Communist bloc. Insights from Eastern Europe, the former Soviet Union, China, and Vietnam pervade the text. A second change is the presentation of new empirical evidence on the role of markets and openness as determinants of growth. In addition to the Syrquin-Chenery study mentioned in the previous edition, Chapter 5 now presents statistical results from recent research by Jeffrey Sachs and Andrew Warner, and evidence on the link between macroeconomic stability and growth, from a study by Stanley Fischer. Third, there are important shifts in emphasis. For example, the text now stresses the gains in factor productivity that come from allowing competitive markets to function. Also, the discussion of restructuring includes a closer look at property rights.

Class Notes. Chapter 5 addresses a fundamental question: what institutional foundation is best for economic development, and why? It is important to get across to students: (1) a balanced view of both the advantages and the shortcomings of market forces, (2) a careful explanation of why controls so often fail and often prove counterproductive as tools for ameliorating market failures, and (3) a grasp of the serious problems associated with the transition to wider reliance on market forces *starting* from a position encumbered by the institutional, political, and economic legacy of pervasive controls. Avoid absolutes, though. Bear in mind that Korea has succeeded despite departures from laissez-faire, and Russia's move to free markets triggered a long and painful adjustment.

   The text is entirely expository, but two key topics are suitable for more analytical treatment in class, using simple applications of supply and demand. First, you can use a supply-and-demand graph to explain the significance of market failure problems. Similarly, supply-and-demand analysis can illustrate how controls create efficiency losses, rent-seeking, and parallel markets. It is easy to construct examples of market failures (private monopolies in the Philippines under Marcos, desertification, conspicuous consumption by elites) and control failures (price controls, quotas and tariffs, industrial licensing). Exercises in the *Study Guide* provide several generic examples. Refer to the 1994 *World Development Report* for a wealth of interesting information on market-oriented innovations in providing infrastructure. Save some examples to toss out for open discussion.

   Another consideration in teaching Chapter 5 is new terminology. It is a safe bet that many students are unfamiliar with export pessimism, outward-looking strategy, conditionality, liberalization, and even terms like real interest rates, import substitution, and wage indexing. Overall, two classes should be an ample time budget for Chapter 5.

Question Bank

Multiple-Choice Questions

1. The defining characteristic of socialism is that

   * a. government owns and controls the means of production.
   b. markets do not play any role in allocating resources.
   c. planning is centralized and nonparticipatory.
   d. government policy depends on a plan.

2. A mixed economy is one in which

   a. there is a proper balance between agriculture and industry.
   b. there are externalities, monopolies, infant industries, and underdeveloped institutions.
   c. the state owns the means of production, while allowing a limited range of market activities.
   * d. government interventions are superimposed on a market-based system.

3. Which of the following is an example of external economies?

   a. Imports of raw materials by local industries
   * b. Government construction of overhead investments, such as roads
   c. The use of protective tariffs to promote infant industries
   d. All the above

4. Which of the following represents an application of letting relative prices move toward reflecting scarcity values?

   a. Applying high tariffs to protect domestic producers from foreign competition
   * b. Raising the price of gasoline to a level that reflects prices in the world markets plus transport and processing costs
   c. Setting interest rates on loans to small farmers below the rates charged to major industrial firms
   d. Introducing minimum wage laws to improve wages for urban unskilled workers

5. The roll call of developing countries undertaking market-oriented reforms during the past two decades includes

   a. China.
   b. Mexico.
   c. Indonesia.
 * d. All the above.

6. Wasteful rent-seeking behavior can best be controlled by

 * a. removing government price and allocation controls that interfere with market outcomes.
   b. constructing more housing units and office buildings.
   c. relying less heavily on markets to allocate resources.
   d. outlawing parallel markets.

7. From their empirical analysis of 75 countries for the period 1970 to 1989, Sachs and Warner conclude that greater market orientation

   a. is the single most important determinant of growth.
   b. does not help poor countries that export mainly primary products.
 * c. is one important factor promoting rapid growth of incomes and productivity.
   d. creates black markets.

8. Why have many LDCs grown disillusioned with central planning?

   a. Centrally planned economies have not adjusted easily to changing economic conditions.
   b. Administrative and managerial skills needed for central planning are very scarce resources in developing countries.
   c. Interventions often create corruption and wasteful rent-seeking behavior.
 * d. All the above.

9. Which of the following is *not* one of the five elements needed to support a well-functioning market system?

 * a. Holding the exchange rate fixed
   b. Achieving a relatively stable macroeconomic environment
   c. Allowing relative prices to reflect relative scarcities
   d. Establishing competition

10. Black markets (or parallel markets) are a natural consequence of

  * a. controls that hold prices below the market equilibrium.
  b. having a single monopoly producer in an industry.
  c. external diseconomies.
  d. inflation.

11. The former Soviet economic system was

  a. quite effective at supplying consumer goods.
  * b. well suited to rapid and massive restructuring of industry, as occurred prior to World War II.
  c. built on the premise that markets could operate only in agriculture, where competition ensured efficiency.
  d. notable for its excellent record in raising factor productivity.

12. At the core of a typical IMF stabilization program is the idea that

  * a. inflation is caused when the domestic money supply grows faster than demand for it.
  b. the government must set a good example by running a budget surplus.
  c. foreign borrowing is the main cause of stagnation.
  d. market failures are pervasive in LDCs.

13. Bolivia's stabilization effort in 1985–86 illustrates that

  a. hyperinflation cannot be reduced without stringent price controls.
  * b. eliminating huge deficits in the government budget is an important part of a credible stabilization program.
  c. hyperinflation is not really such a serious problem.
  d. there is no conflict between restoring growth and repaying foreign debt in full.

14. Structural adjustment programs are designed to

  a. promote the growth of industry rather than agriculture.
  b. assure that scarce foreign exchange is rationed in accordance with a five-year plan.
  * c. dismantle controls that interfere with market allocations.
  d. stop inflation.

15. China and Vietnam are examples of formerly planned economies that

    a. adopted the shock-therapy approach to liberalization.
    b. began their reform programs by privatizing large state-owned industrial enterprises.
    c. suffered severe economic contraction during the transition to a market system.
* d. managed the transition to a market economy in gradual steps.

16. The international organization with responsibility for helping developing countries design and finance *structural adjustment* programs is the

* a. World Bank.
    b. Organization of Petroleum Exporting Countries.
    c. United Nations.
    d. International Monetary Fund.

17. For privatization programs to succeed, it is essential to

    a. declare the old state-owned enterprises bankrupt.
    b. eliminate externalities in the industrial sector.
    c. use tariffs to protect the enterprises from import competition.
* d. cut the ties that bind the enterprises to the government bureaucracy.

18. Heterodox economists criticize IMF-style stabilization programs in Latin America on the grounds that

    a. infant industries will always need protection.
    b. central planning has been quite successful in these countries.
    c. foreign debts must be repaid before reforms can begin.
* d. wages and prices are determined by structural conditions rather than by market forces.

19. Compared to the situation in a competitive market, in a monopolistic market firms generally

    a. use more-efficient technologies.
    b. sell a greater share of output in parallel markets.
* c. produce less output, while charging higher prices.
    d. are more likely to succeed in response to infant industry protection.

20. What East Asia's "four tigers" (Korea, Singapore, Hong Kong, and Taiwan) have in common is that they achieved rapid industrial growth by

    a. eliminating virtually all government interventions.
    b. heavily subsidizing exports, while prohibiting competing imports.
    c. imposing effective central planning.
*   d. fostering conditions in which domestic producers must learn to compete in world markets.

IDs and Paired-Concept Questions

These terms can be used individually as short-answer identification questions, or they can be used in pairs. In the latter case, ask students to explain (1) the meaning and significance of each of the two terms and (2) the relationship between them.

1. Monopoly power, infant industries
2. Import substitution, overvalued exchange rate
3. Stabilization, IMF conditionality
4. Privatization, property rights
5. Heterodox economists, elasticity pessimists
6. Five-year plan, one-year plan.
7. Parallel market, rent-seeking behavior
8. Overvalued exchange rate, liberalization
9. Neoclassical school, factor productivity

Study Guide Applications

Worked Example

The Worked Example applies simple supply-and-demand analysis to show how rent-seeking behavior and parallel markets emerge from price controls.

Exercises

1. Students work through a variation of the Worked Example. This time, supply-and-demand analysis is used to show how parallel markets and rent-seeking behavior emerge from import controls used to protect an infant industry.

2. Calculations based on macroeconomic data for Ghana show how structural adjustment turned around a long-term negative trend; the exercise also provides an example of using a with-and-without comparison to analyze the effectiveness of reforms.

3. Students examine several market failure problems and various distortions created by government controls, in the context of a hypothetical developing country.

4. The last exercise presents simple examples illustrating the five elements needed to support a well-functioning market system, as enumerated in the text.

CHAPTER 6   Planning Models

Chapter Outline

I. Even though central planning is a waning force in most developing countries, economic planning models are still widely used for the analysis of development strategies and policies. Chapter 6 surveys the technical tools. The chapter opens by distinguishing between consistent and optimal model solutions. The distinction is explained using a production possibilities frontier, with community indifference curves representing the objective function or welfare function.

II. The first model presented is a six-equation growth model with a Harrod-Domar supply side, expressed as a first-difference equation in Y (= GDP). The demand side consists of simple Keynesian-style structural equations incorporating domestic and foreign saving as well as imports and exports. This model is used to explain two-gap analysis, in which either saving or foreign exchange can be a binding constraint on investment and growth.

III. The survey of interindustry models begins with a detailed explanation of the structure of input-output tables and the methodology of input-output modeling. The text then describes the format of a social accounting matrix (SAM), which provides a comprehensive framework for quantifying economic flows. Linear programming models and computable general-equilibrium (CGE) models are discussed more briefly and nontechnically—except for an explanation of objective functions for linear programming, plus simple examples of nonlinear equations that can be handled by CGE models. More emphasis is placed on special characteristics and applications of these tools.

IV. The final section examines tools for project appraisal. After presenting discounting techniques, the text explains how to compute net present value and how to apply NPV analysis to project selection. The internal rate of return and the benefit-cost ratio are also covered briefly. The text then explains how the concept of opportunity cost serves as the basis for introducing shadow pricing into economic project appraisal.

In the New Edition. Apart from editorial changes and clarifications, Chapter 6 remains unchanged from the previous edition.

Class Notes. This is one of the most technical chapters in the book. To cover the whole chapter in reasonable detail would require at least three class periods (for topics I and II, topic III, and topic IV, respectively). By reasonable detail, we mean explaining the underlying intuition of each tool and the textbook algebra, plus numerical examples and a discussion of the range of planning applications. On each of these issues, the *Study Guide* Exercises can be especially helpful to your students.

The input-output model should be covered, since input-output logic is used repeatedly later in the book. Work through how to derive Table 6–2 from Table 6–1, and then show how to compute a solution for a simple 2×2 numerical example. It is vital that students understand what interindustry flows are all about, why it is so important to distinguish gross outputs (X) from the final uses (F), and how a solution can be infeasible.

Project appraisal concepts also return in many later chapters. The net present value calculation should be developed carefully, with simple numerical examples. Many students have trouble mastering this tool. Table 6–4 provides a good focus for lecturing on the application of shadow pricing, and students will need your help to understand it.

It is important to emphasize the limitations of these models, but not to the extent of dismissing them. The models are tools to promote more informed and more consistent policy analysis, even though one cannot and should not expect the analysis to provide mechanical technocratic answers. Policy decisions are ultimately a matter of informed judgment.

Question Bank

Multiple Choice Questions

1. A feasible solution to a planning problem must be on

    a. the production possibilities frontier (PPF).
* b. or inside the PPF.
    c. the PPF at the point that maximizes the value of the appropriate welfare function.
    d. the PPF at a point halfway between the two axes.

2. The equation $I_t = S_t + F_t$ in the Keynesian macroeconomic model says that _____ in year t is determined by the amount of domestic saving plus the inflow of foreign _____.

* a. investment, saving
    b. income, exchange
    c. investment, exchange
    d. income, saving

3. What are the two gaps that can constrain growth in the two-gap model?

    a. Saving constraint and investment constraint
    b. Foreign exchange constraint and investment constraint
    c. Food constraint and investment constraint
  * d. Saving constraint and foreign exchange constraint

4. In an input-output table, each row shows how one sector's

  * a. total output is allocated across uses.
    b. total cost breaks down according to type of payment.
    c. value-added breaks down into wages, rents, and profits.
    d. capital stock is allocated across specific product lines.

5. With a discount rate of 10 percent, the present value of a $5,000 income payment to be received in two years is

    a. $500.
  * b. $4,132.
    c. $4,990.
    d. $4,545.

6. What accounts for the difference between total use and final use in an input-output table?

    a. Value-added
    b. Depreciation
  * c. Intermediate use
    d. Profits

7. Let sector 1 = agriculture and sector 3 = manufacturing. Agriculture uses $100 million of manufactured inputs to produce $500 million of output. The input-output coefficient a_{31} equals

  * a. 0.20.
    b. 5.0.
    c. $400 million.
    d. $600 million.

8. In a social accounting matrix, the element shown in the Capital account row and Households column represents

    a. foreign investment by nationals.
    b. bank loans to households
    c. profits.
* d. household savings.

9. In practice, linear programming models are most often used to evaluate the optimum

    a. pattern of foreign trade.
    b. macroeconomic policy.
    c. distribution of income.
* d. design for microeconomic projects.

10. The general expression for the present value $P of a future payment $F to occur at time t using a discount rate i (in decimal units) is

    a. $P = F(1 + i)/t$.
    b. $P = F(1 + t)/i$.
* c. $P = F/(1 + i)^t$.
    d. $P = F/(1 + t)^i$.

11. An economy has an ICOR of $k = 4.0$, a saving rate (net of depreciation) of $s = 10$ percent, and no foreign exchange constraint. If current GNP is $Y = 1,000$, what level of GNP would be forecast for next year?

    a. 1,100
    b. 1,400
* c. 1,025
    d. 1,060

12. Which of the following models best captures possibilities for factor substitution in industry?

* a. CGE model
    b. SAM
    c. Two-gap growth model
    d. Input-output model

13. For an economy faced with a foreign exchange constraint, which of the following changes increases the growth rate?

    a. An increase in the ICOR
* b. An increase in exports
    c. An increase in the domestic saving rate
    d. All the above

14. An agricultural project has an initial cost of Rs1,000 and a net return of Rs600 each year for the next two years. With a discount rate of 8 percent, the net present value of this project is

* a. Rs70.
    b. Rs200.
    c. 6 percent.
    d. 8 percent.

15. The use of which planning tool depends on specifying an objective function mathematically?

    a. Input-output model
    b. Project appraisal
* c. Linear programming model
    d. SAM model

16. Which transaction enters an input-output matrix as an interindustry flow of intermediate goods?

    a. A consumer purchases an imported automobile.
* b. A cannery purchases fresh fruits from farmers.
    c. A textile firm purchases a machine from a local producer.
    d. A peasant farmer buys clothes for his family.

17. In the equation, $X_1 = a_{11} X_1 + a_{12}X_2 + a_{13}X_3 + F_1$, the term a_{13} represents the

    a. income elasticity of demand for good 1 by factor 3.
    b. income elasticity of demand for good 3 by factor 1.
* c. input of good 1 required per unit of output in industry 3.
    d. input of good 3 required per unit of output in industry 1.

18. An irrigation project pays $60 per month to unskilled workers who otherwise would be earning $35 per month. The opportunity cost of labor (per worker on the project) is

    a. $60.
    b. $95.
    c. $25.
*   d. $35.

19. In the project described above, the shadow wage rate would be

    a. $60.
    b. $95.
    c. $25.
*   d. $35.

20. The appraisal of a project to produce shrimp for export reveals that the project is commercially unprofitable. It may still have a high economic rate of return if

*   a. the official exchange rate is well below the shadow exchange rate.
    b. the shadow wage is well above the market wage.
    c. the social discount rate is well above the commercial discount rate.
    d. none of the above; it can't have a high economic rate of return if it is commercially unprofitable.

IDs and Paired-Concept Questions

These terms can be used individually as short-answer identification questions, or they can be used in pairs. In the latter case, ask students to explain (1) the meaning and significance of each of the two terms and (2) the relationship between them.

1. Optimality model, community indifference curves
2. Economic appraisal, social appraisal
3. SAM, fixed-coefficient production function
4. Saving constraint, two-gap model
5. Intermediate use, final use
6. Discount rate, internal rate of return

7. Market price, shadow price
8. Welfare function, priority weights
9. Net cash flow, net present value
10. Interindustry flow matrix, input-output coefficient matrix

Study Guide Applications

Worked Example

The Worked Example is a numerical application illustrating the structure and solution of a three-sector input-output model for the legendary country Planland.

Exercises

1. It's the students' turn to solve a two-sector input-output model and test for feasibility. The last section asks about the structure and use of SAMs.

2. Students examine the consistency, feasibility, and optimality of government plans in Rambonesia, using a production possibilities curve and some unusual welfare functions.

3. Students work through numerical problems applying a simplified version of the Keynesian macroeconomic growth model, both under a saving constraint and under a foreign exchange constraint.

4. This exercise presents a variety of calculations involving discounting and net present value, including a simple project appraisal problem illustrating the role of the discount rate and shadow pricing.

5. [*More difficult*] Students solve a simple two-sector linear programming problem geometrically.

CHAPTER 7   Sustainable Development

Chapter Outline

I. Chapter 7 examines the economics of managing natural resources, including environmental quality. Few developing countries have been able to convert resource wealth into rapid economic growth. Too often, resources are degraded or depleted without producing sustainable development. The inefficiencies stem partly from market failures. For example, open access to a common resource—including forests, fishing stocks, wildlife, aquifers, soils, rangeland, and the air we breathe—leads to excessive depletion. More broadly, the exploitation of natural resources creates external diseconomies, including congestion, erosion, and pollution. With such externalities, competitive markets exploit the resources beyond the point that maximizes net benefits to society.

II. Economic analysis provides rules for the sustainable harvest of renewable resources and for the optimal rate of depletion of nonrenewable resources. The general rule is to maximize the discounted present value of resource rents (net revenues). One implication is that the present generation, with reinvestments, can exploit nonrenewable resources without sacrificing the welfare of future generations. The higher the real return on alternative investments (and thus the discount rate), the greater the warranted rate of exploitation.

III. The fact that externalities cause markets to *over*exploit resources suggests that government controls are needed for an efficient outcome. Most countries respond with arbitrary regulations, but it is difficult for any government to regulate efficiently. A better solution is to *internalize* external costs so market participants will take the costs into account. One way to do this is to confer long-term, transferable property rights. A second device is to impose taxes that approximate the external costs. A more efficient technique is to introduce marketable permits that entitle the holders to use the resource. The permit is a property right with a market value; use of the permit therefore entails an opportunity cost which internalizes the externality. All three of these are ways to *correct* the market rather than regulate it.

IV. Minimizing government intrusion is desirable because *policy* failures are another major cause of resource mismanagement. Through protectionist trade measures, tax breaks, energy subsidies, and poorly appraised infrastructure investments, government interventions often accentuate the wasteful use of scarce resources.

V. Standard measures of national income and product contribute to poor resource management by neglecting the depletion or degradation of natural capital. Thus, national accounts overstate consumable output and growth, particularly for resource-rich developing countries. To correct this, economists have devised a measure of *adjusted net national product* (ANNP), but the adjustment has not yet been widely used.

VI. A final issue is *global* sustainability. Many uncertainties remain concerning the long-term effects of pollution, but history consistently has disproved simple Malthusian views that the world is running out of resources. One reason is that technology has more than kept pace with population. More to the point, neoclassical economics shows that markets respond to scarcity by inducing substitutions, conservation, exploration for new reserves, and development of alternative materials. Hence, a sound strategy for global sustainability is to promote efficient markets, effective property rights, and a minimum of distortionary interventions. Since poverty is a powerful impediment to conservation and prudent management of resources, economic development is itself part of the solution. In this regard, the rich nations have a great stake in promoting development of the poor nations.

Boxed Examples. Chapter 7 presents seven boxed examples, each quite short. (1) Soil erosion problems in the uplands of Java illustrate how markets fail to cope with external diseconomies. (2) A case of communal forest management in West Bengal, India, shows a successful policy experiment in creating property rights. (3) Malaysia sharply reduced water pollution caused by the milling of palm-oil nuts through a fee system akin to pollution permits. (4) Various subsidies to cattle ranchers in the Brazilian state of Rondonia led to widespread destruction of Amazon rainforests, even though the economic rate of return was negative for the investments in ranching. (5) Kerosene subsidies in Indonesia were scrapped after research demonstrated that they were helping the wealthy more than the poor and that far cheaper methods were available to deal with deforestation. (6) The example of an urban park in Bangkok, Thailand, illustrates how an economic value can be placed on environmental amenities. (7) Adjusting national accounts for natural-resource depletion reveals that the Malaysian state of Sabah has been consuming unsustainably by harvesting forest resources without sufficient replacement investment.

In the New Edition. Chapter 7 may bear a superficial resemblance to the previous Chapter 19, but the contents are wholly new. Toss out your old lecture notes on this topic.

Class Notes. This chapter presents a minicourse on the economics of natural resources and pollution, with a steady eye on applications to developing countries (which are fascinating in their own right). The chapter's basic theme is that market-oriented solutions may be the best way to correct market failures and encourage sustainable development. Students find many of the topics to be quite thought provoking—how a market process can lead to extinction of fishery stocks, the concept of optimal pollution, the use of marketable permits, the advantages of *higher* energy prices, and the idea that real resource prices do *not* indicate that we are running out of resources. These issues are topical and highly relevant to industrial countries as well as developing countries.

The text contains a lot of formal analysis. Most of it is basic enough that students will be able to master the details, with reinforcement from your lectures. If you skipped the modeling in Chapter 6, you will have to cover discounting carefully in order to explain the valuation of natural capital and the rules for optimal extraction over time. Figure 7–3, showing harvest options for slow-growth forests, is a good lecture subject; it combines discounting, optimal depletion, and valuation of natural capital, and it is difficult enough to require an explanation.

The basic question of sustainability of worldwide development is a winning topic for discussion, including the respective interests of rich and poor countries. This issue follows neatly from the focus on human welfare in Chapter 4, and it leads naturally into the analysis of population growth in Chapter 8.

If you are not already familiar with the *World Resources* report, published annually by the United Nations Environment Programme and the World Resources Institute, you should look it over carefully in conjunction with Chapter 7. It has excellent international data on many aspects of natural-resource management.

Question Bank

Multiple-Choice Questions

1. Many, if not most, resource-rich developing countries have

   * a. grown more slowly than countries with scarce natural resources.
   b. grown more rapidly than countries with scarce natural resources.
   c. grown at about the same rate as countries with scarce natural resources.
   d. not grown at all over the past three decades.

2. Which of the following is *not* an example of an external cost?

   * a. Payment for an imported input
   b. Congestion caused by additional vehicles entering a roadway
   c. Fertilizer runoff into rivers and streams
   d. Soil erosion from overlogging

3. If the use of a resource creates an external diseconomy, in a free market

    a. the price of the resource will be too high for efficiency.
* b. the resource will be overexploited relative to the efficient outcome.
    c. the use of this resource will be unsustainable.
    d. all the above.

4. For a renewable resource, the difference between the rate of harvest and the rate of growth is called the

    a. social marginal cost.
    b. net marginal benefit.
* c. rate of depletion.
    d. marginal abatement cost.

5. If the discount rate is 10 percent, what is the present value of a marginal net benefit equal to $1,000 earned two years hence?

    a. $200
    b. $980
    c. $909
* d. $826

6. Given present extraction plans and economic projections, a bauxite mining company's marginal net benefit from bauxite production is $300 per ton in 1997 and $345 in 1998. If the company uses a discount rate of 15 percent,

    a. production should be shifted forward from 1998 to 1997.
    b. production should be shifted backward from 1997 to 1998.
* c. the present production plan is optimal.
    d. production in both years should be reduced.

7. The model of fishery economics shows that the economy maximizes *net* revenue at an effort level that is

* a. less than the level that maximizes total revenue.
    b. equal to the level that maximizes total revenue.
    c. more than the level that maximizes total revenue.
    d. likely to cause extinction of the fishery stocks.

8. The basic rule for maximizing sustainable net revenue from a renewable resource is to

    a. equalize output each year.
    b. set the ratio of revenue to cost equal to the discount rate.
    c. equate total cost and total revenue.
* d. equate marginal cost and marginal revenue.

9. One implication of the rule for optimal management of a nonrenewable resource is that more should be exploited by the current generation when the discount rate is

* a. higher.
    b. lower.
    c. positive.
    d. negative.

10. When property rights to a resource are *auctioned* off by the government,

    a. the successful bidders have no incentive to conserve the resource.
* b. most of the resource rents are captured by the government.
    c. there will be no external diseconomies from exploitation of the resource.
    d. all the above.

11. The boxed example of forest management in West Bengal, India, shows that

    a. the forest is worth more in the form of firewood than in the form of standing trees.
* b. communal forest management can succeed in rehabilitating forests.
    c. protecting the forests impoverishes the villagers.
    d. the problem of overcutting was not very serious in the first place.

12. The optimal level of pollution is

    a. zero.
    b. the level at which marginal abatement costs are minimized.
    c. the level at which external costs are so low as to be unnoticeable.
* d. the level at which the sum of the abatement cost and external cost is minimized.

13. A major problem with direct government controls to deal with pollution problems is that

    a. abatement costs are likely to be much higher than necessary.
    b. the amount of abatement stipulated is likely to be quite arbitrary.
    c. private-sector abatement efforts can be difficult to monitor.
 * d. all the above.

14. Compared to the regulatory approach to reducing overuse of a common resource, taxes that internalize external costs have the advantage of

 * a. allowing producers to choose the least-cost method of reducing use of the resource.
    b. preventing the abatement cost from being passed on to consumers.
    c. requiring much less information for monitoring.
    d. all the above.

15. The government of Malaysia succeeded in reducing water pollution from palm-oil processing mills by

    a. nationalizing the mills.
 * b. charging fees per unit of effluent.
    c. taxing palm oil.
    d. privatizing the mills.

16. In which of the following cases did government policy move the market closer to an efficient solution in the presence of an external diseconomy?

    a. Subsidies to cattle ranchers in the Amazon basin of Brazil
 * b. Removal of kerosene subsidies by the government of Indonesia
    c. Banning log exports in Ghana
    d. Fixing a low price for gasoline in Venezuela

17. In the neoclassical view of global sustainability,

    a. the soundest strategy is to move toward more-effective property rights and to end subsidies that encourage resource depletion.
    b. Malthus was wrong; the world is not quickly running out of resources.
    c. growing scarcity induces changes in behavior and technology which ameliorate the problem.
 * d. all the above.

18. The value of a forest can be calculated as the

    * a. discounted present value of future resource rents.
      b. discounted present value of future gross revenues.
      c. sum of the future resource rents.
      d. sum of the future gross revenues.

19. A basic criterion for sustainable development is that

      a. natural capital should be left in place until new reserves are found or substitutes are developed.
      b. the present discounted value of future incomes should be no less than the present year's GNP.
    * c. the depletion of natural capital should be offset by investment in made capital.
      d. population growth should halt.

20. A country's *adjusted* net national product (ANNP) is equal to

    * a. GNP – depreciation of made capital – depletion of natural capital.
      b. GNP + depreciation of made capital + depletion of natural capital.
      c. GNP – depreciation of made capital + depletion of natural capital.
      d. GNP – depletion of natural capital.

IDs and Paired-Concept Questions

These terms can be used individually as short-answer identification questions, or they can be used in pairs. In the latter case, ask students to explain (1) the meaning and significance of each of the two terms and (2) the relationship between them.

1. External diseconomy, pollution
2. Resource rent, depletion
3. Marginal net benefit, present value
4. Transferable property rights, marketable permits
5. Common resource, renewable resource
6. Marginal abatement cost, optimal pollution
7. Malthusian trap, neoclassical theory
8. Adjusted net national product, sustainable growth
9. Debt-for-nature swap, global sustainability
10. Natural capital, made capital

Study Guide Applications

Worked Example

The Worked Example examines a large copper mine in Zambia to show (i) how to value natural resources by computing the present value of the stream of resource rents, (ii) how to adjust the measure of output for depletion, and (iii) the intertemporal condition for defining an optimal time path for depletion of a nonrenewable resource.

Exercises

1. Students apply the tools covered in the Worked Example using variations on the Zambian copper mine story.

2. The problem of achieving an efficient, sustainable harvest of a common renewable resource, with open access, is illustrated in the context of decisions to gather firewood in Madagascar.

3. Students explore the efficiency effect of external diseconomies using the example of coal-fired electrical power generation in Indonesia. The exercise also compares the effects of corrective regulation versus "green taxes" that internalize the externality, and the problem of government interventions that worsen market outcomes.

4. The boxed example of water pollution from palm-oil mills in Malaysia serves as the basis for studying the concept of optimal pollution, and the economic rationale for marketable permits.

5. This exercise probes in detail the methods that have been developed to adjust national accounts for depletion of natural capital; it includes research data on resource accounting in Indonesia in the early 1980s.

6. The final exercise shows students how a debt-for-nature swap works, using Bolivia as the illustration for the analysis.

CHAPTER 8   Population

Chapter Outline

I. This chapter—the first of four treating human resources—presents terminology, facts, theories, and policy options relating to population growth. After introducing some basic demographic terms, the text outlines the history of world population growth. A key feature associated with economic development is the demographic transition, which leads to low birth and death rates and low population growth. Industrial countries have largely completed this transition, and it is well underway in most developing countries as well. Though long-term projections are inherently tenuous, present demographic conditions and trends ensure that the world's population will continue to expand well into the twenty-first century, possibly stabilizing at a bit above 10 billion people.

II. The analysis of what causes population growth starts with Malthus' pessimistic theory. In more modern times, death rates are more or less exogenous. So birth rates are the main behavioral determinant of population growth. The text presents a nontechnical summary of Gary Becker's economic theory of fertility, along with the more eclectic views of demographers like Richard Easterlin and Gary Caldwell, who incorporate changing tastes and social conditions. In general, economic development alters the costs and benefits of childbearing in ways that encourage lower fertility.

III. In analyzing the economic effects of population growth, the text starts with the static concept of optimum population. Emphasis, however, is on the dynamics of economic-demographic interactions. The text outlines the influential model of India by Ansley J. Coale and Edgar M. Hoover; in this model, population growth reduces per capita income growth as rising dependency ratios cut savings, while investment is diverted to capital widening rather than capital deepening. The text also reviews subsequent research, including more recent work challenging the Coale-Hoover conclusions. In fact, empirical studies do *not* reveal a clear negative relationship. Hence, a new consensus has been emerging: slower population growth would benefit many developing countries, but slower population growth is neither a necessary nor a sufficient condition for economic development.

IV. Population policy interventions can be justified on the grounds that family planning improves the health of mothers and children, that government programs can help couples to achieve their preferred family size, and that individual decisions impose external costs, though such costs are difficult to assess. The text evaluates various means to slow down population growth.

These include family planning, population redistribution, measures that alter the incentives to bear children, and simply concentrating on economic development to hasten the demographic transition. In general, family planning and economic development are mutually reinforcing.

Boxed Examples. Three case studies—Kenya, China, and Indonesia—are used to illustrate several approaches to population policy. In Kenya, the lack of effective demographic policy led to extremely rapid population growth until recently, when fertility has started to decline as a result of economic development and stronger government support for family planning. In contrast, China introduced increasingly severe population controls which have led to a rapid decline in fertility. There is now hope that China's population will stabilize early in the next century. The case of Indonesia demonstrates how an ambitious family planning program can succeed even in a low-income country, without requiring the strong controls used in China.

In the New Edition. All the statistics have been updated through 1992. More important, the tone has changed. The text no longer hedges on whether developing countries are undergoing the demographic transition or whether the world population will be stabilizing. Recent data reveal widespread declines in fertility, even in many parts of Africa. As an example of the new tone and the new statistics, the case study of Indonesia reports that the total fertility rate has fallen from 5.5 in 1970 to 2.9 in 1992; the previous edition simply said that the government *hoped* to cut fertility in half. Another important change is that the topic of sustainable development is covered ahead of population growth. This makes it easier to link a discussion of world population dynamics with the problem of world resource management.

Class Notes. Population growth is one of the most controversial issues of development policy since it touches on sensitive matters relating to family and religion. The topic becomes less emotional if one downplays government *interventions*, while emphasizing aspects like opportunities for women, helping couples to achieve their own family preferences, and family planning as an instrument to improve maternal and infant health.

This is also a complicated topic, since the interactions are complex; this makes it a challenge to teach clearly. Although the material in Chapter 8 is presented mostly in an expository manner, it is still useful to cover the three main analytical topics in class—the causes of rapid population growth, the effects of such growth, and the policy options.

To many students, childbearing as an economic decision is alien thinking. You should clarify this notion and emphasize that empirical studies strongly confirm the importance of economic factors as determinants of fertility. I find it useful to develop the theory of fertility using a budget line that reflects the choice between family size and "other goods." This is a convenient framework for discussing the trade-offs, the role of preferences, and deviations between actual and desired family size. In the same context one can discuss the effects of changes that accompany economic development, the effects of family planning, and policies that alter incentives to bear children.

The theory of optimum population is a simple tool to clarify the meaning of "overpopulation" and to show how demographic momentum can lead a country to overshooting the desired size. On the dynamics, I start by analyzing population growth using tools from Chapter 3: the Harrod-Domar model (which one can readily generalize to explain the Coale-Hoover model); the growth accounting model; and the Fei-Ranis model. Such cross-chapter linkages are always useful to reinforce major learning objectives. These models each imply that rapid population growth has a negative effect on development. This leads into a discussion of potential positive effects or ameliorating factors, since the empirical evidence does not reveal a strong negative association between population growth and economic development.

Question Bank

Multiple-Choice Questions

1. In 1992 Uganda had a crude birth rate of 54, a crude death rate of 22, and an infant death rate of 109. What was the rate of natural increase of the population?

   a. 32 percent
 * b. 3.2 percent
   c. 2.45 percent
   d. 5.5 percent

2. The text cites three basic preconditions for a significant decline in the marital fertility rate. Which of the following is not one of them?

 * a. The average age at which people marry must be defined by cultural standards.
   b. Fertility must be subject to conscious choice.
   c. Reduced fertility must be perceived as beneficial to the parents.
   d. Effective fertility reduction methods must be available.

3. One direct implication of the view that childbearing decisions are influenced by economic benefits and costs is that

    a. people will not have additional children unless they can earn a profit from doing so.
    b. social factors do not affect childbearing decisions.
    c. compulsory education will increase fertility by raising each child's prospective earnings.
 * d. fertility should fall with improved opportunities for women to work in jobs outside the home.

4. The total fertility rate in Ethiopia was 7.5 in 1992. This means that

    a. there were 7.5 live births per 100 women of childbearing age.
    b. there were 7.5 live births per 100 women.
    c. there were 7.5 live births per 100 people.
 * d. given prevailing age-specific fertility rates, the average woman bears 7.5 children during her reproductive years.

5. Which of the following is *not* characteristic of the demographic transition?

    a. Both the birth rate and death rate are initially high.
    b. The rate of natural increase is initially low.
 * c. The birth rate increases rapidly as people move to urban areas.
    d. Early in the transition process the death rate falls sharply.

6. In 1992, ____ percent of humanity lived in what are now developing countries, and this percentage will rise sharply in the future.

 * a. 85
    b. 95
    c. 40
    d. 66

7. A country's "optimum population" will increase as a result of

    a. an increase in per capita income.
 * b. the discovery of new reserves of natural resources.
    c. an increase in the fertility rate.
    d. any of the above.

8. The World Bank estimates that fertility rates in Zambia will drop to
   the replacement level by the year 2040, but the population may grow
   by another 50 percent after that date, before leveling off. This is an
   example of

   a. the futility of birth control.
 * b. the phenomenon of demographic momentum.
   c. the demographic transition.
   d. Becker's economic theory of fertility.

9. The case study of Indonesia shows

   a. that population control is not important in a country that is
      experiencing rapid economic growth.
   b. that population growth in a densely inhabited region can be stopped
      by transmigration to outlying provinces.
 * c. that a well-managed family planning program operating through
      village institutions can succeed even in low-income rural areas.
   d. all the above.

10. According to the text, most analysts still believe which of the following
    positions?

    a. Most developing countries remain underpopulated, because of the
       enormous gains in productivity made possible by modern science.
  * b. Slower population growth would permit per capita income to rise
       more rapidly in nearly all developing countries.
    c. High rates of population growth benefit economic development.
    d. There is no economic rationale for government intervention in
       population growth since individuals properly balance the costs and
       benefits when making decisions about family size.

11. From 1980 to 1992 the urban population in Turkey grew by nearly 5.6
    percent per year. If this growth continues, Turkey's urban population
    will double every _____ years and quadruple in about _____ years.

  * a. 12.5, 25
    b. 12.5, 156.3
    c. 17.8, 35.6
    d. 17.8, 316.8

12. In recent years the world population has been growing by

    a. 0.5 percent per year.
    b. 3.8 percent per year.
  * c. 1.7 percent per year.
    d. 6.2 percent per year.

13. The "three reproductive norms" promoted in China's *wan xi shao* program after 1971 included which of the following elements?

  * a. Families should plan for longer spacing between births.
    b. Families should continue bearing children until a male child is born, and then stop.
    c. China can care for all children through revolution plus production.
    d. Having no children is best.

14. To economist Julian Simon, population growth is beneficial because the ultimate resource is

  * a. human ingenuity.
    b. family ties.
    c. military power.
    d. children.

15. The worldwide empirical record supports which of the following generalizations?

    a. Higher rates of population growth are strongly associated with lower rates of economic growth.
    b. Low-income countries have low dependency ratios.
  * c. Low-income countries have high rates of population growth.
    d. All the above.

16. In 1987 the world's population surpassed

  * a. 5 billion people.
    b. 2 billion people.
    c. 15 billion people.
    d. 40 billion people.

17. Family planning programs work best in countries where

  * a. at least a significant portion of the population desires smaller families.
    b. infant mortality rates are high.
    c. per capita incomes are low.
    d. all the above.

18. The child-replacement thesis implies that

  * a. health programs that lower child death rates can cause fertility rates to decline.
  b. parents would prefer having two children, on average, if effective birth-control devices were available.
  c. as incomes rise parents choose to have more material goods and fewer children.
  d. child "quality" replaces child "quantity" as a parental objective as countries develop.

19. If the labor force grows 3 percent per year and the capital stock grows 2 percent per year, does "capital deepening" take place?

  a. Yes, because the capital stock is still growing.
  * b. No, because capital per worker is declining.
  c. Maybe; the answer depends on the initial capital per worker.
  d. Maybe; the answer depends on the rate of technical change.

20. By 1992, the total fertility rate in China had fallen below the replacement level. This indicates that the population will stabilize early in the next century and is a clear example of

  a. the natural effect on individual fertility decisions due to economic development.
  * b. successful birth control through heavy-handed government interventions.
  c. the theory of optimum population.
  d. the effectiveness of monetary incentives to reduce family size.

IDs and Paired-Concept Questions

These terms can be used individually as short-answer identification questions, or they can be used in pairs. In the latter case, ask students to explain (1) the meaning and significance of each of the two terms and (2) the relationship between them.

1. Crude birth rate, total fertility rate
2. Crude death rate, demographic transition
3. Dependency ratio, demographic momentum
4. Rate of natural increase, optimum population
5. Infant death rate, life expectancy
6. Coale-Hoover model, capital widening
7. New household economics, child quality
8. Population redistribution, family planning
9. Replacement level of fertility, child replacement thesis
10. Positive checks, preventive checks

11. Revolution plus production, one-child campaign
12. Implicit costs of children, incentives to have children

Study Guide Applications

Worked Example

The Worked Example illustrates the economic effects of an increase in the fertility rate using a year-by-year numerical application of the Harrod-Domar model, along the lines of the Coale-Hoover model.

Exercises

1. Students get an empirical look at the demographic transition by plotting and interpreting group-average data on birth and death rates for countries at various income levels for 1970 and 1992.

2. A series of questions tests student comprehension of the economic theory of fertility and the theory's implications for population policy.

3. Using a worksheet to keep track of year-to-year changes, this exercise explores the relationship between infant mortality, age structure, population growth, and demographic momentum.

4. Drawing on the analysis from the Worked Example, students use demographic data from Exercise 3 to evaluate the economic effects of rapid population growth.

5. The last problem examines optimum population using a graph of the relationship between population and per capita income; students are also asked to identify the effect of various exogenous changes on a country's optimum population.

CHAPTER 9   Labor's Role

Chapter Outline

I. Chapter 9 opens by surveying basic characteristics of developing-country labor markets. This survey touches on rapid labor supply growth, heavy concentration of labor in agriculture, large wage differentials, and widespread underutilization of labor. The text explains how labor markets in many developing countries are segmented into an urban formal sector, an urban informal sector, and a rural sector. Not uncommonly, urban formal-sector wages exceed market-clearing levels due to institutional constraints or efficiency-wage considerations. The section closes with a discussion of the complex problem of measuring labor supply and labor underutilization. Familiar unemployment statistics are quite inadequate in most developing countries, where disguised unemployment is the most prevalent form of labor underutilization.

II. The reallocation of labor is the next topic. First, the text explains why the opportunity costs of labor reallocation are nearly always positive, in contrast to simple labor-surplus assumptions. The opportunity cost of urban job creation includes externalities associated with urban growth, as well as induced migration of labor from rural areas. Migration behavior is analyzed using a simple version of the Harris-Todaro model. Also examined are the costs and benefits of international migration of both skilled labor (the brain drain) and unskilled labor.

III. Turning to employment policy, the most pressing need is to expand productive employment opportunities. The text uses a simple formula (Equation 9–5) to show that the industrial sector in most developing countries absorbs only a fraction of the growing labor force. To accelerate productive employment creation, developing countries need more labor-intensive industrialization. To this end, policies to correct factor price distortions are especially important. The effectiveness of such policies depends on the elasticity of factor substitution. The text explains this technical concept and reviews the debate between elasticity optimists and pessimists. Other policy issues relating to job creation include promoting appropriate technologies, redistributing incomes, undertaking investments (like irrigation) that complement labor, promoting small-scale industry, and adopting food-for-work projects.

IV. The chapter concludes that policies to accelerate the creation of productive employment are important components of an equitable growth strategy, but the pertinent policies differ according to a country's size and economic structure.

Boxed Example. A case study of informal-sector employment summarizes research on the productivity of pedicab operators, waste scavengers, and curbside hawkers in Jakarta, Indonesia.

In the New Edition. The only substantive revision to this chapter is that the data have been updated.

Class Notes. Most of the material in Chapter 9 requires explanation in class. Fortunately, the topics are enjoyable to teach in that they neatly combine economic analysis and insights about developing countries. This comment applies to labor market segmentation, disguised unemployment, the Harris-Todaro model, the formula for industrial employment creation (be careful to explain the *units* here), factor price distortions, and the elasticity of substitution. If you wish to be selective, make clear which topics students need to know.

Chapter 9 is a pivotal chapter that ties together earlier material, while foreshadowing later coverage of financial markets, trade policy, and sectoral development. This perspective can be integrated into your lectures. For instance, you can refer to two-sector growth models when discussing labor underutilization and industrial employment creation. You can spotlight the link between employment and equity. You can preview the importance of trade strategies for promoting appropriate factor choices. And so forth.

Note: In Chapter 18, the term "appropriate technology" refers to the production techniques that minimize cost, given factor prices that reflect factor scarcity. The use of the term in Chapter 9 is somewhat broader but also somewhat murkier. You may find it useful to draw on the definition from Chapter 18.

Question Bank

Multiple-Choice Questions

1. The labor force in the developing countries is currently growing at an average rate of about

  a. 0.7 percent per year.
* b. 2.0 percent per year.
  c. 4.8 percent per year.
  d. 7.6 percent per year.

2. On average, industrial employment represents what share of total employment in countries with less than $1,000 per capita income (in 1990 PPP dollars)?

    * a. 8 percent.
    b. Less than 1 percent.
    c. 26 percent.
    d. 44 percent.

3. The textbook defines disguised unemployment to include workers who

    a. pretend to work while actually having no job.
    b. falsify credentials when looking for a job.
    c. stay in school rather than try to look for work.
    * d. have a job, but one with very low productivity and very low pay.

4. Which statement correctly describes the urban informal-sector labor market in most developing countries?

    a. All workers are recent migrants to the city.
    b. There is a long queue of workers seeking informal-sector jobs.
    * c. The wage is basically market determined.
    d. All the above.

5. Which statement about the rate of visible unemployment in developing countries is broadly valid?

    * a. It significantly underestimates the extent of labor under-utilization.
    b. It is determined primarily by conditions in the rural labor market.
    c. It is the best available measure of poverty.
    d. All the above.

6. Say that unskilled workers in the urban formal-sector earn 50 shillings per day. Each year 5,000 jobs open up, but 10,000 job-seekers are hunting for such positions. A migrant entering this job market faces an *expected* wage of

    a. 50 shillings per day.
    b. 100 shillings per day.
    * c. 25 shillings per day.
    d. zero, since the number of job seekers already exceeds the number of job openings.

7. Suppose rural workers earn 10 rupees per day. In the urban labor market there is a 5 percent probability of finding a job paying 25 rupees per day. The Harris-Todaro model predicts

    a. a slow flow of rural-to-urban migration.
    b. a rapid flow of rural-to-urban migration.
    c. a rapid increase in the rural wage rate.
* d. none of the above.

8. The textbook concludes its discussion of factor pricing by stating that _____ promotes appropriate factor choices.

    a. industrialization
    b. planning
* c. open competition
    d. a ceiling on interest rates

9. In low-income countries, on average, the elasticity of industrial employment with respect to industrial value-added is approximately equal to

    a. 0.09.
* b. 0.60.
    c. 2.10.
    d. 7.10.

10. Which of the following changes would increase labor intensity in industry?

    a. A decline in the cost of credit
* b. A decline in the minimum wage rate
    c. A decline in the elasticity of substitution
    d. All the above

11. A policy change reduces the wage-rental ratio by 20 percent and thereby causes the capital-labor ratio in industry to decline by 20 percent. The elasticity of substitution equals

* a. 1.
    b. 20.
    c. 0.
    d. an amount that cannot be computed from the data given.

12. A slowdown in the growth of _____ leads to reduced labor force growth, but only after 15 years or so.

    a. wages
    b. government spending on health care
    c. the elasticity of substitution
*   d. population

13. The efficiency wage theory helps to explain

    a. why rural wages are so low.
    b. why wages in the urban informal sector generally exceed wages in rural labor markets.
    c. why low-income countries have a comparative advantage in products that involve labor-intensive technologies.
*   d. why wages may exceed market-clearing levels in the urban formal sector, even in the absence of wage controls.

14. If the elasticity of substitution is 1.3, then a 10 percent decline in the _____ causes a 13 percent decline in the _____.

    a. capital-labor ratio, capital-output ratio
    b. urban-rural wage ratio, rate of migration
    c. exchange rate, trade balance
*   d. wage-rental ratio, capital-labor ratio

15. The boxed example of the urban informal sector in Jakarta, Indonesia, reveals that

    a. the marginal product of labor in the informal sector is essentially zero.
*   b. informal-sector earnings compare favorably with what many of the workers could earn in the urban formal sector.
    c. the total number of informal-sector jobs is far less than previously believed.
    d. informal-sector operations use surprisingly modern technology.

16. Surveys from many countries show that recent rural-to-urban migrants are usually

*   a. better-off than rural workers.
    b. faced with long periods of destitution while seeking urban jobs.
    c. too undernourished to work productively.
    d. seeking the bright lights of urban life, rather than economic gains.

17. In poor countries the lowest income stratum typically consists of

    a. those who are visibly unemployed in urban areas.
    b. unskilled workers in the urban informal sector.
    c. unskilled workers in the urban formal sector.
*   d. unskilled rural workers.

18. The term "brain drain" refers to

    a. efficiency losses caused by shortages of skilled workers and managers.
    b. high dropout rates from primary schools in rural areas.
*   c. the loss of highly educated workers through international migration.
    d. skills and talents lost because of high mortality rates due to poor health conditions.

19. Technologies imported from industrialized countries are often inappropriate for low-income countries in that

    a. they are overly capital-intensive for the recipient countries.
    b. they produce the wrong type or grade of product for impoverished consumers.
    c. they require skills that are very scarce in low-income countries.
*   d. all the above.

20. A government project will expand both output and employment only if the marginal product of labor on the project is greater than

*   a. the social opportunity cost of labor.
    b. zero.
    c. the cost of feeding the workers.
    d. the wage paid.

IDs and Paired-Concept Questions

These terms can be used individually as short-answer identification questions, or they can be used in pairs. In the latter case, ask students to explain (1) the meaning and significance of each of the two terms and (2) the relationship between them.

1. Labor force, discouraged worker
2. Disguised unemployment, visible unemployment

3. Urban formal sector, urban informal sector
4. Indirect job creation, secondary job creation
5. Induced migration, brain drain
6. Expected urban wage, Harris-Todaro model
7. Factor price distortion, appropriate technology
8. Wage-rental ratio, elasticity of substitution
9. Price-incentive school, elasticity pessimists
10. Opportunity cost of labor, costs of urbanization

Study Guide Applications

Worked Example

The Worked Example illustrates how relative factor prices affect labor intensity, using an isoquant diagram. The example also shows how to calculate the elasticity of substitution.

Exercises

1. It is the students' turn to analyze how relative factor prices affect factor proportions, using an isoquant diagram. The problem also leads students through a calculation of the elasticity of substitution and a consideration of policies affecting relative factor prices.

2. The example from Exercise 1 continues, with a focus on how factor prices influence the product mix and incentives for innovation.

3. A final extension of the same example uses supply and demand to analyze interactions between labor markets in the urban formal sector, the urban informal sector, and the rural sector.

4. Exercise 4 presents a set of numerical problems applying Equation 9–5 from the textbook (which is used to calculate the extent of industrial employment creation).

5. In the context of a hypothetical case study, students work through a numerical application of the Harris-Todaro model of rural-urban labor migration.

CHAPTER 10   Education

Chapter Outline

I. Whereas Chapter 9 dealt with the quantity of labor, Chapters 10 and 11 focus on the quality of human resources and the investment in human capital. The introductory section of Chapter 10 explains that governments in most developing countries devote 15 to 20 percent of their budgets to education because schooling is in great popular demand and because education is highly correlated with productivity and earnings.

II. The second section distinguishes between formal, nonformal, and informal education, and then examines empirical record, particularly for formal education. In most developing countries, rapid growth in primary school enrollment led to subsequent problems such as teacher shortages, low achievement-test scores, excess demand for secondary-school facilities, high dropout rates, unemployment among school leavers, and regional inequalities. The text also discusses the tendency for credentials to become more important than learning ("diploma disease") and the problem of curriculum irrelevance.

III. In view of popular demand and the important socioeconomic role of education in development, governments cannot satisfy all educational needs at once. Education policy must be conceived on a rational economic basis. In this context, the text outlines manpower planning techniques and offers a critical evaluation of the methodology.

IV. The use of cost-benefit analysis in education planning is treated in more detail. The text explains the divergence between private and social rates of return to education, and implications for education policy. Empirical studies indicate that rates of return on education are generally high in developing countries, especially for basic literacy and numeracy. The text also explains why cost-benefit analysis and rate-of-return computations cannot be used mechanically as tools for planning educational investments.

V. Finally, the text reviews several alternative viewpoints on education policy in developing countries. These include the contention that education is basically a socialization and screening mechanism, the idea that education "vouchers" should be used to let the market determine education priorities, and proposals for expanding vocational and nonformal education.

Boxed Examples. One boxed example examines education policy in Indonesia. This case study explains how access to education spread rapidly during the 1970s and how success at the primary level created bottlenecks at higher levels of education in the 1980s. A second boxed example contrasts educational policies in Kenya and Tanzania. The contrast reveals that manpower planners in Tanzania seriously underestimated the productive potential of expanding secondary education.

In the New Edition. Data tables and examples in the text have been updated for the fourth edition of the text. New estimates of the rates of return to education (in Table 10-4) provide evidence that the rates of return to education tend to diminish as countries become more developed.

Class Notes. In terms of technical analysis, this is an easy chapter for students. It is helpful to highlight the concept of education as investment in human capital and the simple point that education is a matter for economic analysis, as is any other policy decision affecting investment and resource allocation. Scarcity and the need to choose efficiently are hard realities that poor countries can ill afford to neglect when considering costly education decisions. In this regard, the divergence between private and social rates of return to education is of major importance. You can explain the issue neatly using supply-and-demand analysis, augmented to show externalities and subsidies.

The application of cost-benefit analysis to evaluating education investment is the analytical crux of Chapter 10. You can cover this material at a broad intuitive level or provide a more thorough technical treatment. The latter approach takes more time, but it is necessary if you want students to understand the techniques. The *Study Guide* applications can serve as a basis for your lectures here. By planning ahead, you can include education among the applications of input-output analysis and project appraisal covered in the lectures on Chapter 6.

One of the opening lines in Chapter 10 notes that the accumulation of human capital is a significant growth determinant that was missing from the growth accounting model in Chapter 3. Its effect was therefore buried in the residual. The present revision does not elaborate on the point, though a great deal of research has been done recently on the topic, in the literature on new growth economics. This is an issue that you might deal with more fully in class to supplement the text.

Question Bank

Multiple-Choice Questions

1. In low-income countries, the demand for education is

  * a. tremendous across all segments of the population.
   b. confined mostly to urban areas.
   c. confined mostly to social elites, both urban and rural.
   d. not very strong, due to poverty and hopelessness.

2. In 1990 what was the percentage of adults who were illiterate in countries with per capita GNP below $1,000 (PPP)?

   a. 95 percent
  * b. 61 percent
   c. 24 percent
   d. 12 percent

3. Lifetime earnings curves for most developing countries show that

   a. earnings from primary education are nearly the same as earnings from secondary education.
   b. less-educated workers have shorter life expectancies.
   c. there is not much of a payoff from primary education alone.
  * d. more schooling yields higher earnings at every level.

4. Using standard methods to measure benefits and costs, the private rate of return to education cannot be less than the social rate of return because

   a. benefits of education accrue to the individual, not to society.
   b. individuals would otherwise choose not to go to school.
  * c. social costs include public-sector outlays as well as private costs of schooling.
   d. all the above.

5. When the private rate of return to education is much higher than the social rate of return,

* a. it is not economically efficient to expand education to the point of fully satisfying private demand.
  b. school tuition charges need to be raised.
  c. funds should be reallocated from other types of investment to more investment in education.
  d. the market wage exceeds the shadow price of labor.

6. The boxed example of education in Indonesia illustrates a case in which

  a. school fees were used to reduce demand for education in rural areas to a level that could be satisfied.
  b. primary education became widely available in urban areas, but not in rural areas.
* c. the primary-school enrollment rate rose from 54 to 95 percent in just one decade due to a concerted government effort.
  d. overexpansion of higher education led to a high unemployment rate among university graduates.

7. The term "educational deepening" refers to

  a. increasing the number of qualified teachers.
  b. improving the curriculum to make it more relevant to practical needs of students in developing countries.
  c. expanding school facilities into more remote locations.
* d. using people with more schooling for jobs that previously were done by people with less schooling.

8. According to those who are labeled in the textbook "radical critics,"

  a. manpower planning and cost-benefit analysis should be more widely used for education planning
  b. education vouchers should be used to reduce inequalities.
  c. school curricula in low-income countries should emphasize vocational skills.
* d. education serves mainly to get individuals to accept their social class roles, not to raise productivity.

9. In low-income countries, the social rate of return is generally highest for investment in

    a. university education.
* b. primary education.
    c. vocational education.
    d. adult education.

10. Which criticism of manpower planning methodology is invalid?

* a. It is a purely macroeconomic approach that fails to take into account an economy's industrial structure.
    b. It uses fixed coefficients to model relationships that are far from fixed in reality.
    c. It does not take into account costs.
    d. None of the above.

11. In the early 1990s, governments in developing countries typically spent what fraction of total GNP on education?

    a. Less than 0.5 percent.
* b. 2 to 5 percent.
    c. 15 to 20 percent.
    d. Over 20 percent.

12. The term "nonformal education" refers to learning that

    a. takes place at home, within the family.
    b. does not enhance productivity.
    c. occurs on the job.
* d. takes place in organized programs, but not in schools.

13. In most developing countries, primary-school enrollments began to grow very rapidly

    a. in the late 1800s.
    b. between World War I and World War II.
* c. in the 1950s.
    d. in the 1980s.

14. Spending on education has been inefficient in many developing countries because

    * a. dropout and repeat rates are high as a result of poverty.
    b. school fees paid by parents are too low to cover costs.
    c. manpower planning methods have not been widely used.
    d. all the above.

15. The text explains that many developing-country governments became disillusioned with the push for universal, compulsory, and free primary education because

    a. of the resulting budget strains.
    b. of rising unemployment among school leavers.
    c. expanding capacity at the primary level created an unquenchable demand for secondary schooling.
    * d. all the above.

16. To apply manpower planning to education, one estimates GNP growth, then the sectoral structure of output, employment by sector, employment by _____ category, and finally the corresponding _____ requirements.

    a. educational, earnings
    * b. occupational, educational
    c. earnings, educational
    d. earnings, occupational

17. For the students' families in developing countries, the main *implicit* cost of secondary education is

    a. required school fees.
    * b. earnings or work at home forgone when the student attends school.
    c. the cost of textbooks.
    d. incidental costs like school uniforms and transportation.

18. The internal rate of return on investment in education is defined as

    * a. the discount rate that equates the net present value to zero.
    b. the interest rate on educational loans.
    c. the ratio of earnings potential with the education to earnings potential without the education.
    d. the ratio of after-tax earnings to before-tax earnings.

19. The main problem one faces in calculating the private rate of return to education is

    a. figuring out the opportunity cost of capital for the student's family.
*   b. predicting how the structure of earnings will change.
    c. measuring all the explicit costs of sending a child to school.
    d. estimating how much of the extra earnings will be remitted to the parents.

20. The case study of educational policy in Kenya and Tanzania illustrates the point that

    a. education contributed far more to equity in Tanzania, because of the country's commitment to socialism.
    b. special vouchers can be used effectively to assure the poor of equal access to education.
*   c. restricting secondary schooling to the predicted need for high school graduates can be very inefficient.
    d. vocational education is more productive than a standard academic curriculum.

IDs and Paired-Concept Questions

These terms can be used individually as short-answer identification questions, or they can be used in pairs. In the latter case, ask students to explain (1) the meaning and significance of each of the two terms and (2) the relationship between them.

1. Informal education, nonformal education
2. Investment in human capital, enrollment ratios
3. Private rate of return, age-earning profiles
4. Cost-benefit analysis, net present value
5. Social rate of return, educated unemployment
6. Explicit costs of schooling, implicit costs of schooling
7. Manpower planning, educational deepening
8. Education vouchers, vocational education

Study Guide Applications

Worked Example

The Worked Example uses a simple set of (two-period) lifetime earnings profiles to illustrate how to compute the private and the social rates of return to education and how there can be a large gap between the two.

Exercises

1. Students calculate private and social rates of return to education using a simple set of (three-period) lifetime earnings profiles.

2. As a follow-up to Exercise 1, students see why current earnings differentials can be very misleading as a guide to the benefits of education.

3. The third exercise is a step-by-step numerical application of the Tinbergen-Parnes method for manpower planning, incorporating two sectors and two skill categories. The exercise also leads students to examine weaknesses of the manpower-planning methodology.

CHAPTER 11   Health and Nutrition

Chapter Outline

I. Health and nutrition go hand in hand as basic human needs and as basic investments in human capital. The first section of Chapter 11 reviews trends and patterns in health conditions. Most developing countries have achieved impressive gains in life expectancy and infant mortality through a combination of rising income, improved health technology, rising literacy, and specific health and nutrition policies. Still, mortality and morbidity rates remain relatively high due to the continued prevalence of infectious, parasitic, and respiratory diseases, as well as malnutrition.

II. Health expenditures can be productive investments that allow the population to lead more productive and longer working lives, in addition to the direct value of health as an end in itself. Yet it is difficult to evaluate the economic rate of return on health projects because the benefits are hard to measure. In addition, health improvements are often a joint outcome of medical, environmental, and nutritional factors. Serious environmental health problems include unsafe drinking water, inadequate sanitation, and squalid housing.

III. The discussion of malnutrition starts with an outline of how food supplies compare with nutritional requirements, using national food balance sheets. National aggregates, however, reveal little about malnutrition, since food insecurity is caused mainly by unequal distribution of entitlements, not by inadequate food supplies. At the household level, nutrition depends on income, food prices, tastes, and distribution decisions within the family. Although food quality choices may be far from optimal, the main diet problem in developing countries is calorie-protein malnutrition; the main victims are infants and children.

IV. Governments can improve both the quantity and quality of food consumption through nutrition interventions. Particularly useful is food distribution linked to maternal and child health care. Food subsidies too often prove to be wastefully expensive, as a large portion of the benefits wind up accruing to the nonpoor. Well-designed programs targeted to the needy tend to be far more cost-effective.

V. The last topic is the delivery of medical services. Health care in most developing countries is poorly funded, heavily skewed to favor urban areas, and too concerned with curative rather than preventative care. The experiences of countries like Sri Lanka, China, and Cuba prove that these problems can be overcome by committed governments. To help finance medical care, some economists advocate charging user fees. This device is suitable for curative services aimed at the nonpoor, but user fees should be imposed with great care so they do not exclude the poor from primary treatment.

In the New Edition. The only changes to Chapter 11 (formerly Chapter 10), are data updates in the text and tables.

Boxed Examples. There are two boxed examples. The first shows how Sri Lanka achieved remarkably good health status through a combination of disease control, widely distributed medical facilities, near-universal literacy, food price subsidies, and equitable income distribution. The second explains how Cuba, despite an unprecedented outflow of medical personnel after 1959, made great strides in health through a reorganized and well-distributed health care system, supported by high literacy levels and an equitable distribution of food and other basic goods.

Class Notes. While famine grabs the headlines, health and nutrition problems in developing countries are far broader in scope and vastly more prevalent than what one sees in the headlines. Chapter 11 views health conditions broadly, covering the facts, the development effects, and the policy considerations. This material is presented in a nontechnical manner that students can easily follow. One exception is the analysis of income and substitution effects, which might confuse some students. The textbook simplifies this by forgoing the use of indifference curves.

The text touches on two other analytical points that can be expanded into lecture topics: national food balance sheets and the application of cost-effectiveness analysis to health and nutrition policy evaluation. You will find examples in the *Study Guide*.

Chapter 11 covers many provocative topics that you can discuss in class: the remarkable health progress achieved by most developing countries; how life expectancy is linked to infant mortality rates; the types of health problems prevalent in low-income countries (most of which will be unfamiliar to your students); the interaction between health care, environmental conditions, and nutrition; the concept of food entitlements; the disadvantages of food subsidies; and the gains that can be achieved through primary health care and preventative medicine. And, of course, famine. For up-to-date statistics, see the latest edition of the United Nation's *Human Development Report*.

Question Bank

Multiple-Choice Questions

1. What happened to the life expectancy at birth in developing countries between 1965 and 1992?

    * a. It increased substantially.
       b It increased very slightly.
       c. It fell.
       d. It increased sharply in middle-income countries, but fell slightly in low-income countries.

2. Health statistics on morbidity refer to the

       a. incidence of mental-health problems.
    * b. incidence of sickness.
       c. fraction of deaths caused by preventable disease.
       d. incidence of unnatural death due to accidents, crime, and war.

3. Even in countries where average calorie consumption exceeds the minimum requirements, one still finds widespread malnutrition because

       a. the statistics on calorie consumption don't adjust for food that is exported or wasted.
    * b. some people consume more than average, so others consume much less.
       c. malnutrition is caused primarily by vitamin deficiency, not calorie deficiency.
       d. all the above.

4. The case of Cuba under Castro is one in which

       a. the emigration of medical personnel caused the health status to decline for more than two decades.
       b. life expectancy remains abnormally low despite health-care facilities that are widely available.
       c. health care is excellent in urban areas, but poor in rural areas.
    * d. excellent health has widely shared due to the equitable distribution of health services, education, and basic necessities.

5. An increase in the price of a particular food creates an income effect in that it causes

    a. greater problems for the poor than for the rich.
    b. labor market adjustments that boost the equilibrium wage.
* c. a decline in the purchasing power of household incomes.
    d. increased earnings for farmers.

6. How is an increase in life expectancy likely to affect the rate of return to investments in education?

    a. Not at all, because the two issues are separate.
* b. The rate of return should increase because better health permits people to work longer.
    c. The rate of return should decline because the impact of education is spread over more years.
    d. The rate of return should increase for middle-aged people, but not for young people.

7. According to statistics, what happens to the quantity and the nutritional quality of food consumption as household incomes rise?

* a. Quantity and quality both improve.
    b. Quantity increases but quality deteriorates as people buy more junk foods.
    c. Quantity and quality stay roughly the same but people buy more expensive brands.
    d. Quantity changes little but quality improves.

8. Oral rehydration therapy (ORT) is a simple and inexpensive treatment that can prevent most deaths from

    a. drowning.
* b. diarrhea.
    c. malaria.
    d. roundworm parasites.

9. The World Health Organization (WHO) defines health as

    a. the absence of illness or disability that prevents one from engaging in normal functions.
    b. a condition of physical well-being, consistent with the standards of one's national culture.
* c. a state of complete physical, mental, and social well-being.
    d. the absence of a serious need for medical attention.

10. In developing countries, major gains in life expectancy have been achieved primarily by reducing mortality rates for what population group?

    a. The elderly
    b. Rural workers
* c. The very young
    d. Women of childbearing age

11. In countries with per capita GDP below $1,000 (PPP) in the early 1990s, public-sector expenditure on health care averaged

* a. about $12 per person per year.
    b. about $50 per person per year.
    c. under $1 per person per year.
    d. about $100 per person per year.

12. The textbook authors accept the idea of imposing user fees for medical services where

    a. there are large external benefits from improved health.
* b. the fees are imposed on curative services aimed at the rich.
    c. demand for medical care is inelastic.
    d. the fees are imposed on preventive care as well as curative care.

13. Sri Lanka is often cited as an outstanding example of good health despite low incomes. What were health conditions like in Sri Lanka at independence in 1948?

* a. Already unusually good compared with other Asian countries
    b. Among the worst in the world
    c. Not much better or worse than in most other low-income countries
    d. Quite good for the rich, but quite poor for everyone else

14. Compared to the economic returns on education, the returns to investment in health tend to be

    a. much higher.
    b. much lower.
    c. about the same, since investments in health and education equally affect the stock of human capital.
* d. more difficult to measure.

15. The main economic effect of trypanosomiasis (African sleeping sickness) is to

* a. prevent large areas of land from being used productively for raising livestock.
    b. sap labor productivity by making workers very lethargic.
    c. increase mortality rates among the elderly and the very young.
    d. make the water undrinkable.

16. Typhoid, dysentery, and cholera are leading examples of

* a. water-borne diseases.
    b. parasitic diseases transmitted by mosquito.
    c. diseases that cause long-term morbidity rather than mortality.
    d. diseases that have been eliminated through WHO programs.

17. Which nutrition factor is not tabulated in a national food balance sheet?

    a. Imported food supplies
    b. Food stock losses to rodents and spoilage
* c. The extent to which food supplies fail to reach the poor
    d. Food supplies distributed through public-sector programs rather than sold through the market

18. If a poor urban household spends 30 percent of its income on rice, a 20 percent increase in the retail price of rice amounts to a _____ percent cut in the household's purchasing power.

    a. 50
    b. 33
    c. 10
* d. 6

19. The goal of food security means making sure that

    * a. all people at all times have access to enough food to permit them to lead active, healthy lives.
       b. the country's food stockpile equals or exceeds one year's minimum nutritional requirements.
       c. people can get jobs that pay at least enough that they can afford adequate diets.
       d. the government is strong enough to quell disturbances that could disrupt food production and distribution.

20. Food price subsidy programs in developing countries are often not cost-effective because

    * a. the subsidies are not targeted to the poor.
       b. the subsidies do not lower the price enough to make much of a difference to consumers.
       c. poor families do not take price into account when buying food.
       d. providing more food to the poor has little effect on their health unless medical care improves at the same time.

IDs and Paired-Concept Questions

These terms can be used individually as short-answer identification questions, or they can be used in pairs. In the latter case, ask students to explain (1) the meaning and significance of each of the two terms and (2) the relationship between them.

1. Morbidity, parasitic conditions
2. Life expectancy, environmental health problems
3. National food balance sheet, calorie deficit
4. Protein-calorie malnutrition, food security
5. Income effect, substitution effect (of food prices)
6. Barefoot doctors, primary health care
7. Food quality, food supplementation
8. Cost-effectiveness, food price subsidy
9. User fees, preventive medicine
10. Famine, food entitlements

Study Guide **Applications**

Worked Example

The Worked Example illustrates how a national food balance sheet is constructed and explains some pitfalls in interpreting such aggregate data.

Exercises

1. Students complete a sample national food balance sheet and examine the nutritional problems that lurk behind the national averages.

2. Students analyze and interpret empirical relationships on health and nutrition using cross-section data for 23 low-income countries in 1992.

3. Students appraise a malaria control project, which typifies the difficulties faced in evaluating rates of return on health investments.

4. This exercise uses supply-and-demand analysis to demonstrate differences in the cost-effectiveness of two alternative policies to provide better nutrition for the poor.

CHAPTER 12   Capital and Saving

Chapter Outline

I. Even though capital fundamentalism is no longer the center of the development universe, saving and investment are still essential to income growth. The effective use of capital is equally important. The text illustrates this point with a numerical simulation of growth and investment using different ICOR values. The ICOR is related to factor intensity, which in turn is influenced by development strategy and factor prices. The empirical record shows that many developing countries had difficulty maintaining investment at 20 percent or more of GDP during the 1980s, even though some of the most rapidly growing countries achieved investment ratios above 30 percent.

II. The next section introduces the main components of total savings—government saving, private saving, and foreign saving; these complementary forms of finance will be considered in detail in the next three chapters. The degree of success in mobilizing domestic saving varies widely across countries. Early development economists thought that government saving would be the primary source of domestic saving. Though most countries have increased tax ratios over the past quarter century, the public sector's marginal propensity to consume has been high. As a result, the expansion of government saving has not been a significant source of development finance in most countries.

III. Given the importance of private saving, the text examines five theories of household behavior: the simple Keynesian absolute income hypothesis, the relative income hypothesis, the permanent-income hypothesis, the precautionary-saving hypothesis, and Nicholas Kaldor's class-savings hypothesis. Corporate saving is treated only briefly, since the corporate sector accounts for a small share of total income in most developing countries. The text points out, however, that noncorporate businesses may be the major source of private saving. In most countries' national accounts these enterprises are consolidated with the household sector.

IV. Finally, the chapter considers the short-run and long-run mobility of capital. International capital inflows provide foreign savings for development finance. But capital can also be mobile in the outward direction. In some countries stabilization problems have stimulated massive capital flight. Also, hostile investment climates lead to a long-run outflow of domestic savings. Attempts to control capital outflows are widely evaded. Although capital mobility is far from perfect, particularly in the short run, governments should not ignore these considerations when formulating policy.

In the New Edition. The only revision to this chapter (formerly Chapter 11) is that the numbers have been updated in both the text and the tables, generally to 1992.

Class Notes. Three fundamental ideas need to be driven home in lectures. First, growth is fostered not merely by achieving high investment rates, but also by keeping the ICOR low (meaning high investment productivity). Both of these growth factors are influenced by government policy. Second, the three components of savings—government, private and foreign—are central to the study of development finance. This taxonomy of saving forms the outline for the next three chapters. Third, international capital flows work both ways. Policies that ignore the outward mobility of capital can seriously erode the supply of finance for development, while supportive policies can attract net foreign financing to augment domestic resources and boost investment.

It is a good idea to keep the most recent *World Development Report* (*WDR*) handy to provide updated statistics for the class. Updates are particularly useful for savings rates, which are calculated as a residual and are notoriously volatile from year to year. Note that ICORs can be approximated using data from the World Development Indicators appendix to the *WDR*, using tables showing GDP growth and gross investment. Government saving can be estimated from the tables presenting government revenue, government expenditure, and government consumption. (The *WDR* data won't provide exact figures because some of the tabulations are for central government, while others are for general government; also some figures are given as percentages of GDP, others with respect to GNP.)

If time is short, you may be inclined to skip the theories of saving. Be aware, however, that the permanent-income hypothesis reappears a number of times in later chapters.

Question Bank

Multiple-Choice Questions

1. To achieve a growth rate of 5.0 percent per year, a country's investment ratio must equal _____ if the ICOR equals 3.0. If the ICOR were 4.0, an investment ratio of _____ would be required.

   a. 1.33 percent, 1.25 percent
   b. 2 percent, 1 percent
   c. 8 percent, 9 percent
 * d. 15 percent, 20 percent

2. A low-income country will have a higher ICOR if its

   * a. development strategy emphasizes capital-intensive production.
       b. development strategy emphasizes labor-intensive production.
       c. domestic saving rate is high.
       d. domestic saving rate is low.

3. Excluding China and India, low-income countries in 1992 had an average ratio of gross domestic investment to GDP of 17 percent, yet the gross domestic saving rate averaged 8 percent. This means that

       a. GDP was declining.
       b. there was enormous capital flight from these countries.
   * c. foreign savings provided the main source of development finance.
       d. the tax ratio averaged 9 percent for these countries.

4. Country X has a tax ratio equal to 20 percent. This means that total tax revenues are equal to 20 percent of

       a. total government expenditures.
       b. gross domestic savings.
   * c. GNP.
       d. the national debt.

5. According to the permanent-income hypothesis, the household saving rate will be higher the larger the fraction of income that is

       a. permanent.
   * b. transitory.
       c. taxed.
       d. consumed.

6. In most developing countries the main source of domestic savings growth has been from

       a. the savings of state enterprises.
       b. government budget savings.
       c. corporate savings.
   * d. household savings.

7. In a country that is experiencing a significant outward movement of capital, _____ will exceed _____.

  * a. gross domestic savings, gross domestic investment
  b. foreign savings, zero
  c. foreign savings, gross domestic savings
  d. household savings, government savings

8. The Keynesian absolute income hypothesis is inconsistent with the observed tendency of household saving rates to

  a. rise and fall with changes in disposable income.
  b. be much higher in rich countries than in poor countries.
  * c. be roughly constant over time within a given country.
  d. exceed government saving rates.

9. The data presented in the textbook show gross domestic saving rates for developing countries ranging from as low as ____ percent to as high as ____ percent in 1992.

  a. −10, +10
  * b. −1, +39
  c. 3, 20
  d. 20, 31

10. Private saving is not a function of per capita income only. Studies show that private saving rates also tend to be higher the greater the

  a. percentage of the population consisting of younger families.
  * b. percentage of incomes earned by rural households.
  c. rate of inflation.
  d. tax ratio.

11. Comparing the data for low-income and middle-income countries, one finds that, on average,

  a. low-income countries have a higher domestic saving rate.
  b. low-income countries have higher tax ratios.
  c. middle-income countries have higher ICORs.
  * d. middle-income countries depend much less on foreign savings.

12. The ICOR measures the

    a. additional income generated by one more unit of investment.
* b. additional capital needed to produce one more unit of output.
    c. ratio of investment to GDP.
    d. ratio of investment to GNP.

13. Country A has a lower ICOR and a lower investment ratio than country B. From this information we can conclude that

    a. GNP is growing faster in country A.
    b. GNP is growing faster in country B.
* c. either country could have the higher growth rate.
    d. country A is less dependent on foreign savings.

14. Using the notation of the text, which of the following is correct?

    a. $S = S_d + S_f$.
    b. $S = S_p + S_g + S_{fo} + S_{fp}$.
    c. $S = S_{ph} + S_{pc} + S_{gb} + S_{ge} + S_{fo} + S_{fpd} + S_{fpe}$.
* d. All the above.

15. Government budgetary saving is the difference between

* a. government revenues and government consumption expenditures.
    b. government revenues and government expenditures.
    c. government assets and government debts.
    d. the government deficit and government borrowing from abroad.

16. In developing countries over the past three decades, the percentage share of private consumption in GDP has

* a. fallen.
    b. risen.
    c. stayed constant at about 80 percent of GDP.
    d. stayed constant at about 60 percent of GDP.

17. The Keynesian absolute income hypothesis asserts that $S = a + bY$, where

    a. a is the marginal propensity to consume and Y is disposable income.
* b. b is the marginal propensity to save and Y is disposable income.
    c. a is the marginal propensity to consume and Y is permanent income.
    d. b is the marginal propensity to save and Y is permanent income.

18. James Duesenberry's relative income hypothesis relates current consumption to

    a. disposable income and the previous peak level of income.
* b. disposable income and the previous peak level of consumption.
    c. permanent income and last year's income.
    d. permanent income and last year's consumption.

19. Corporate saving in low-income countries makes up a small share of domestic savings because

    a. most businesses are not incorporated.
    b. many corporations are loss-making state-owned enterprises.
    c. the advantages of incorporation are small without enforceable property rights and reliable legal recourse.
* d. all the above.

20. The textbook cites a study showing that the real after-tax return to capital is close to 7.5 percent in both rich and poor countries. This is given as evidence that

    a. the before-tax rate of return on capital is higher in developing countries.
    b. governments can boost domestic investment by encouraging savings.
* c. capital is internationally mobile.
    d. constraints on capital mobility are effective.

IDs and Paired-Concept Questions

These terms can be used individually as short-answer identification questions, or they can be used in pairs. In the latter case, ask students to explain (1) the meaning and significance of each of the two terms and (2) the relationship between them.

1. Capital fundamentalism, investment ratio
2. Effective use of capital, ICOR
3. Foreign savings, private domestic savings
4. Government's marginal propensity to consume, tax ratio
5. Transitory income, class-savings hypothesis
6. Gross domestic investment, gross domestic savings
7. Government savings, budget deficit
8. Absolute income hypothesis, relative income hypothesis
9. Precautionary motives for saving, capital flight
10. International capital mobility, capital controls

Study Guide Applications

Worked Example

The Worked Example explains in detail the computations underlying textbook Table 12–2, which illustrates the interaction between investment, the ICOR, and GDP growth. The example also shows how to extend the projections.

Exercises

1. Students are led through an application of the methodology from the Worked Example, in the context of a five-year projection of investment and growth for country B from textbook Table 12–2.

2. This exercise investigates saving, investment, and growth relationships for a sample of 19 developing countries. Students must supply half the data from the textbook tables.

3. National accounts data for Thailand provide the raw material for calculating government and private savings and the marginal propensity to consume for each sector. The exercise also examines Thailand's tax ratio, the applicability of the Please effect, and sources of finance for investment.

4. Simple examples are given of the Keynesian absolute income hypothesis and the permanent income hypothesis to analyze household saving behavior.

CHAPTER 13   Fiscal Policy

Chapter Outline

I. Broadly defined, fiscal policy covers all aspects of government revenue and expenditure policy. This chapter looks at why government spending is needed and how governments finance their activities. One basic theme is the economic effects of fiscal policy, especially with respect to public saving, private saving, economic efficiency, and the distribution of income.

II. The free market fails to allocate resources efficiently to provide public goods. Such goods display two traits: nonrivalness (my consumption does not subtract from yours) and nonexclusion (it is impossible or prohibitively expensive to exclude nonpayers). Governments everywhere are involved in providing such goods, which include defense, primary education, mosquito spraying, and police protection. In addition, most countries have expanded the size of the public sector to pay for income redistribution, public owner-ship of productive enterprises, and other more debatable activities. Wagner's law asserts that the relative size of the public sector has an inherent tendency to grow as per capita income increases. The empirical evidence broadly supports this notion, as governments in wealthier countries are more likely to expand welfare and subsidy programs, especially for social security.

III. Is there much scope for poor countries to increase public saving by restraining expenditure? Spending on services and nondurable goods usually accounts for half of all recurrent expenditure, mostly for salaries. In most countries this category of spending is chronically underfunded. Indeed, in-sufficient spending for maintenance and repairs leads to unduly rapid decay of the public infrastructure, while inadequate wages for the civil service hamper the effectiveness of all government operations. Other major categories of recurrent expenditure are subsidies, intergovernmental transfers, interest pay-ments on debt, and often-costly payments to cover the deficits of state-owned enterprises. Only the last of these provides ready scope for significant com-pression of recurrent expenditures. Usually, when governments need to reduce spending for purposes of stabilization, it is capital outlays and subsidies intended to help the poor that are cut the most.

IV. If it is difficult to compress expenditures, perhaps governments can aug-ment public saving by increasing revenues. The obvious policy of imposing higher tax rates often produces little or no revenue because of economic sub-stitution effects and problems with tax evasion and corruption of tax officers. Other means of raising revenue include the introduction of new taxes and improvements in tax administration. In most countries tax administration is poor, so improvements could yield large revenue gains; but effective actions are very hard to implement. In recent years quite a number of developing countries have introduced fundamental tax reforms; typical components include widening the base of the personal income tax while lowering the top marginal rate, introducing a VAT-type sales tax, reducing the corporate tax rate while limiting tax holidays, and strengthening tax administration.

V. Taxes also affect the incentives for private saving. In this regard, consumption-based taxes are generally considered as more favorable than income-based taxes. Payroll taxes that fund a pay-as-you-go social security system typically reduce total domestic savings; this adverse effect can be avoided if social security operates on a provident fund basis. In a world of increasing capital mobility, high taxes on corporate profits encourage capital to move abroad.

VI. The fiscal system also has a major influence on the distribution of income. On the tax side, the personal income tax falls mainly on the top 20 percent of the income distribution; luxury excise taxes are also progressive. Surprisingly, the incidence of the corporate income tax may not fall on the rich, since capital owners have the option of exporting their capital to avoid the tax. Hence, the burden ultimately may fall on workers and consumers. Overall, tax policy may have only marginal effects on reducing income inequality, but tax policy can at least be designed to prevent taxes from making the poor worse off.

VII. Policies to assist the poor are often much more effective on the expenditure side of the budget, through spending on primary education, investments such as irrigation that increase the demand for rural labor, and subsidies that favor poorer households. Not all programs established under the banner of equity, however, actually serve such ends. In many instances, the nonpoor turn out to benefit more than the poor. In any case, policies on land tenure, factor pricing, and rural-urban terms of trade may be more potent than fiscal measures for promoting distributional goals.

VIII. The chapter concludes with a discussion of how tax policy affects economic efficiency. Taxes carry administrative costs, which are frequently high, and they also impose an excess burden by distorting market outcomes. An efficient tax system would minimize the excess burden, but this standard is costly and impractical to administer. Hence the text favors the principle of tax neutrality, whereby taxes are designed so as to create minimal distortions to relative prices. This entails relying on uniform tax rates that apply over a broad tax base.

In the New Edition. There are no major changes in this chapter (which used to be Chapter 12). Of course, all the tables and statistics have been updated. Beyond this, there are numerous minor revisions. These include a new table (Table 13–3) to highlight the problem of high military expenditures, an expansion of the section on subsidies, and a new boxed example on tax administration.

Boxed Examples. There are four boxed examples in Chapter 13. Two of them deal with Colombia. The first of these tells how a 100 percent duty on cigarettes produced widespread smuggling and little revenue; when the duty was reduced to 30 percent, tax revenues rose. The second discusses Colombia's ambitious and partly successful 1974 tax reform program, which aimed at improving growth, equity, stability, and efficiency in one package of reforms. A third boxed example reports on research that found that government expenditure on rice irrigation in Asia has had favorable equity effects, contrary to the prevailing opinion that such programs benefit primarily the larger and wealthier farmers. Finally, there is a new boxed example on tax administration in India and Bolivia in the 1980s. This mini-case study shows that there can be relatively enormous revenue losses due to poor tax administration, and corresponding revenue gains when governments take effective measures to simplify and improve tax administration.

Class Notes. Chapter 13 contains a formidable amount of material. The central themes are how government can raise budgetary savings and how the structure and level of taxes affect private saving and investment, income distribution, and economic efficiency. Nothing in the chapter is technical, except for the analysis of excess burden in the concluding section. But several other items are conceptually tricky enough to give students a hard time, including taxable capacity; how high tax rates can backfire and reduce revenue; how the tax structure affects private domestic savings, including the provision of pay-as-you-go social security; tax incidence; neutral versus efficient taxes; and even the basic notion of public goods.

If development finance is not a major focus of your course, you will probably want to be selective in covering this material, despite the fact that many of the topics are excellent examples of applied economics in action. With selective coverage it is important to tell students just what they are responsible for. However be sure to cover, even if briefly, the essential jargon to help them with the reading. Few things are more dismaying than finding out at exam time that many students don't know what "fiscal policy" means, even though it is the title of the chapter.

Question Bank

Multiple-Choice Questions

1. Which of the following policy instruments does not fall under the category of fiscal policy?

   * a. Interest rate controls
   b. Tax rates
   c. Tax structure
   d. Government subsidies

2. Government budget saving is defined as the excess of government _____ over government _____.

   a. revenues, debt
   b. total expenditures, revenues
   * c. revenues, recurrent expenditures
   d. capital expenditures, deficits

3. High tax rates often encourage taxpayers to engage in illegal maneuvers to avoid paying taxes. The term used for this behavior is

   a. revenue elasticity.
   b. tax avoidance.
   * c. tax evasion.
   d. excess burden.

4. An increase in tariff rates may cause tariff revenues to drop. Which of the following is *not* one of the reasons for this?

   a. Higher tariffs increase incentives for smuggling.
   * b. Higher tariffs encourage more government spending.
   c. Higher tariffs stimulate domestic production of the imported product.
   d. Higher tariff rates cause a decline in demand for the imported product.

5. The primary difference between excise and sales taxes is that only excise taxes are

   * a. imposed on specifically enumerated items.
   b. paid by the consumer rather than the seller.
   c. progressive.
   d. revenue elastic.

6. The text's case study of Colombia's 1974 tax reform program illustrates a situation in which comprehensive tax reform

   a. increased tax revenues, but only by sacrificing tax equity and efficiency.
   b. never reached implementation because of political resistance.
   c. totally failed to increase tax revenues.
   * d. was highly successful only in the short run.

7. Data on the ratio of government expenditures to GDP are consistent with Wagner's law: in 1992 the average percentage was ____ for low-income countries and ____ for high-income countries.

   a. 11 percent, 11 percent
   b. 30 percent, 28 percent
   * c. 17 percent, 32 percent
   d. 8 percent, 45 percent

8. Which of the following statements best captures the textbook's conclusions about using fiscal policy to promote equity in developing countries?

   a. Equity is not a proper goal for fiscal policy.
   * b. Economic and administrative realities limit the scope for achieving income redistribution through the tax system.
   c. Highly progressive taxes can and should be used to promote equity and efficiency simultaneously.
   d. Tax policy is far more effective than expenditure policy as an instrument for income redistribution.

9. A neutral tax system is one that

   a. generates no excess burden.
   b. affects government savings and private sector investment decisions equally.
   c. balances the government budget.
   * d. relies, as far as possible, on uniform tax rates.

10. Public goods are goods that

   a. are provided by government to prevent the private sector from charging too much.
   * b. are nonrival in consumption.
   c. should be paid for by charging fees.
   d. are mainly produced by state-owned enterprises.

11. Taxable capacity

  a. is measured by a country's tax ratio.
 * b. is positively related to the size of foreign trade relative to GNP.
  c. measures how successful a country is at raising taxes.
  d. all the above.

12. As GNP rises, which of the following revenue sources increase most rapidly?

  a. Taxes on international trade
  b. Profits of state-owned enterprises
 * c. Social security and payroll taxes
  d. Commodity taxes

13. As usually applied, the Value-Added Tax (VAT) is a

  a. form of excise tax.
  b. tax on income.
 * c. tax on consumption.
  d. tax on domestic production.

14. Heavy taxes on alcohol and tobacco are favored because

  a. they are progressive.
  b. they display a high price elasticity of demand.
 * c. most governments want to discourage consumption of these items.
  d. all the above.

15. Changes in tax administration can potentially increase total tax revenue in low-income countries because

  a. trained tax administrators are readily available.
  b. evasion is easy to detect.
  c. tax rates are very high.
 * d. income is widely underreported.

16. All the following are key ingredients of tax reform, *except*

  a. broadening the tax base.
  b. introducing a VAT form of the sales tax.
  c. lowering corporate income tax rates.
 * d. offering more tax holidays.

17. The VAT form of the sales tax is preferred in many developing countries because

   * a. a large share of VAT revenue is collected prior to the retail level.
     b. the VAT can be levied at a higher rate.
     c. firms have no way to suppress information on their purchases and sales.
     d. there is no need to conduct periodic audits to ensure compliance.

18. The introduction of a social security system will typically increase the national savings rate if

     a. it is organized on a pay-as-you-go basis.
   * b. it is set up on a provident fund basis.
     c. benefits are provided to the older citizens from the very beginning.
     d. it is paid for from general government funds.

19. The cost of a corporate income tax (CIT) will *not* fall on rich households if

   * a. capital is internationally mobile.
     b. capital is internationally immobile.
     c. there is a noncorporate sector that does not pay the CIT.
     d. the domestic CIT rate is below the CIT rate in the United States.

20. Which of the following is budgeted as a capital expenditure rather than a recurrent expenditure?

     a. Nurses' salaries
     b. Maintenance of public buildings
   * c. A road construction project
     d. Military land mines

IDs and Paired-Concept Questions

These terms can be used individually as short-answer identification questions, or they can be used in pairs. In the latter case, ask students to explain (1) the meaning and significance of each of the two terms and (2) the relationship between them.

1. Fiscal policy, financial policy
2. Tax ratio, taxable capacity
3. Tax rates, tax evasion
4. Import duty, excise tax

5. Public saving, recurrent expenditures
6. Consumption-based taxes, saving incentives
7. Tax haven, tax holiday
8. Tax incidence, progressive tax
9. Public good, Wagner's law
10. Tax neutrality, efficient tax system
11. Payroll tax, provident fund
12. VAT, sales taxes

Study Guide Applications

Worked Example

The Worked Example uses a hypothetical case study of tariff rates to analyze how higher tax rates can reduce tax revenues. The example involves both an elastic demand curve and a domestic supply response—what the text calls accidental protection.

Exercises

1. The first exercise lets students examine the issue of tax rates and tariff revenues in more detail. The exercise also compares the effects of a selective import duty with the effects of a corresponding excise that applies equally to imports and domestic supplies.

2. Students plot and analyze data relating to Wagner's law, tax ratios, and tax capacity.

3. Exercise 3 demonstrates the basic mechanics of a value-added tax and explains why the VAT has been a favored element in many tax reform programs.

4. Two excise tax examples are used for a graphical analysis of tax incidence, highlighting the role of price elasticity.

5. [*More difficult*] The graphs from Exercise 4 provide the raw material for an evaluation of the excess burden of an excise tax. The exercise demonstrates that equal tax rates do not assure equal excess burdens.

CHAPTER 14   Financial Policy

Chapter Outline

I. Financial policy in developing countries encompasses all measures intended to influence the size, structure, and operation of financial markets and the system of financial intermediaries. The financial system plays a key role in development by supplying financial assets (including money, variously defined), by mobilizing and allocating savings (financial intermediation), by distributing risk, and by providing monetary authorities with tools for managing economic stability. The ratio of broad money (M2) to GDP is a common measure of financial development.

II. The most obvious problem of financial policy in developing countries has been controlling inflation. The text distinguishes between chronic, acute and runaway (hyper-) inflation, and then reviews the sad history of high-inflation episodes over the past half century. Usually, the source of inflation can be traced to unmanageable government budget deficits.

III. Some economists argue that inflation can be beneficial, as it forces the mobilization of savings by effectively taxing money balances. Some also contend that inflation may be tolerable as a by-product of keeping aggregate demand buoyant to stimulate investment. Yet high inflation probably has the opposite effects. First, the inflation tax only augments domestic savings if the government has a higher marginal propensity to save than the private sector, which is improbable. In any case, inflation is a very distortionary form of tax. Second, high inflation is often associated with negative real interest rates. While the link between interest rates and savings is weak, there is no doubt that negative real interest rates strongly affect the *form* in which savings are held. In particular, negative real interest rates reduce the demand for liquid assets; this impedes monetization and financial intermediation. In addition, negative real interest rates mean that financial institutions must resort to nonprice rationing of funds. Finally, inflation interferes with price signals and adds to investment risks. On balance, high inflation almost certainly has an adverse effect on the level and efficiency of investment.

IV. Indeed, negative real interest rates is a hallmark of a shallow financial system. Shallow finance results from policies involving repressive interventions, which retard development of the financial system. In contrast, deep finance can be achieved by liberalizing financial markets and avoiding sharply negative real interest rates and rapid inflation. A deep finance strategy puts the financial system to work mobilizing and allocating savings. It also accelerates the development and efficiency of the financial system and helps reduce dependence on informal credit markets.

V. The final section examines the relationship between monetary policy and inflation. From the balance sheet for the banking system, one can derive the fact that money supply growth is determined by the expansion of domestic credit and changes in international reserves: $\Delta M \equiv \Delta DC + \Delta IR$. This shows that money supply expansion, and thus inflation, are linked to credit expansion for financing government deficits and private investments and to the balance of payments. The second term on the right-hand side of this identity implies that monetary policy is affected by the choice of exchange-rate regime. In a small open economy with a fixed exchange rate, the monetary authority must buy and sell international reserves to stabilize the foreign exchange market; but this means that it cannot independently control the money supply. Similarly, the need to finance large fiscal deficits may cause the central bank to lose control of money supply growth. To the extent that monetary authorities have an independent role in stabilization policy, they influence the volume and cost of credit by determining reserve requirements and the rediscount rate, by managing credit controls, and by using moral suasion to influence the banking system.

Boxed Examples. There are two boxed examples in Chapter 14. The first tells the sobering tale of Peru's destructive hyperinflation. By 1989, the inflation rate was up to 2000 percent, mainly because of huge government deficits. The inflation caused great hardships affecting daily life and brought the economy to a virtual standstill. The second boxed example describes successful schemes in Bangladesh (Grameen Bank) and Indonesia (Bank Rakyat Indonesia) to develop savings and credit institutions that serve the financial needs of very small-scale clients throughout the countryside.

In the New Edition. The second boxed example is new. All the data are updated, with concomitant revisions to the text. Other changes are largely editorial.

Class Notes. The importance of Chapter 14 stems from the fact that many developing countries have been dogged by high inflation. Even more have pursued poor policy with regard to developing financial markets. The essence of the chapter can be distilled into three points. First, the financial system plays a central role in mobilizing and allocating private domestic savings. Second, rapid inflation, negative real interest rates, and other repressive interventions damage the effectiveness and the growth of the financial system (shallow finance). Third, rapid inflation is driven by rapid money supply growth, which is attributable to large fiscal deficits, excessive expansion of credit, or rapid accumulation of foreign exchange reserves. Each of these points merits emphasis and explanation in class, though the degree of detail is your choice.

There are also three items of technical analysis: (1) the calculation of real interest rates, with and without income tax; (2) the determinants of demand for liquid assets; and (3) the sources of change in the money supply. Several other technicalities are introduced in footnotes. You may or may not want to deal with these: (4) calculation of the inflation tax; (5) the revenue elasticity of a tax system; and (6) the money multiplier. In addition, you can use simple supply-and-demand analysis to illustrate the adverse effects of interest rate controls and negative real interest rates. You can also use supply-and-demand analysis to show why interventions are needed in the market for foreign exchange in order to maintain a pegged exchange rate, and so to lead to endogeneity of the money supply in a fixed-rate regime.

Question Bank

Multiple-Choice Questions

1. Decisions on which of the following items would not be categorized as financial policy?

   a. Interest rate controls
   * b. The allocation of government capital expenditures
   c. Credit ceilings
   d. The growth rate of the money supply

2. Which of the following is not a liquid financial asset?

   a. Currency in circulation
   b. Time deposits
   c. Demand deposits
   * d. Foreign aid

3. During the period since 1950 the majority of developing countries have experienced

   a. chronic inflation.
   b. acute inflation.
   c. runaway inflation.
   * d. none of the above.

4. In 1992 the inflation rate in Nigeria was 65 percent, while the nominal interest rate on time deposits averaged 8 percent. What was the real interest rate on deposits?

   a. −57 percent
 * b. −35 percent
   c. +73 percent
   d. −86 percent

5. Evidence clearly shows that a period of sharply negative real interest rates will cause

   a. private domestic savings to drop to zero.
 * b. the growth of financial intermediaries to slow or even turn negative.
   c. a major boom in domestic investment.
   d. gross domestic savings to become negative.

6. Which of the following is essential to a strategy of deep finance?

   a. Avoiding a government budget deficit
   b. Maintaining very high real interest rates
 * c. Avoiding strongly negative real interest rates
   d. All the above

7. What is the basic contribution of a healthy and competitive financial system to the development process?

 * a. Mobilizing private domestic savings and channeling the funds to productive investments
   b. Financing the government budget deficit
   c. Allowing business to escape the grips of traditional moneylenders
   d. Providing a large base for the inflation tax to operate on

8. Under a system of fixed exchange rates, a large increase in export revenues (without a corresponding jump in imports) has what effect on the domestic money supply?

 * a. The money supply will increase.
   b. The money supply will decline.
   c. The money supply will not be affected.
   d. The answer depends on whether the central bank has imposed credit controls on the commercial banks.

9. A monetary policy instrument that is used far more widely in low-income countries than in high-income countries is

   a. reserve requirements.
   b. open market operations.
* c. interest rate controls.
   d. tariff rates.

10. Which of the following terms refers to the fraction of economic activity transacted using money?

   a. Medium of exchange
   b. Exchange rate
* c. Monetization ratio
   d. Demand for liquid financial assets

11. An inflation tax is imposed when

   a. inflation leads to higher income taxes by pushing people into higher tax brackets.
   b. inflation boosts government sales tax revenue as a result of higher prices for goods and services.
* c. holders of money lose purchasing power.
   d. governments are compelled to increase tax rates to reduce the deficit and end the inflation.

12. Defined precisely, the real interest rate is

   a. $i - p$.
   b. $i - E(p)$.
* c. $(1 + i)/[1 + E(p)] - 1$.
   d. $[i(1 - t) + p]/(1 + p)$.

where i is the nominal interest rate, p is the inflation rate, $E(p)$ is the expected rate of inflation, and t is the tax rate on interest.

13. Which of the following is *not* a major function of the financial system?

   a. Supplying money to facilitate payments and transactions
* b. Collecting taxes to finance government expenditures
   c. Mobilizing domestic savings
   d. Distributing risks through pooling and diversification

14. The ratio of broad money (M2) to GDP

    a. is smaller than the ratio of narrow money M1 to GDP.
 * b. is below 50 percent in most low-income countries.
    c. tends to rise under conditions of shallow finance.
    d. is higher in countries where real interest rates are low.

15. Total liquid assets (M3) include all the following *except*

    a. time deposits.
 * b. holdings of gold.
    c. cash on hand.
    d. checking deposits.

16. Countries with a tradition of high inflation tend to have

 * a. a low financialization ratio.
    b. a high monetization ratio.
    c. small government budgetary deficits.
    d. a slow expansion of domestic credit and international reserves.

17. What is the real interest rate, net of income tax, if the tax rate on interest is 20 percent, expected inflation is 15 percent, and the nominal interest rate is 26.5 percent?

    a. 10.0 percent
    b. 11.5 percent
 * c. 5.4 percent
    d. 14.5 percent

18. The demand for broad money (M2) is negatively related to

    a. real income.
    b. the real interest rate on savings and time deposits.
 * c. the real return on nonfinancial assets.
    d. the soundness of the banking system.

19. Nominal interest rate ceilings accompanied by rapid inflation hurt economic growth for all but one of the following reasons. Which is the exception?

   * a. Low real interest rates discourage investment demand.
   b. Banks ration credit to safe and well-connected firms rather than to projects with a higher social rate of return.
   c. Banks avoid taking risks because they cannot charge a risk premium.
   d. Banks lend less to small firms, even when the returns on such loans are high.

20. The central bank can most easily control the money supply in a country with a

   a. fixed exchange rate regime and no government deficit.
   * b. floating exchange rate regime and no government deficit.
   c. fixed exchange rate regime and a large government deficit.
   d. floating exchange rate regime and a large government deficit.

IDs and Paired-Concept Questions

These terms can be used individually as short-answer identification questions, or they can be used in pairs. In the latter case, ask students to explain (1) the meaning and significance of each of the two terms and (2) the relationship between them.

1. Medium of exchange, M2
2. Commercial banks, financial intermediation
3. Hyperinflation, government budget deficit
4. Inflation tax, forced savings
5. Shallow finance, informal credit market
6. Financial assets, nonfinancial assets
7. Real interest rate, deep finance
8. Interest elasticity of savings, interest elasticity of demand for liquid assets
9. Pegged exchange rate, floating exchange rate
10. Open-market operations, moral suasion
11. International reserves, imported inflation
12. Domestic credit expansion, credit ceilings

Study Guide Applications

Worked Example

The Worked Example illustrates the calculation of real interest rates on financial assets, with and without income taxes, and the rate of the inflation tax on money balances.

Exercises

1. The first exercise gives students a shot at calculating real interest rates and inflation tax rates using data on nominal interest rates and inflation for five developing countries.

2. The exercise uses a two-family graphical example to illustrate the efficiency gains from financial intermediation and the efficiency costs of shallow finance.

3. A simple numerical problem demonstrates the relationship between the rate of growth of the money supply and the rate of inflation.

4. The problem set up in Exercise 3 is extended to explore determinants of the rate of growth of the money supply, with emphasis on the role of the government budget deficit.

5. The fifth exercise lets students examine the relationship between real interest rates and private saving rates by plotting data for 14 developing countries; the link between real interest rates and financial deepening (as measured by the growth of M2/GDP) is also assessed using historical data for Indonesia.

6. The final exercise uses basic principles of supply and demand to show how efforts to peg the exchange rate lead to changes in international reserves and endogenous changes in the money supply.

CHAPTER 15   Foreign Capital and Debt

Chapter Outline

I. Investment may be financed by domestic or foreign savings; Chapter 15 examines the latter, focusing in turn on the three main components—foreign aid, foreign direct investment, and commercial borrowing. The chapter opens with an explanation of basic terminology and a review of recent trends in the flow of foreign savings to developing countries. The net resource flow totaled $157 billion in 1992, or 3.3 percent of GDP, for these countries; this was down from 4 percent of GDP in 1970, despite the fact that the net resource flow more than doubled over this time period in constant-dollar terms. Of the total flow in 1992, 35 percent was official development assistance (ODA), 30 percent was foreign direct investment (FDI), and 35 percent came in other forms including 12 percent in commercial bank loans.

II. The post-World War II evolution of foreign aid is surveyed, with attention to the rationale for aid, donor goals, and patterns of aid flows. Smaller and poorer countries get proportionally larger amounts of concessional aid. The text reviews the main multilateral and bilateral aid agencies and the various forms in which aid is packaged. The substantive part of the discussion is the impact of aid on development. This is analyzed using the Harrod-Domar model and neoclassical sources-of-growth model; the discussion then emphasizes the scope for substitution effects (fungibility). Ultimately, aid can foster development by providing resources for investment or consumption, by providing technical assistance, by pushing countries to change their policies as a condition for obtaining funds, and by supporting an establishment of specialists whose thinking about economic development gradually influences practice.

III. Foreign Direct Investment (FDI) has generated considerable controversy because it involves foreign management of productive enterprises. FDI typically provides a package that includes equity finance, management skills, technology, and access to world markets. The review of the empirical record and institutional characteristics of multinational corporation (MNC) operations challenges some common misconceptions, such as the belief that MNC investments are mostly for manufacturing that takes advantage of cheap labor. The effect of MNC operations depends greatly on policies adopted by the host countries, including performance requirements, trade protection, and incentives such as tax holidays. The text emphasizes that granting MNCs protection from competition and tax holidays often results in large benefits to foreigners and few to the host country. However the text's basic point is that foreign direct investment can be of benefit to the host countries, especially with suitable policies to maximize positive effects.

IV. Commercial bank borrowing has declined in relative importance since the debt crisis, which is a focus of the final section. Between 1970 and 1983 commercial bank lending to developing countries tripled in real terms. Several countries overborrowed and were unable to service their loans when interest rates rose and world economies slid into a deep recession. To a large extent, though, the crisis can be traced to poor policies on the part of debtor-country governments. Many countries mismanaged their macroeconomic balances and used borrowed funds unproductively. The text analyzes the conditions for sustainable borrowing in the framework of a two-gap model. It considers several means that have been used to alleviate the debt burden, including interest capitalization, rescheduling, buybacks, and debt-equity swaps. Countries which suffered from the debt crisis typically needed to undertake large adjustments for macroeconomic stabilization and structural adjustment.

In the New Edition. Apart from the usual updating of data, the main change is that the section on commercial borrowing declares that the debt crisis has passed. In the section on FDI, an entire subsection on MNC objectives has been dropped. Other parts of the chapter have also been trimmed. For example, what formerly were Tables 14–5, 14–6 and 14–8 are gone. In addition, the data updates entail some notable changes of substance, such as the strong rise in FDI flows in recent years. Not much is said about portfolio flows, however.

Boxed Example. There is one boxed example, which sketches the origins and aftermath of Mexico's debt crisis. It notes that the Mexican economy grew faster during the 17 years prior to the 1973 oil boom than it did after oil prices soared. Adjustment in the 1980s was slow and painful, as per capita income and real wages fell and inflation accelerated. By the early 1990s Mexico had succeeded in achieving a strong recovery. (The case study ends prior to the 1994–95 crisis that was brought on by misalignment of the exchange rate and overreliance on short-term capital flows to cover a large savings-investment gap.)

Class Notes. Chapter 15 deals with important links between developing and developed countries. The subject matter has also been a source of controversy. Moreover, many students have an intrinsic interest in financial markets. For all these reasons, this is enjoyable material to present in class. The fundamental story is that foreign savings in any form can benefit the recipient host country if it manages the resources and its economic policies prudently. Each form of foreign capital flow, however, has distinct advantages and disadvantages that you may probe with varying degrees of depth and emphasis.

Three topics are technical: a graphical treatment of foreign aid fungibility, the graph showing how developing countries can be disadvantaged by offering MNCs tax holidays and monopoly rights; and the formal treatment of conditions for sustainable foreign borrowing, with reference to both the trade gap and the savings-investment gap. These are important parts of the story and are also fine examples of applied economics.

While the chapter mentions the need for macroeconomic stabilization and structural adjustment for countries with a debt crisis, it does not treat this subject in much detail. For relatively advanced classes this might be the right point at which to introduce the more rigorous analysis of Chapter 20.

The discussion in Chapter 15 pays virtually no attention to "dependency theory" points of view. You may want to augment the text's analysis of aid, MNCs, and debt with more discussion of leftist critiques.

Question Bank

Multiple-Choice Questions

1. During the late 1980s and early 1990s the component of foreign savings that grew most rapidly was

   a. official development assistance.
   b. export credits.
   * c. foreign direct investment.
   d. commercial bank lending.

2. In countries most heavily dependent on foreign savings, such as Ethiopia, Tanzania, and Mali, official development assistance amounted to what percentage of GDP in 1991?

   a. 1 to 2 percent.
   b. 4 to 6 percent.
   c. 10 to 12 percent.
   * d. Over 15 percent.

3. In the late 1960s and early 1970s foreign aid donors became increasingly concerned with

   * a. goals such as poverty alleviation, basic human needs, and rural development.
   b. using the Harrod-Domar model to evaluate the economic effects of aid projects.
   c. using aid to build basic infrastructure such as dams and port facilities.
   d. environmental degradation.

4. What is the International Development Association (IDA)?

    a. A group of major bilateral donor countries who meet to coordinate aid programs
    b. The U.S. government agency responsible for administering foreign aid programs
* c. The World Bank affiliate that dispenses soft loans to the poorest developing countries
    d. An organization of Third-World countries that deals with problems relating to aid, debt, and foreign investment

5. Foreign savings is

* a. the amount by which investment exceeds domestic savings.
    b. the amount by which exports exceed imports.
    c. the total of foreign aid.
    d. all the above.

6. Suppose that in the absence of foreign savings a country would save 16 percent of GDP. Considering substitution effects, an inflow of foreign aid equal to 4 percent of GDP is likely to cause this country's total savings to

    a. drop below 16 percent of GDP.
* b. increase to a level between 16 and 20 percent of GDP.
    c. increase to a level somewhat above 20 percent of GDP.
    d. increase to 20 percent of GDP.

7. Foreign private savings includes all the following *except*

    a. foreign direct investment.
    b. portfolio investment.
    c. commercial bank lending.
* d. official development assistance.

8. The net resource flow to a developing country (i.e., net foreign savings) is given by

   a. imports of goods *less* exports of goods.
   b. imports of goods and nonfactor services *less* exports of goods and nonfactor services.
   * c. imports of goods and all services *less* exports of goods and all services, including income payments for factor services.
   d. c *plus* repayments of principal on debt.

9. Many studies conclude that income tax holidays to attract foreign direct investment are bad policy because

   * a. the incentives cost a lot and mostly go for investments that would have taken place anyway.
   b. developing countries are better-off without the multinationals.
   c. multinational investments are much more capital intensive than comparable investments by local companies.
   d. all the above.

10. The textbook states that foreign borrowing is consistent with development when

    * a. the additional investment and imports are put to productive use.
    b. it increases total imports.
    c. it increases total savings.
    d. a country can afford the debt service payments.

11. Which of the following was not a significant factor contributing to the debt crisis in the early 1980s?

    * a. A rapid decline in interest rates
    b. A sharp decline in the availability of new bank loans
    c. A decline in export earnings due to a deep recession in the industrial economies
    d. Failure by developing countries to channel prior commercial credits into productive investments

12. If foreign savings equal $5 billion, then a country's gross domestic
    _____ can exceed gross domestic _____ by $5 billion.

    a. savings, investment
* b. investment, savings
    c. consumption, savings
    d. investment, consumption

13. Which of the following is true?

    a. In 1992 official development assistance (ODA) accounted for just over half the net resource flow to developing countries.
    b. In 1992 bank lending was a larger percentage of the net resource flow to developing countries than in the 1970s.
* c. Foreign direct investment accounted for about 30 percent of net resource flows in 1992.
    d. The net resource flow amounts to about 1 percent of GDP for developing countries, overall, in 1992.

14. As a fraction of GNP, developing countries tend to get most ODA if they are

    a. large.
* b. poor.
    c. former British colonies.
    d. in Latin America.

15. Which of the following organizations makes equity investments in private corporations in developing countries?

    a. UNDP
    b. IDA
* c. IFC
    d. IMF

16. Suppose that aid amounts to 5 percent of GDP, the average capital-output ratio is 2.5, and capital's share of GDP is 40 percent. Then if all the aid is used for extra investment, GDP should rise by about

    a. 0.5 percent.
* b. 0.8 percent.
    c. 1 percent.
    d. 5 percent.

17. The package provided by multinational corporations includes all the following *except*

    a. equity finance.
    b. access to world markets.
    c. management expertise.
 * d. soft loans.

18. Which of the following statements is true?

    a. MNCs have created over 10 percent of the jobs in most developing countries.
    b. MNCs transfer technology at low cost because they have already earned a return on their research and development expenditures.
 * c. Developing countries have increasingly sought to unbundle the MNC package of equity, management, technology, and marketing.
    d. MNCs from developing countries are more likely to be in resource sectors than in manufacturing.

19. Which of the following countries devotes the *smallest* share of its GNP to foreign aid (official development assistance)?

    a. Canada
    b. France
    c. Japan
 * d. United States

20. A country has a foreign debt of $30 billion at an average interest rate of 5 percent; its imports are $5 billion and its exports are $4 billion. To cover the foreign exchange gap, this country's debt must

 * a. rise by $2.5 billion per year.
    b. fall by $0.5 billion per year.
    c. fall by $2.5 billion per year.
    d. fall by 25 percent per year.

IDs and Paired-Concept Questions

These terms can be used individually as short-answer identification questions, or they can be used in pairs. In the latter case, ask students to explain (1) the meaning and significance of each of the two terms and (2) the relationship between them.

1. Foreign private savings, foreign direct investment
2. Multilateral aid, World Bank
3. Official Development Assistance, soft loan
4. Commercial bank lending, IFC
5. Aid conditionality, aid fungibility
6. Net resource flow, gross resource flow
7. Multinational investment package, unbundling
8. MNC performance requirements, joint ventures
9. Savings-investment gap, foreign exchange gap
10. Capitalization of interest, rescheduling of principal
11. Portfolio investment, export credits
12. Debt service ratio, sovereign debt

Study Guide Applications

Worked Example

Nigeria had to reschedule its foreign debt in the 1980s whereas Indonesia did not. The Worked Example seeks to explain the difference by analyzing macroeconomic data relating to the external shocks facing the two countries and the internal policies each pursued. The analysis shows that Nigeria maintained an overvalued exchange rate, failed to encourage agriculture, and developed a shallow financial system which contributed to a lower saving rate and higher ICOR.

Exercises

1. The first exercise probes in greater depth the comparison between Indonesia and Nigeria, using data from the Worked Example.

2. This exercise analyzes the economic impact of foreign aid, initially with the simple Harrod-Domar equation. Then substitution effects are introduced using a graphical analysis of the production possibilities frontier and social indifference curves.

3. Students analyze information on foreign aid, foreign direct investment, and overall foreign savings to test the validity of statements in the text that:

    Large countries receive proportionately less aid than small countries.

    Poor countries receive proportionately more aid than rich countries.

    Foreign Direct Investment increases with per capita income.

    Countries which suffered from heavy debt loads in the 1980s were compelled by a reduction in net resource flows to undertake major macroeconomic adjustments.

4. Students do calculations applying the debt dynamics equations from the text, using data from four heavily indebted developing countries.

5. The last exercise works through the impact of foreign aid on economic growth using a neoclassical sources-of-growth model. This elaborates on the calculation that is discussed at length in the text but only covered formally in footnote 6.

CHAPTER 16   Agriculture

Chapter Outline

I. Chapter 16 focuses on agricultural production. After an introductory summary of the sector's special characteristics, the first section of the chapter examines the multifaceted role of agriculture in economic development. Agriculture makes key contributions in relation to welfare, nutrition, urbanization, labor, capital, foreign exchange, and demand. The text also considers whether food self-sufficiency is an appropriate policy objective, in view of the fact that world supplies of food for export have been expanding.

II. The second section deals with land tenure and property rights. The section begins by describing how various tenure arrangements influence welfare, political stability, incentives, and efficiency. One notable issue is how free rider problems arise under collective tenure. Covered next are land reform measures, ranging from modifying rent contracts to expropriating land. The text probes political motives for land reform, along with the mixed record of land reform in terms of its effects on productivity and equity.

III. The third section surveys production technologies, beginning with the evolution of traditional agriculture. The text emphasizes that traditional cultivation practices were efficient adaptations to available technologies and inputs. The distinctive character of modern agriculture lies in the pace of change and the scientific basis for progress. Agricultural research must be specific to local growing conditions and factor endowments. Technological innovations include both *mechanical packages* and *biological packages* (Green Revolution). The latter is a primary source of higher yields, whereas the former serves to release labor from agriculture over the course of development. The book uses isoquant analysis to describe features of both packages.

IV. In addition to agronomic research, increased agricultural production also depends on mobilizing labor and capital and on disseminating the new technologies. Accordingly, the next section surveys issues relating to rural public works projects, rural financial markets, agricultural extension services, and the development of markets and transport systems.

V. The chapter ends with an analysis of agricultural pricing policies. This section emphasizes that price effects on food production and real incomes can be rapid and profound. Depending on the policies pursued, these effects can be positive or negative. Food price subsidies, marketing subsidies, fertilizer subsidies, and the effects of an overvalued exchange rate are all examined using basic microeconomic tools.

Boxed Example. There is one case study on labor mobilization in Chinese communes, which exemplify work-reward problems in agriculture.

In the New Edition. This chapter is virtually unchanged. Apart from updating the data, the one substantive revision is repeated emphasis on the importance of exclusive, secure, enforceable, and transferable property rights.

Class Notes. There are four essential elements to the story conveyed in Chapter 16: (1) agriculture is a pivotal sector in the development process; (2) institutional conditions such as land tenure arrangements, credit institutions, and marketing channels have a powerful influence on productivity and growth in this sector; (3) agriculture is a dynamic sector with special technological characteristics; and (4) pricing policies have a profound impact on agriculture. By highlighting these ideas, your lectures can help students grasp the basic lessons.

   Much of the detail in this chapter is simple enough not to require elaborate explanation in class. So you can select a few issues to probe, according to taste. My preference is to place highest priority on the economics of pricing policies, and in particular the analysis of how (and why) many developing countries adopted policies that discriminated against agriculture. This topic provides an interesting application of economic tools. I also enjoy discussing what the Green Revolution is all about, how efficient adaptations to factor endowments can lead to great differences in land and labor productivity, and how land tenure arrangements influence incentives. For stimulating class discussions, ask students about their opinions on agricultural self-sufficiency, land reform, and the role of middle traders!

Question Bank

Multiple-Choice Questions

1. It's a fact that world food production

* a. is not even remotely close to the world's biological production capacity.
   b. is failing to keep pace with world population growth.
   c. has kept pace with population growth, but only with increasingly high real prices for food in the world market.
   d. has been declining steadily due to the depletion of soil nutrients and diversion of land to nonfarm uses.

2. The system of land tenure in which tenant farmers pay a fixed share of their crop to landowners is called

    a. communal farming.
* b. sharecropping.
    c. peasant farming.
    d. latifundia.

3. Most of the successful cases of land reform have involved

* a. little or no compensation to landlords for confiscated assets.
    b. full compensation to landlords for confiscated assets.
    c. consolidation of small farms into large collective farms.
    d. strict enforcement of short-term land rental contracts.

4. The term Green Revolution refers to

    a. the growing international awareness of ecological problems in agriculture.
    b. farm mechanization to release labor from agriculture.
* c. the use of improved seed varieties that dramatically increase farm yields.
    d. political changes that lead to fundamental land tenure reforms.

5. The three basic components of a biological package are use of improved plant varieties, application of _____, and timely supply of _____.

    a. credit cooperatives, tractors
* b. chemical fertilizers, water
    c. land reform, education
    d. subsidies, labor

6. The large margin between farm product prices in the city and the prices paid to farmers results generally from

    a. monopoly power on the part of rural traders.
* b. high marketing costs due to undeveloped transport networks and distribution systems.
    c. high levels of illiteracy among farmers.
    d. the lack of agricultural extension systems.

7. Study after study has found that when crop prices change, peasant farmers

  a. revert to subsistence production to avoid risk.
  b. are too tradition-bound to alter production decisions.
  c. are unaffected, since they produce only for their own consumption.
* d. alter production decisions in much the same way as would any other businessperson.

8. In many of the poorer developing countries 60 to 70 percent or more of the labor force works in agriculture, compared to _____ in developed economies.

* a. less than 10 percent
  b. 10 to 20 percent
  c. 20 to 30 percent
  d. 30 to 40 percent

9. An essential objective of agricultural development is to

  a. eliminate any need for food imports.
* b. release labor for use in the modern sector.
  c. serve as the primary source of domestic savings.
  d. maximize output per unit of land.

10. The free-rider problem tends to arise in agriculture when

  a. governments heavily subsidize transportation of grain to the market.
  b. farm workers are paid on a piece-rate basis.
  c. there is surplus labor in rural areas.
* d. land is owned as a common resource.

11. In which country did the upper-income ruling class use land reform to keep rural unrest from blowing up into a violent revolution?

  a. China after 1949
  b. Japan after World War II
  c. United States during the Great Depression
* d. Mexico after 1911

12. The basic difference between traditional and modern agriculture is that

     a. yields per unit of land were always lower using traditional farm methods.
     b. traditional farming involved less response to price changes.
*   c. the pace of change in modern agriculture is more rapid and is based on scientific research.
     d. all the above.

13. The biological package of agricultural technology refers to raising yields through using

*   a. improved plant varieties such as hybrid corn.
     b. greenhouse germination to shorten the time to harvest.
     c. contour plowing.
     d. biological defenses against insect pests.

14. Rice yields per acre are far higher in Japan than in the United States. This difference reflects the fact that Japanese rice farmers

     a. are far more efficient.
     b. are more mechanized.
*   c. face a higher price of land relative to capital and labor.
     d. have access to better technology.

15. Institutions like IRRI in the Philippines and CIMMYT in Mexico make major contributions to agricultural development by

*   a. developing new varieties of rice and maize.
     b. financing rural transport systems.
     c. extending credit to small farmers.
     d. serving farmers as agricultural marketing agents.

16. The use of modern high-yielding varieties of wheat and rice in developing countries

     a. is still confined largely to experimental farms.
     b. is rarely seen among small farmers who need help the most.
*   c. expanded swiftly over the past two decades.
     d. requires heavily mechanized farming techniques.

17. In a country with low wages due to an abundance of labor relative to capital, efficient agriculture is characterized by

   * a. labor-intensive farming techniques.
     b. highly mechanized farming techniques.
     c. production of food rather than export cash crops.
     d. collectivized farming.

18. Where has food production per capita declined since 1980?

     a. Worldwide, with scattered exceptions
     b. Only in a few scattered locations
   * c. In much of Africa
     d. In most developing countries, but not in the industrialized economies

19. One clear lesson from experience in Chinese communes is that

   * a. incentive and managerial problems become more serious the larger the collective unit.
     b. the free-rider problem makes it all but impossible to mobilize labor voluntarily for rural public works projects.
     c. increased food production requires providing farmers with access to credit.
     d. farmers work best when they share equally from the harvest.

20. Which of the following statements is an appropriate summary of the textbook's conclusions about agricultural policy?

     a. Because agriculture is so tradition bound, policies to promote this sector have little impact.
     b. To hasten structural change, policies promoting farm mechanization should have highest priority.
   * c. Agricultural pricing policies have a profound effect on both farm production and standards of living.
     d. Dramatic increases in agricultural production can best be achieved with an overvalued exchange rate and government control of marketing channels.

IDs and Paired-Concept Questions

These terms can be used individually as short-answer identification questions, or they can be used in pairs. In the latter case, ask students to explain (1) the meaning and significance of each of the two terms and (2) the relationship between them.

1. Food self-sufficiency, Green Revolution
2. Sharecropping, land reform
3. Communal farming, free-rider problem
4. Slash-and-burn cultivation, shortening of fallow
5. Mechanical package, biological package
6. IRRI, extension services
7. Farm profit maximization, price of fertilizer
8. Food subsidies, overvalued exchange rate
9. Moneylenders, credit cooperatives
10. Marketing boards, middle traders
11. Economies of scale, transport costs
12. Pricing policies, chemical fertilizer

Study Guide Applications

Worked Example

The Worked Example uses data for a hypothetical production function relating rice output to fertilizer and labor inputs, to illustrate the microeconomic analysis of the farm production decision.

Exercises

1. The student works through numerical variations on the Worked Example to see how changes in the price of rice and the price of fertilizer alter the farm production decision.

2. This exercise extends the analysis of the farmer's decision problem to show the effects of technical change and of risk.

3. One last variation on the Worked Example investigates how different land tenure arrangements affect farmers' production decisions.

4. Supply and demand curves for grain are used to analyze the economic effects of food subsidy policies.

5. The last exercise applies isoquant analysis to show how factor proportions and factor productivity levels in agriculture depend on relative factor prices.

CHAPTER 17   Primary Exports

Chapter Outline

I. This important chapter opens with an explanation of comparative advantage, and then focuses on the role of primary product exports in economic development. The gains from trade are illustrated with a simple numerical example, and then shown in general equilibrium terms using the production possibilities frontier. This analysis establishes that the potential to gain from trade depends simply on having relative world prices differ from those that would prevail domestically in the absence of trade. Even though all countries can gain from trade, opposition may arise from groups whose interests are hurt by trade, such as consumers of export goods and producers of import-competing goods.

II. A brief empirical review shows that the ratio of exports to GDP tends to rise with per capita income, with considerable cross-section variance depending on size, resource endowments, and government policies. The export earnings of many developing countries are dominated by a handful of primary products.

III. Primary product trade can serve as an effective "engine of growth" when it puts to productive use resources that would otherwise be idle or underutilized ("vent for surplus"). More broadly, primary exports can also expand factor endowments by attracting capital and labor and by increasing domestic savings. Finally, primary exports can create backward and forward linkages, as well as consumption and fiscal linkages.

IV. It is widely believed, though, that world trade barriers impede development based on primary exports. These barriers include sluggish growth of world demand, declining terms of trade, and instability of markets for primary products. In addition, some primary exports involve enclave production that limits favorable linkage effects. The facts bear out the claim that demand for primary products, overall, grows more slowly than total world trade; nonetheless, some countries have had great success in using primary exports as a stepping stone to development. A review of long-term evidence on the terms of trade for primary exporters concludes that the pessimistic views of Paul Prebisch and Hans W. Singer are not confirmed; in this context, three different measures of the terms of trade are introduced. The analysis of export instability explains that volatile incomes may increase saving rates, according to the permanent-income hypothesis. Yet a positive effect on savings may not translate into higher growth, since instability tends to reduce the efficiency of investments (the *signaling* effect). The empirical evidence supports these hypotheses.

V. Over the past three decades, numerous arrangements have appeared on the world stage to support the markets for primary exports. These include international commodity agreements, buffer stock funds, producer cartels, and funds to stabilize export earnings. The text evaluates these arrangements carefully, pointing out analytical and pragmatic problems.

VI. The most serious problem facing primary exporters may, ironically, be the after effects of a commodity boom that triggers the syndrome known as Dutch disease. The problem is that a commodity boom tends to appreciate the real exchange rate, with adverse consequences for other producers of tradables. Also, the foreign exchange inflows and fiscal revenues stemming from a commodity boom often get monetized, and so lead to inflation. Some primary exporters, like Nigeria, may find that they would have been better-off without the boom. Yet some countries, like Indonesia, have avoided the syndrome through prudent management of the exchange rate, combined with conservative monetary and fiscal policies.

Boxed Examples. There are four case studies in Chapter 17. The first is a review of Malaysia's successful experience with primary-export-led growth; starting from a heavy dependency on rubber and tin, Malaysia converted its primary export revenues into a diversified export base and strong, sustained economic growth. The second case study reports on Ghana's tragic failure to exploit its resource potential, prior to a reversal of its import-substitution policies in the mid 1980s. The last two cases contrast Nigeria's severe case of Dutch disease with Indonesia's success in coping with the same oil boom in the 1970s.

In the New Edition. In the process of bringing the empirical record up to date, the new edition modifies the conclusion on export instability. The text previously cited empirical evidence indicating that export instability is positively correlated with investment and growth. New evidence shows that export instability tends to enhance saving rates but not growth rates, because instability may reduce the efficiency of investment by creating uncertainty about relative-price signals. Note, too, that references to the New International Economic Order and the Common Fund for buffer-stocks have been dropped.

Class Notes. Many students will need help to understand Figure 17–1, showing the gains from trade in a general equilibrium context. This is time well spent, since comparative advantage is fundamental and powerful. Emphasize that trade inherently involves mutually beneficial transactions and that potential gains from trade depend on just one condition: relative prices in world markets must differ from relative prices prevailing at home for at least some pairs of goods.

On balance, the text reaches a favorable verdict on exports of primary products. Despite the barriers, some of which are more apparent than real, primary exports can serve as an effective engine of growth. The supporting discussion provides useful samples of applied economic analysis, including the different measures for evaluating terms of trade, and the application of the permanent income hypothesis to export instability effects. In addition, you can apply basic supply and demand analysis to elaborate on the text's discussion of buffer stock operations and cartel arrangements. The analysis of real exchange rates and Dutch disease is also enjoyable to teach. These are important topics that students will probably find very stimulating, because they combine solid analysis with insights that are often counterintuitive.

Question Bank

Multiple-Choice Questions

1. The relative lack of made and human capital in developing countries indicates that these countries

   a. do not gain from trading with industrialized countries.
   * b. should import capital-intensive goods.
   c. should heavily protect capital-intensive industries.
   d. cannot produce at points on their production frontier.

2. Based on his analysis of data for the period 1900 to 1988, what did Cuddington conclude about the net barter terms of trade facing primary exporters?

   a. The long-term trend is distinctly negative.
   b. The long-term trend is distinctly positive.
   * c. The terms of trade have fluctuated widely, but there is no distinct long-term trend.
   d. The terms of trade fell steadily until the 1950s, but have risen since then.

3. Begonia produces the optimal combination of radios and onions in the absence of trade. The local price of radios is twice the price of onions. In neighboring Magnolia the price of radios is 3 times the price of onions.

* a. Begonia can benefit by trading radios for onions.
   b. Begonia can benefit by trading onions for radios.
   c. One cannot tell which trade pattern would benefit Begonia without knowing absolute price levels and exchange rates.
   d. Begonia cannot benefit from trade if it is already producing the optimal combination of outputs.

4. In general, when a country moves to more open international trade and specialization,

   a. everyone in the country becomes better off.
* b. producers of the product to be imported may be hurt.
   c. consumers of the product to be imported may be hurt.
   d. the capitalists gain at the expense of the workers.

5. The empirical record shows that

   a. trade is relatively more important to large countries than to small countries.
   b. most low-income countries depend on one or two primary products for over 95 percent of their export earnings.
   c. world demand for primary exports from developing countries has declined steadily since the 1950s.
* d. none of the above.

6. The case of Malaysia represents an example of a country that has grown

   a. slowly, due to reliance on primary exports.
* b. rapidly,with growth led by primary exports.
   c. rapidly, due to policies that minimized its reliance on primary exports.
   d. slowly, due to policies that failed to exploit its primary-product export potential.

7. The opening of export markets for primary products can provide employment for previously underutilized land, labor, and natural resources. The term for this is

* a. vent for surplus.
   b. enclave export.
   c. forward linkage.
   d. buffer stock.

8. Which of the following is a *fiscal* linkage effect of producing tea for export?

    * a. The increase in government revenues from taxing tea plantations
    b. The improvement in the balance of payments
    c. The effect of tea exports on the exchange rate
    d. The increase in demand for tools and implements used on the tea plantations

9. Which is a correct formula for calculating the income terms of trade (using notation from the textbook)?

    a. $P_m/(P_x \times Q_x)$
    b. $P_x/(P_m \times Q_m)$
    * c. $P_x \times Q_x/P_m$
    d. $P_m \times Q_m/P_x$

10. As applied to the analysis of primary export instability, the permanent-income hypothesis states that

    a. it is not rational to sacrifice growth for more stable export earnings.
    * b. the savings rate may be higher when export earnings are less stable.
    c. primary exports lead to a permanent increase in income.
    d. all the above.

11. A buffer stock that stabilizes commodity prices would reduce exporters' earnings when

    * a. supply declines.
    b. supply expands.
    c. demand declines.
    d. none of the above; a buffer stock always stabilizes export earnings as well as export prices.

12. Which statement is true of commodity cartel arrangements to raise export earnings for primary producers?

    * a. They work only if demand is price inelastic.
    b. They work only if price goes up without any decline in export volume.
    c. They succeed if producers cooperate, regardless of the demand elasticity.
    d. None of the above.

13. A weakness of the theory of comparative advantage is that the theory cannot explain

    a. why political opposition arises to free trade.
    b. how resource-poor countries can gain from trade.
* c. the process of structural change that alters efficient trade patterns over time.
    d. the choice of products to export and products to import.

14. From 1980 to 1990 the average price of Senegal's exports rose 4 percent, the average price of Senegal's imports fell 4 percent, and export volume rose 37 percent. What happened to the net barter terms of trade?

    a. They fell 8 percent.
    b. They remained unchanged.
* c. They rose 8 percent.
    d. They rose 48 percent.

15. Econometric tests reveal what correlation between the instability of export earnings and economic growth?

* a. Higher instability is correlated with higher investment ratios but lower GDP growth.
    b. Higher instability is correlated with higher investment ratios and higher GDP growth.
    c. There is no correlation between export instability and growth.
    d The correlation is positive for large countries and negative for small countries.

16. The case of Ghana illustrates a country that

* a. failed to exploit its potential as a primary exporter.
    b. fell prey to Dutch disease due to the rapid growth of its primary exports.
    c. successfully promoted growth through primary exports based on comparative advantage.
    d. grew rapidly despite declining terms of trade.

17. The purpose of the Stabex scheme established by the European Community was to

   a. finance buffer stock operations to stabilize commodity prices.
* b. compensate low-income primary exporters for fluctuations in export earnings.
   c. promote free international trade in primary products.
   d. restrict production and raise world prices for primary products.

18. Between 1980 and 1990, Pakistan's income terms of trade rose by 89 percent. This means that

   a. the world price of Pakistan's exports rose by 89 percent.
   b. the world price of Pakistan's exports rose by 89 percent relative to the world price of imports.
   c. the world price of Pakistan's imports rose by 89 percent relative to the world price of its exports.
* d. Pakistan's total export earnings (price times quantity) rose by 89 percent relative to the price of its imports.

19. Many symptoms of Dutch disease can be traced to the fact that a commodity boom generates a large inflow of foreign exchange, which causes the

   a. nominal exchange rate to appreciate.
   b. nominal exchange rate to depreciate.
* c. real exchange rate to appreciate.
   d. real exchange rate to depreciate.

20. Between 1980 and 1990, Singapore's nominal exchange rate went from 2.09 to 1.74 (in Singapore dollars per U.S. dollar). At the same time, Singapore's price level rose to 125 while world prices rose to 164 (both measured as index numbers with 1980 = 100). Thus, Singapore's *real* exchange rate

   a. appreciated by 9 percent.
   b. appreciated by 37 percent.
* c. depreciated by 9 percent.
   d. depreciated by 37 percent.

IDs and Paired-Concept Questions

These terms can be used individually as short-answer identification questions, or they can be used in pairs. In the latter case, ask students to explain (1) the meaning and significance of each of the two terms and (2) the relationship between them.

1. Comparative advantage, factor endowment
2. World terms of trade, gains from trade
3. Enclave export, backward linkage
4. Permanent-income hypothesis, buffer stock
5. Consumption linkage, fiscal linkage
6. Vent for surplus, export pessimism
7. Net barter terms of trade, income terms of trade
8. Commodity cartel, price elasticity of demand
9. Tradable goods, primary exports
10. Dutch disease, real exchange rate

Study Guide Applications

Worked Example

The Worked Example walks students step by step through an analysis of comparative advantage and gains from trade, similar to Figure 17–1 in the textbook.

Exercises

1. It is the students' turn to work through an application of comparative advantage and gains from trade, following the analysis illustrated in the Worked Example.

2. The second exercise contains a series of numerical and analytical questions on the different terms-of-trade concepts and the real exchange rate, using data from Colombia and Malawi.

3. Students apply a simple supply-and-demand graph to examine the source of export instability, the operation of a buffer stock, and the effects of commodity cartels.

4. The final exercise uses a hypothetical case study to illustrate in detail the mechanisms that turn a commodity boom into a bad case of Dutch disease.

CHAPTER 18   Industry

Chapter Outline

I. Empirically, industry is a leading sector in that the share of GDP originating in manufacturing tends to rise with per capita income, up to income levels around $10,000 (1992 PPP$). Manufacturing tends to be more prominent in large countries than in small ones, due to the size of the domestic markets. Cross-country variations in the development of manufacturing also relate to resource endowments and to the choice of development strategy. To serve as a leading sector in a functional sense, industrial growth should generate rich linkage effects. Standard measures of linkages bear this out, but such measures are based on fixed input-output coefficients; as such, they provide little useful guidance about which interindustry relationships are efficient.

II. Industrialization is also strongly associated with urbanization. The text surveys the benefits of urban growth, including economies of agglomeration, as well as the costs, which include infrastructure requirements and congestion effects. Many governments have attempted to provide inducements for dispersing industrial development, to reduce the growth of major urban centers. Depending on the circumstances, the benefits of such policies do not always outweigh the economic costs. In the long run, the best approach is to achieve a balance between policies that encourage rural development as well as urban industry.

III. A fundamental issue in industrialization is the choice of technology. Empirical studies reveal a wide range of technology choice in many industries, with large differences in factor intensities. Factor price distortions and engineering biases in noncompetitive protected industries typically promote inappropriate, capital-intensive technologies. This results in high social costs and lost opportunities for productive job creation.

IV. A related aspect of industrial technology is the extent of scale economies. The text explains the meaning, the source, and the empirical significance of scale economies. Most developing countries have small domestic markets; consequently, many products cannot be manufactured efficiently without cultivating export markets.

V. Many simple products, though, can be produced by small-scale enterprises, which tend to be very labor-intensive. Development specialists often argue for programs to promote small-scale industry. Efforts to evaluate the efficiency of small versus large firms yield mixed results, but it appears that few cottage and small-scale enterprises have much potential for growth and development.

Consequently, costly subsidies to promote small-scale enterprises may be wasteful in the long run. The best policy is to establish a market environment in which efficient small businesses can thrive, without special subsidies.

VI. The chapter concludes with some basic themes. Industrial productivity is a key to improved standards of living, but industrialization should not be pursued at the neglect of rural development. Industrial development should be pursued efficiently. In many countries, however, political objectives outweigh economic considerations in the design of industrial policy.

Boxed Example. The chapter has one boxed example explaining how China, in the 1970s, promoted rural small-scale industry at the same time as it developed large-scale urban manufacturing. The discussion deals with the pros and cons of this policy of "walking on two legs."

In the New Edition. The one major change to this chapter is that it now precedes the discussion of trade policies for promoting industrialization. As usual, the empirical record is updated. In addition, some elements have been edited out in the new edition. These include a table presenting GDP shares for early, middle, and late industries and outdated estimates of urbanization costs.

Class Notes. Three technical issues are covered in Chapter 18: the measurement of linkage effects, technology choice, and scale economies. For each, the economic implications merit as much attention as the tools themselves. With regard to the choice of technique, students may be quite familiar with isoquant analysis by now. You can emphasize the huge empirical differences in factor proportions across alternative technologies, and the importance of pursuing policies to promote efficient technology choice.

The chapter touches on several interesting topics for discussion, including the pros and cons of urbanization, noneconomic considerations influencing the choice of technique, policies to support small-scale industry, and the reciprocal relationship between industrialization and rural development.

Question Bank

Multiple-Choice Questions

1. On average, for small countries, as per capita income quintuples from $1,000 to $5,000 (PPP), manufacturing value-added rises from

   a. 1 to 4 percent of GNP.
 * b. 7 to 17 percent of GNP.
   c. 55 to 70 percent of GNP.
   d. 35 to 56 percent of GNP.

2. Large developing countries typically produce a wider range of industrial goods than small ones with similar income levels. The main reason is that large countries

    a. take more advantage of gains from international trade.
* b. take advantage of scale economies within the domestic market.
    c. attract more foreign investment.
    d. invest more in urban infrastructure.

3. If value-added accounts for 23 percent of the value of cotton textile output and imported inputs account for 14 percent of the value of output, then direct backward linkages represent

    a. 23 percent of the value of output.
    b. 77 percent of the value of output.
* c. 63 percent of the value of output.
    d. an amount that cannot be determined from the information given.

4. In branches of industry such as cotton spinning, brickmaking, and sugar processing, the most capital-intensive technology has a capital-labor ratio _____ times higher than that of the appropriate technology.

    a. 1.1 to 1.5
    b. 2 to 3
* c. 5 to 15
    d. 40 to 50

5. The boxed example on China in the 1970s illustrates a case in which small-scale industry

* a. allowed regions to be self-reliant in providing farm inputs, equipment, and consumer goods for rural consumers.
    b. became overly capital-intensive due to distorted factor prices.
    c. was concentrated in major urban centers.
    d. disappeared rapidly because large factories could take advantage of scale economies.

6. Which of the following is a *forward*-linkage effect of expanding the tractor industry?

    a. Increased demand for tractor motors.
    b. Increased incomes for workers in the tractor industry.
    c. The loss of jobs in agriculture caused by mechanization.
* d. The potential increase in agricultural output made possible by having more tractors made available.

7. Some countries, like Colombia and Mexico, have a smaller-than-average share of GDP produced by the manufacturing sector because

    a. the governments have been concerned primarily with rural development.
    b. factor price distortions have rendered manufacturing unprofitable.
    c. they have suffered from long periods of civil war.
* d. they are relatively well endowed with natural resources.

8. Scale economies are characterized by

* a. falling long-run average costs.
    b. rising long-run average costs.
    c. falling marginal costs.
    d. rising marginal costs.

9. When there are substantial scale economies, as in the production of durable consumer goods, manufacturing in a small low-income country can still be viable and efficient only if

* a. the industry serves export markets as well as the domestic market.
    b. the government provides protection from competing imports.
    c. the local industry is a monopoly.
    d. all the above.

10. Empirical studies find that small-scale manufacturing firms in developing countries tend to

    a. use more modern production techniques than large firms.
* b. use more labor-intensive technology than large-scale firms for most, but not all, products.
    c. operate very inefficiently.
    d. all the above.

11. A high index of backward linkages is especially characteristic of

    a. agriculture and mining sectors.
* b. early-developing manufacturing sectors.
    c. capital-intensive manufacturing enterprises.
    d. cottage industries.

12. In their study of 18 industries in five developing countries, Yotopoulos and Nugent calculated that the leather industry had the highest total backward-linkage index. This means that

    a. leather production is more labor-intensive than the other industries studied.
    b. the leather industry is the most efficient industry in these five countries.
*   c. an additional dollar of leather output generates a large demand for domestic inputs of all kinds, directly and indirectly.
    d. leather production is more capital-intensive than the other industries studied.

13. Industries that locate in urban areas benefit from economies of agglomeration. This term refers specifically to

*   a. the proximity of many firms providing a wide range of inputs and services.
    b. the high saving rates of urban households, which reduce the cost of financing investments.
    c. the social and cultural amenities of urban life in developing countries.
    d. the presence of large, concentrated groups of consumers.

14. In general, the "appropriate" choice of technology for industrial development is the technology that

    a. minimizes the incremental capital-output ratio (ICOR).
    b. maximizes the labor-intensity of production.
    c. maximizes total backward linkage effects.
*   d. minimizes the cost of production, evaluated at nondistorted factor prices.

15. The best approach for stemming overly rapid urban growth is to

    a. pass regulatory laws for dispersing industrial investments to smaller urban centers.
    b. reduce public-sector spending on urban infrastructure and housing.
    c. provide incentives for more capital-intensive industrial investments in urban areas.
*   d. encourage rural development as actively as industrialization.

16. Many industrial plants in developing countries have been too capital intensive, in part because

    a. factor-market distortions raised the price of capital relative to the price of labor.
    b. firms in developing countries have not been able to afford more appropriate machinery.
* c. managers in protected industries often have a bias toward using the most modern machinery.
    d. all the above.

17. Scale economies in manufacturing arise for several reasons. Which of the following is not *one* of the reasons?

    a. High fixed costs can be spread over a larger volume of output.
* b. Larger firms are more capital-intensive.
    c. Longer production runs reduce the number of times equipment must be set up or readjusted.
    d. Larger producers can obtain quantity purchase discounts when they procure inputs.

18. The minimum efficient scale (MES) is defined as a plant size that is large enough

* a. so no further scale economies are achieved by building a larger facility.
    b. to take advantage of the most modern technology.
    c. to qualify for bank credit.
    d. to break even, given the prices that prevail for both inputs and outputs.

19. Cottage shops and small enterprises employ _____ of all manufacturing-sector workers in many low-income countries, while accounting for _____ of value-added in the manufacturing sector.

    a. about one-third, about one-half
* b. over one-half, about one-fourth
    c. nearly 90 percent, nearly 90 percent
    d. less than one-fourth, nearly one-half

20. The most efficient approach for promoting small-scale enterprise is for the government to

    a. provide subsidized credit and technical services.

* b. eliminate policies discriminating against small firms and provide supporting institutions, while otherwise letting the market determine the outcomes.

    c. require that government agencies and large firms purchase a minimum percentage of inputs from small-scale suppliers.

    d. impose protective tariffs on competing imports.

IDs and Paired-Concept Questions

These terms can be used individually as short-answer identification questions, or they can be used in pairs. In the latter case, ask students to explain (1) the meaning and significance of each of the two terms and (2) the relationship between them.

1. Industrialization, urbanization
2. Direct backward linkages, total backward linkages
3. Economies of scale, economies of agglomeration
4. Urban external economies, costs of congestion
5. Appropriate technology, labor-intensive technology
6. Long-run average cost, minimum efficient scale (MES)
7. Capital-intensive technology, factor prices
8. Urban infrastructure, industrial dispersion

Study Guide Applications

Worked Example

The Worked Example uses input-output data from Chapter 6 to demonstrate how to compute and interpret backward linkage indices for two of Planland's three sectors.

Exercises

1. Students replicate the analysis of direct and total backward linkage effects, focusing on the service sector in Planland. The exercise also examines the index of forward linkages.

2. In this exercise, students analyze the technology-choice problem in the context of a hypothetical case study with three alternative technologies, and different factor prices for modern and informal-sector firms.

3. Students use a graph of long-run average costs to evaluate scale economies and consider the implications for industrialization policy.

CHAPTER 19   Trade and Industrialization

Chapter Outline

I. Nearly all developing countries try to accelerate the pace and influence the pattern of industrialization. Two main trade strategies have been pursued for this purpose: inward-looking import-substitution and export-led outward-looking industrialization. The core premise of import substitution is that infant industries need protection to survive, while the premise of outward-looking industrialization is that domestic producers must become competitive.

II. Import substitution was nearly universal in the 1960s and remained widespread until quite recently. This strategy entails identifying large domestic markets served by imports, assessing the technical feasibility of domestic production, and then erecting protective barriers to shield ostensible infant industries from import competition. After an initial burst of growth, import substitution generally bogs down because domestic markets are limited in size and infant industries remain too uncompetitive to penetrate export markets. In contrast, the export-led strategy of East Asia's "tigers" has been outstandingly successful. These countries have been interventionist and protectionist to varying degrees, but they shared four key characteristics: a disciplined focus on policies to promote rapid economic development, prudent management of macroeconomic policy and exchange-rate policy, flexible factor markets, and insulation of exports from domestic price distortions.

III. Governments have four basic policy instruments at their disposal to influence the industrialization process: tariffs on imports, quantitative restrictions on trade, various forms of subsidy, and exchange-rate policy. Protective tariffs involve significant efficiency losses, particularly when effective rates of protection are quite high. Import quotas have similar effects, with the added disadvantage of bestowing monopoly power and scarcity rents on favored firms. Subsidies and other market preferences can achieve similar ends, with less of a deadweight loss to the economy. The above instruments can be applied to very specific products or firms. Exchange-rate policy, however, affects all tradables producers in a more evenhanded fashion. An overvalued real exchange rate renders exports less profitable and imports less expensive, while an undervalued real exchange rate has the opposite effects. Ironically, efforts to shield domestic producers from import competition discriminate, through exchange-rate effects, against exports as well as against imports.

IV. Where these instruments have been geared to protect import-substitution industries they typically impose heavy costs on consumers, discourage exports

147

(limiting import capacity), induce excessively capital-intensive investments, discourage backward linkages, promote political rent-seeking activity in lieu of competitive market adjustments, and ultimately lead to arrested growth. Where the instruments have been used to encourage outward-looking industrialization, the result has generally been rapid growth in income and productivity, though the direction of cause-and-effect remains uncertain.

V. To induce domestic entrepreneurs to commit capital to new industries, there may well be a need for some form of protection, but it should be used selectively to support infant industries that show clear promise of growing up and becoming competitive. Not all developing countries, of course, have the capacity to intervene so judiciously. In any case, once competitive production is within reach, no further protection is justified.

VI. The spread of outward-looking trade strategies, together with multilateral agreements to reduce barriers to international trade, has sparked rapid growth of manufactured exports from developing countries after 1965. This trend benefits all trading countries. Yet within each country, trade creates losers as well as gainers. Since the benefits of trade tend to be widely spread, while the costs are narrowly borne by particular sectors, shifts in comparative advantage have bred political pressures in many industrial economies to impose new non-tariff barriers to trade. Such reactions are quite costly to the developed country itself, but even more so for developing countries that lose access to large export markets. One response to the threat of protectionism has been greater trade between developing countries and moves to establish regional trade arrangements, such as customs unions and free-trade areas. There is also a movement toward regional trading blocs. These arrangements can lead to trade diversion as well as trade creation. Hence, the effects of these trends on developing countries remain uncertain.

Boxed Examples. There are two boxed examples in Chapter 19. The first describes how Kenya's import-substitution policies led to rapid initial industrial growth. By the end of the 1970s the bloom had faded from this strategy because the domestic market was too small to support sustained industrial growth which depended on protectionism. In response, Kenya has slowly moved toward a more outward-looking industrialization strategy. The second case study explains the radical transformation of trade policies in Mexico during the late 1980s. To emerge from the depth of its debt crisis, the Mexican government switched from a heavily protective trade strategy to a bold program of encouraging trade. These reforms culminated in the North American Free Trade Agreement (NAFTA), which took effect at the beginning of 1994.

In the New Edition. Chapter 19 in the Fourth Edition of the textbook is an amalgam of the two former chapters covering import substitution and outward-looking trade strategy, respectively. The consolidated chapter edits out some details, such as the analysis of domestic monopoly with import quotas, and the matrix of distortions and interventions. On the other hand, the revision adds information on the results of the Uruguay Round of GATT talks and the establishment of the World Trade Organization. Also revised is the discussion of the policy mix used by Asia's most successful economies.

Class Notes. Chapter 19 vies with Chapters 3, 6, and 20 as the most challenging in the book, in terms of technical concepts and tools. Yet the material bears emphasis because trade looms large in the panoply of development issues, not least of which is the impact of world development on jobs and living standards in the United States and other industrialized countries. In addition, many of today's pressing policy concerns in the developing countries, such as neglected agricultural development, low capital productivity, serious balance-of-payments constraints, and low rates of job creation, are at least in part a legacy of inefficient trade policies. This story needs telling. Since most students start out with a tendency to accept the argument for heavy protectionism, they can gain a great deal from seeing a detailed analysis of the costs of trade interventions and the relative efficacy of tariffs, quotas, and subsidies.

Much of the analytical insight can be conveyed with nothing more difficult than supply and demand graphs. Of the technical topics, the one I most enjoy teaching is the effective rate of protection. This is a powerful tool for showing the extent of the inefficiencies that can be bred by modest-looking tariffs. The effective rate of subsidy (ERS) and the real effective exchange rate (REER) are broader gauges of policy effects, but the basic point about distorted incentives can be established well enough in terms of the ERP. For lecturing on any of these technical points, it is important to give examples that illustrate the key lessons.

Question Bank

Multiple-Choice Questions

1. Effective rates of protection in developing countries typically

   a. are very high for manufactured consumer goods.
   b. differ widely from industry to industry.
   c. discriminate against the agricultural sector.
 * d. all the above.

2. Malawi's currency, the kwacha, is overvalued when the kwacha price of foreign exchange rate is

   a. too high compared to the equilibrium free-trade exchange rate.
* b. too low compared to the equilibrium free-trade exchange rate.
   c. rising.
   d. falling.

3. Zawana faces world prices for finished radios and for radio components which are 100 shillings and 95 shillings, respectively. There is a 30 percent tariff on imported radios and no tariff on imported components. What is the effective rate of protection for the radio assembly industry in Zawana?

   a. 30 percent
   b. 60 percent
* c. 600 percent
   d. 5 percent

4. The effective rate of protection measures how much

   a. investment will be drawn into the protected industry.
   b. profit can be earned by producing the protected product.
* c. the margin of price over input cost for domestic producers can exceed the margin at world market prices.
   d. the price of the product increases due to the tariff.

5. What effect do high *import* tariffs have on a country's *export* industries?

* a. Tariffs reduce the demand for foreign exchange, so the home currency appreciates; this hurts exports.
   b. Tariffs reduce the demand for foreign exchange, so the home currency depreciates; this boosts exports.
   c. Tariffs reduce the demand for foreign exchange, so the home currency appreciates; this boosts exports.
   d. Tariffs do not affect exports, just imports.

6. The boxed example of Kenya illustrates a country where import-substitution policies

   a. led to declining agricultural output.
* b. promoted industries that manufactured at too high a cost to permit sustained growth through exports.
   c. produced thirty years of rapid growth for the economy.
   d. were never used because the domestic market was too small to support local manufacturing.

7. Other things being equal, the effective rate of protection for domestic producers of steel nails will be higher,

    a. the lower the tariff on imported nails.
* b. the lower the tariff on imported steel.
    c. the higher the value-added in converting steel to nails.
    d. all the above.

8. When the government auctions import licenses it captures the quota rent. Who gets the quota rent when the government administratively allocates import licenses?

    a. The foreign producer of the imported product
* b. The importers
    c. The domestic consumer
    d. The domestic producers of the import substitutes

9. Suppose Kenya imports film at a border price of $5 per roll. If there are 70 Kenyan shillings to the dollar and Kenya imposes a 50 percent tariff on imported film, then the domestic price of the imported film per roll is

    a. 350 shillings.
    b. 105 shillings.
* c. 525 shillings.
    d. 400 shillings.

10. The text mentions that "the industrial landscape is littered with infants that never grew up." This refers to infant industries that

* a. require protection from import competition indefinitely.
    b. remain labor-intensive instead of adopting modern technology.
    c. are not successful in the export market.
    d. cannot earn profits even with protection from import competition.

11. The essence of outward-looking development is that it

    a. relies on primary exports until domestic industry is efficient enough to compete in export markets.
    b. gets prices right and lets the free market dictate the development of manufactured exports.
* c. establishes an incentive system that induces firms to seek export markets.
    d. subsidizes export-oriented manufacturing firms.

12. To minimize deadweight efficiency losses, protection for infant industries should be provided through

  * a. subsidies.
    b. quotas.
    c. tariffs.
    d. an overvalued exchange rate.

13. In 1986, Peru's official exchange rate remained fixed, while domestic prices rose 78 percent and world prices rose 2 percent. What happened to Peru's real exchange rate (RER) and the profitability of its exports?

    a. The RER appreciated, so export profitability rose.
    b. The RER depreciated, so export profitability fell.
  * c. The RER appreciated, so export profitability fell.
    d. The RER depreciated, so export profitability rose.

14. What credit-market policy did the Korean government use to promote exports during the 1970s?

    a. The government liberalized financial markets and let market forces allocate credit.
    b. The government set high interest rates on loans to exporters to screen out low-productivity investments.
    c. The government cut off credit to exporters to make them compete for loans overseas.
  * d. The government used low-interest-rate loans as a form of indirect subsidy to exporters.

15. Between 1965 and 1991 what happened to the total volume of manufactured exports from developing countries?

    a. It grew very slowly.
  * b. It expanded by 18 percent per year.
    c. It declined.
    d. Intra-South volume grew rapidly, but manufactured exports to industrial countries declined.

16. Suppose a country devalues its official exchange rate by 50 percent and simultaneously cuts the average tariff rate from 80 to 20 percent. If domestic inflation equals world inflation, what happens to the REER for importables?

* a. The REER remains unchanged.
  b. The REER depreciates by 50 percent.
  c. The REER appreciates by 10 percent.
  d. The REER depreciates by 125 percent.

17. In an outward-looking trade policy regime, the effective rate of subsidy (ERS) is generally

* a. no lower for exports than for import-substitution activity.
  b. positive for exports and negative for import-substitution activity.
  c. negative for exports and positive for import-substitution activity.
  d. near zero for all industries.

18. What does one call an agreement to eliminate tariffs among associated countries while levying a common set of tariffs on imports from nonassociate countries?

* a. Customs union
  b. Free-trade area
  c. Common market
  d. Trade diversion

19. Economists generally prefer the use of subsidies instead of protective tariffs because

  a. subsidies create smaller deadweight losses.
  b. subsidies can be targeted more carefully.
  c. the visible cost of subsidies creates an automatic incentive to phase out protection.
* d. all the above.

20. Which policy change reduces the ERS for steel producers?

    a. Increasing the tariff on competing imports of steel
* b. Increasing the tariff on iron ingots used for producing steel
    c. Providing special credits at reduced interest rates
    d. All the above

21. The textbook says that a crawling-peg system of exchange-rate management is commonly employed as part of an outward-looking policy regime. What is the purpose of a crawling peg?

    a. To avoid devaluation of the home currency
    b. To reduce the domestic-currency price of imported inputs
* c. To avoid appreciation of the real exchange rate
    d. To maximize government tariff revenues

22. Which of the following is *not* an argument in favor of export-oriented development over import substitution?

    a. International competition compels domestic producers to become more efficient.
    b. Exposure to world markets enhances opportunities to learn new technologies.
    c. Producing for export permits greater specialization.
* d. Outward-looking development favors firms that are better at rent-seeking.

23. What was GATT?

* a. An international organization that oversaw multilateral trade negotiations and tariff policies.
    b. A voluntary export restriction agreement governing international trade in textiles.
    c. A free-trade area in southeast Asia.
    d. An eastern European trading bloc that disbanded in the early 1990s.

24. New protectionism to save jobs in declining industries in the industrial countries hurts whom?

    a. Consumers in the industrial countries
    b. Export industries in the industrial countries
    c. Export industries in the developing countries
* d. All the above

IDs and Paired-Concept Questions

These terms can be used individually as short-answer identification questions, or they can be used in pairs. In the latter case, ask students to explain (1) the meaning and significance of each of the two terms and (2) the relationship between them.

1. Import substitution, infant industry
2. Effective rate of protection (ERP), effective rate of subsidy (ERS)
3. Tariff revenue, quota rent
4. Import quota, deadweight loss
5. Overvalued exchange rate, import-GDP ratio
6. Rent-seeking, import licensing
7. Outward-looking strategy, crawling peg
8. Real effective exchange rate (REER), overvalued exchange rate
9. GATT, most-favored-nation principle
10. Voluntary export restrictions, non-tariff barriers
11. Customs union, free-trade area
12. Trade diversion, dynamic gains from integration

Study Guide Applications

Worked Example

The Worked Example investigates the effects of a 50 percent protective tariff on production, consumption, price, trade, and efficiency, using the framework presented in Figure 19–1 of the textbook. The Example also touches on broader points such as the effect of an equivalent import quota, and reasons behind the lack of long-run success for many import-substitution programs.

Exercises

1. The first exercise gives students a chance to work through the economic effects of protective tariffs and quotas, using the same approach as the Worked Example.

2. Several numerical examples show students how to calculate and interpret the effective rate of protection.

3. A supply-and-demand graph of the market for foreign exchange shows students how an overvalued exchange rate can be used to foster import-substitution industrialization and how a protective tariff discriminates against exports through its effects on the equilibrium exchange rate.

4. The fourth exercise provides applications of the formula for the effective rate of subsidy (ERS) and shows how ERS differentials distort the allocation of resources.

5. Students get to work through applications of the formula for the real effective exchange rate (REER), which combines the effects of exchange-rate policy and other trade-related policies.

6. The sixth exercise is an application of the textbook discussion of the short- and long-run effects of import substitution in a general equilibrium context, using the production possibilities frontier.

7. The final exercise illustrates the concepts of trade diversion and trade creation from formation of a free-trade area, in the context of a three-good, three-country numerical example.

CHAPTER 20   Managing an Open Economy

Chapter Outline

I. Although most development policies relate to long-term outcomes, short-run stabilization problems often dominate the policy agenda. Serious macroeconomic imbalances can arise from external or internal shocks or from the cumulative effects of prior mismanagement. Stabilization problems were especially widespread during the 1970s and 1980s following wide swings in oil prices, real interest rates, major exchange rates, and the availability of foreign financing.

II. The basic model for analyzing stabilization policies in developing countries is the Australian model, which starts from the presumption that most developing countries are small, open economies. They are small in the sense of being price takers in the world markets for tradable goods (including both importables and exportables). They are open in that the domestic economy is heavily affected by international trade and finance. Nontradables, including most services, also account for a substantial share of output. The domestic price of tradables is determined by the world price and the official exchange rate, while the price of nontradables is a function of domestic supply and demand conditions. The relative price of tradable to nontradable goods measures the real exchange rate (P) in this model.

III. *External balance* is defined as equality between the supply and demand for tradables. With zero net foreign financing, this is equivalent to a zero balance of trade; with a net inflow of foreign savings, a corresponding balance-of-trade deficit is consistent with external balance. External *imbalance* can take the form of an unsustainable trade deficit or, less critically, an excessive trade surplus. In like fashion, *internal balance* is defined as equality between the supply and demand for nontradables. Internal *imbalance* can take the form of inflationary excess demand or contractionary excess supply, which idles factors of production and leads to excessive unemployment. These concepts are easy to depict using supply-and-demand analysis for tradables and nontradables, with P as the price variable.

IV. Two key variables determining the macroeconomic outcome are aggregate expenditure (absorption) and the real exchange rate. A rise in absorption increases demand for both tradables and nontradables. A rise in the real exchange rate, by altering relative prices, induces a shift in consumption toward nontradables and a shift in production toward tradables. Although the markets possess self-correcting tendencies, structural rigidities can render the adjustments too slow to solve short-run crises; in addition, the automatic adjustments can be counteracted by inappropriate policy responses.

V. The model reveals which combination of changes in absorption (A) and real exchange rate (P) are needed to restore macroeconomic balance, starting from any initial situation of external and/or internal imbalance. To simplify the analysis, the model is presented in the form of a phase diagram with A and P on the axes. In this diagram, the external balance line (EB) delineates combinations of A and P for which the tradables market has a balance, a surplus, or a deficit. Similarly, the internal balance line (IB) shows the combinations of A and P for which the market for nontradables has a balance, a surplus of capacity (unemployment), or excess demand (inflation).

VI. Two main instruments are available to the government to help move the system toward overall balance. First, monetary and fiscal policies directly affect absorption; second, official exchange-rate policy affects the real exchange rate.

VII. The Australian model is used to analyze the nature of macroeconomic imbalances and the mix of policies needed to achieve stabilization. In general, both policy instruments must be used in a coordinated fashion to reach the equilibrium. The essence of stabilization policy is to identify the disequilibrium condition and then determine the warranted policy adjustments. For countries suffering large external deficits and high domestic inflation, the indicated response is austerity plus a real depreciation. This is the standard IMF prescription. One important detail is that aid inflows ease the adjustment process by reducing the necessary dose of austerity and devaluation. The model also provides a basis for analyzing Dutch disease, the nature of the debt repayment problem, and the macroeconomic effects of drought.

Boxed Examples. Chapter 20 has three boxed examples. The first surveys Chile's rocky road to stabilization over the period 1973 to 1984. Since Chile was a pioneer in this endeavor, the problems it encountered proved to be very instructive for countries that later adopted stabilization programs. One of the most important lessons was the need to coordinate fiscal and monetary policies with exchange-rate policies. The second case study tells how Ghana, starting in 1983, went about recovering from a decade of mismanagement. The adjustment program focused on exchange-rate reforms, fiscal adjustment, and monetary controls. The third boxed example involves a very different situation, namely, Taiwan's adjustments following a period of excellent domestic performance with a large trade *surplus*. In this case the adjustment problem was to reduce the buildup of foreign exchange reserves without hampering growth.

In the New Edition. The initial section of Chapter 20 replicates some of the two-good general equilibrium analysis from the Appendix to the Third Edition of the textbook. Otherwise, this chapter is absolutely new.

Class Notes. Chapter 20 is quite different from the rest of the text in two respects. First, the material is more advanced. If your class includes a lot of mathphobes who have trouble with analytical tools, then it would be a good idea to skip this material. (Though you could let the top students tackle it as an extra-credit assignment, using the exercises in the *Study Guide* as a homework assignment.) Second, Chapter 20 develops and applies a single model, the Australian model of external and internal balance in a small, open economy. Other chapters, in contrast, surveyed a variety of approaches or aspects of a thematic topic. The introductory analysis in Chapter 20 uses the production frontier to set up some basic concepts, but this tool gets very messy (as one can see by referring back to the Appendix in the Third Edition). This leads to a more complete presentation of the model in terms of supply and demand for tradables and nontradables. Then the model is recast into a phase diagram focusing on the instrument variables A and P.

The phase diagram provides a convenient map for examining various cases of comparative statics and identifying the appropriate policy adjustments to cure any combination of imbalances. But there are several more subtle details that students might not grasp without your help. First, be sure to clarify the difference between shifts in *EB* and *IB* versus movements along these curves due to changes in A or P. Second, hammer home the fact that P goes *up* with a devaluation and *down* with appreciation. In this regard, don't let your students get confused by seeing supply and demand curves in the market for nontradables that seem to have the wrong slopes. These are perfectly ordinary behavioral relationships; the unusual thing is that the vertical axis is the inverse of the relative price of nontradables. Third, give the students a clear explanation of the *switching* effects of a real change in the exchange rate, with reference to movements along the production frontier. Finally, you might elaborate on the market's self-correcting tendencies, including how they operate in this context and why they might not work well enough or fast enough to resolve short-run stabilization crises.

Question Bank

Multiple-Choice Questions

1. During the 1970s and 1980s, many economies became unbalanced because of external shocks, including

   a. unstable oil prices.
   b. world recession.
   c. rising real interest rates.
   * d. all the above.

2. The two main policy approaches for correcting macroeconomic imbalances are

   * a. changes in aggregate expenditure and adjustments to the exchange rate.
   b. changes in expenditure and price controls.
   c. adjustments to the exchange rate and price controls.
   d. price controls and trade restrictions.

3. For purposes of macroeconomic analysis, a country is small when

   a. its population is less than 20 million.
   * b. it is a price taker in world markets for its exports and imports.
   c. its macroeconomic imbalances have no significant effect on other countries.
   d. its domestic economy is not significantly influenced by international trade and financial flows.

4. Which of the following should be classified as a nontradable?

   * a. Rural road construction services
   b. Wheat production that is wholly consumed within the country
   c. Computer equipment that cannot be produced locally
   d. All the above

5. Using the notation from the textbook, the domestic price of a tradable good is determined by which equation?

   a. $P_t = e/P_t^*$.
   b. $P_t = P_t^*/e$.
   * c. $P_t = eP_t^*$.
   d. $P_t = e - P_t^*$.

6. The defining characteristic of equilibrium in the Australian model is that

   a. the economy is operating on its production frontier.
   b. the market for nontradables is in equilibrium.
   c. the market for tradables is in equilibrium.
 * d. both the market for nontradables and the market for tradables are in equilibrium.

7. If the world price of cotton is $0.75 dollars per pound and Mexico's exchange rate is 6 pesos per dollar, then the peso price of cotton in Mexico (in the absence of distortionary policies) is

   a. P0.08 per pound.
   b. P0.125 per pound.
 * c. P4.50 per pound.
   d. P8 per pound.

8. If the world price of tradables remains unchanged while the official exchange rate rises by 20 percent and domestic prices for nontradables rise by 50 percent, then the real exchange rate (as defined in the Australian model)

   a. rises by 30 percent.
   b. falls by 30 percent.
 * c. falls by 20 percent.
   d. rises by 70 percent.

9. In terms of national income accounting concepts, absorption is defined as GNP

 * a. *plus* imports *minus* exports.
   b. *plus* exports *minus* imports.
   c. *plus* imports *plus* exports.
   d. *minus* investment expenditures *minus* exports.

10. At any point to the left of the *EB* line in the phase diagram,

   a. there is inflationary pressure.
 * b. there is an external surplus.
   c. fiscal and monetary policies are too loose.
   d. all the above.

11. Starting from an equilibrium in both markets, an increase in absorption will cause

    a. the supply curve to shift to the left for both tradables (T) and nontradables (N).
  * b. the demand curve to shift to the right for both T and N.
    c. the demand curve to shift to the right for N and to the left for T.
    d. no shifts in the curves, but the economy moves to a position of inflation and external deficit.

12. Starting from equilibrium in both markets, an increase in the real exchange rate will cause

    a. the supply curve to shift to the left for both tradables (T) and nontradables (N).
    b. the demand curve to shift to the right for both T and N.
    c. the demand curve to shift to the right for N and to the left for T.
  * d. no shifts in the curves, but the economy moves to a position of inflation and external surplus.

13. A *depreciation* of the real exchange rate (as defined in the Australian model) means that the

  * a. price of tradables rises relative to the price of nontradables.
    b. price of tradables falls relative to the price of nontradables.
    c. official exchange rate (defined as local currency per unit of foreign currency) falls.
    d. official exchange rate rises more slowly than the average price of nontradables.

14. Which of the following events will cause the external-balance line in the phase diagram to shift to the left?

    a. An appreciation of the exchange rate
    b. A decline in the interest rate on foreign debt
    c. A decline in absorption
  * d. A decline in export earnings

15. For an economy suffering from high inflation and a large external deficit, the standard prescription for stabilization entails fiscal

  * a. austerity to reduce demand and a real devaluation.
    b. austerity to reduce demand and a real appreciation.
    c. stimulus to expand supply and a real devaluation.
    d. stimulus to expand supply and a real appreciation.

16. For an economy that is experiencing internal balance with a large external deficit, which package of stabilization measures is warranted?

    a. A real devaluation, with no change in absorption
    b. A real appreciation, with no change in absorption
* c. A real devaluation, with fiscal austerity
    d. A real appreciation, with fiscal austerity

17. Which of the following is a self-correcting tendency in the market, when an economy is in the inflation-and-deficit zone?

    a. The loss of foreign exchange reserves compels the government to impose price controls and trade controls.
    b. The macroeconomic imbalances cause international lenders to increase the interest rate on the country's external debt.
* c. Domestic inflation reduces the real exchange rate.
    d. All the above.

18. Using the exchange rate as an *anchor* for an adjustment program means

    a. letting the market set the nominal exchange rate.
    b. maintaining a crawling peg such that the real exchange rate remains fixed.
* c. fixing the official, nominal exchange rate.
    d. imposing strict controls over foreign exchange transactions.

19. An *unexpected* feature of Chile's stabilization program in the 1970s was that

    a. export growth was weak after the real exchange rate appreciated.
    b. the economy stabilized without requiring fiscal austerity.
    c. the market's self-correcting mechanisms worked smoothly and quickly to eliminate the imbalances.
* d. inflation stayed high despite tight monetary policy and a big drop in the fiscal deficit.

20. The onset of Dutch disease is represented in the Australian model as

    a. a shift of the external-balance (*EB*) line to the left.
* b. a shift of the *EB* line to the right.
    c. a shift of the *EB* line to the left combined with a shift of the internal balance (*IB*) line to the left.
    d. a shift of the *EB* line to the right combined with a shift of the *IB* line to the left.

IDs and Paired-Concept Questions

These terms can be used individually as short-answer identification questions, or they can be used in pairs. In the latter case, ask students to explain (1) the meaning and significance of each of the two terms and (2) the relationship between them.

1. Tradable goods, real exchange rate
2. Nontradable goods, absorption
3. Official exchange rate, devaluation
4. Fiscal policy, austerity
5. Internal balance, inflation zone
6. Stabilization program, crawling-peg exchange rate regime
7. International Monetary Fund, balance of trade
8. Exchange-rate anchor, monetary policy
9. Phase diagram, self-correcting tendencies
10. Small economy, open economy

Study Guide Applications

Worked Example

The Worked Example provides a detailed explanation of one common source of macroeconomic imbalances—populist mismanagement of fiscal and monetary policies. The analysis of macroeconomic imbalances, including the cure, is framed in terms of the supply and demand for tradables and non-tradables; at the end of the example the analysis is restated using the phase diagram.

Exercises

1. The first exercise gives students lots of practice in dealing with the mechanics of the model—shifts in curves, movements along curves, the meaning of imbalances—using both supply and demand and the phase diagram.

2. Following a hypothetical story line, students have to trace the effects of various macroeconomic shocks and analyze the appropriate policy responses; the tool for analysis here is the phase diagram.

3. Finally, students are asked to match points on a phase diagram to seven real-world examples of macroeconomic imbalances and to identify the appropriate policy responses for each case.

**ANSWERS
TO THE
*STUDY GUIDE
AND
WORKBOOK* EXERCISES**

CHAPTER 1   **Introduction**

Exercise 1

a. CMR = 117.6; *Y* = $1,295.
    CMR = 90.9; *Y* = $2,714.
    CMR = 39.3; *Y* = $6,556.

b. (i) See the three data points and the connecting lines in Figure 1–2a.

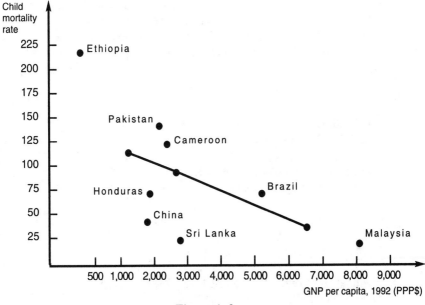

Figure 1–2a

(ii) The figure shows that child mortality rates decline sharply as GNP per capita rises.

c. (i)

	CMR	*Y*
Ethiopia	216	$ 340
China	43	$ 1,910
Honduras	70	$ 1,930
Pakistan	142	$ 2,130
Cameroon	124	$ 2,300
Sri Lanka	24	$ 2,810
Brazil	76	$ 5,250
Malaysia	20	$ 8,050

(ii) See the eight points plotted on Figure 1–2a.

(iii) Government policy certainly has an important effect on child health conditions. Another determinant of whether a country's child mortality rate is above or below average for its income level is education levels, especially for women. The distribution of income may be another factor contributing to favorable or unfavorable outcomes, relative to the underlying "pattern." Can you think of other factors?

d. Yes and no! Differences across countries cannot be explained solely on the basis of GNP per capita (serving as a proxy for development). Individual countries do not follow a set pattern; child mortality rates are influenced by country-specific factors at least as much as by general tendencies. Still, strong regularities undoubtedly exist on average, so one can speak of underlying "patterns" of development.

Exercise 2

a. K113 billion/8.1 million people = K13,951.
   K13,951/K29 per US$ = $481.

b. K218 billion/8.4 million people = K25,952.
   K25,952/K65 per US$ = $399.

c. $481
   $399
   Lower by 17 percent

d. Nominal GDP 1990 = K3,150 million; 1991 = K6,300.
   GDP = $900 million in 1990.
   GDP = $900 million in 1991.
   GDP per capita = $450 in 1990.
   GDP per capita = $429 in 1991.

Exercise 3

a. The pattern is that primary-school enrollments rise as a function of GNP per capita, and the whole relationship involved higher enrollment rates in 1995 than in 1965. Hence:

Percentage of age group
   enrolled in primary school = A
GNP per capita = D
1965 = C
1995 = B

b. Energy   line *B*
   Adult literacy   line *B*
   Life expectancy   line *B*
   Population in rural areas   line *A*
   Industry share of GNP   line *B*
   Access to clean water   line *B*

Exercise 4

Only a sketch of possible answers will be provided here.

a. The Malay girl works long hours in a factory for $2.50 per day so she can save $20 per month to send to her family. The girl in Massachusetts goes to high school and may have a part-time job to earn money to spend at the mall. The Malay is concerned with putting aside small amounts of money to improve her prospects for the future, not with school, clothes, and boy friends. She shares in a one-bedroom squatter house with seven other factory workers, rather than having her own room with a telephone and stereo.

b. In Mozambique the old lathe breaks down frequently. The workshop is hot and crowded, with a dirt floor and a tin roof. Product standards are crude. The worker walks home each night to a very small cement-block home with no electricity, no running water. He gets paid $50 per month. His Japanese counterpart works on a modern precision lathe which is carefully maintained. The workshop has climate control and good lighting. Product standards are extraordinarily precise. The worker takes the subway home each night to a small, comfortable flat. He gets paid $2,000 per month.

c. The farmer in Malawi has a small plot of land with simple hand tools, not a tractor. She lives in a small hut made of sticks and crumbly clay-soil bricks, not a small wood-frame house with central heating and a television. She worries about whether the year's maize harvest can last through the hunger season, rather than whether the year's crop income can be adequate to buy a new car. She owns tattered clothes and a few crude chairs and doesn't even dream of owning a television. She hopes that some of her eight children will be able to complete elementary school, not about getting them to college.

Exercise 5 [Optional]

a.

	Growth rate (%)	Doubling time (years)
India	1.9	37
Sri Lanka	2.9	24
Honduras	0.5	140
Ghana	−1.4	Unattainable!
Korea, Rep. of	7.1	10

b.

	Time required to grow eightfold (years)	GNP per capita after growing eightfold ($)
India	$37 \times 3 = 111$	9,680
Sri Lanka	$24 \times 3 = 72$	22,480
Honduras	$140 \times 3 = 420$	15,440
Ghana	Unattainable!	15,120
Korea, Rep. of	$10 \times 3 = 30$	71,600

CHAPTER 2   Starting Modern Economic Growth

Exercise 1

There are several acceptable ways to answer these questions. The answers provided here suggest some of the possibilities.

a. Large numbers of influential workers and managers are dependent on bloated staff levels and inefficient operations, supported by the subsidies. Without the subsidies many of these companies might be forced into bankruptcy. Under such conditions, removing subsidies is politically difficult and potentially destabilizing.

b. This is a universal political problem. No one wants funding for *their* programs cut, or *their* taxes raised. So inflation results by default, and implicitly taxes those who lack the power to adjust their nominal incomes and those who hold domestic-currency balances. A weak government that is dependent on groups that benefit from low taxes and high expenditures would account for the inflation.

c. Government officials themselves, not to mention the industrialists and the generals, want top-notch health care. The fact that little money is left over to provide better health care for the masses is an unfortunate side effect of decisions motivated by the self-interest of the elites.

d. Two groups benefit greatly from the red tape: the bureaucrats, and the owners and workers in enterprises that already have licenses (and for whom added competition would be a threat). These are important interest groups that most governments find difficult to alienate.

Exercise 2

There are numerous ways to answer parts a and b. The answers given here are suggestive only.

a. Three advantages of "backwardness":
   1. Knowledge of modern science is readily available to be applied or adapted to productive uses.
   2. Management techniques and administrative skills have already been discovered and are available to those who seek to learn.
   3. History has provided a great deal of evidence about the advantages and disadvantages of different systems of social and economic organization.

b. Three disadvantages of "backwardness":
1. The legacy of colonialism may have left a developing country with few indigenous entrepreneurs, managers, or skilled workers, at least initially.
2. Leaders may emulate the lifestyles of the high-income countries and divert scarce resources into luxury consumption.
3. Trained personnel such as doctors or engineers may emigrate to countries with higher pay scales.

c. (i) Several developing countries have performed poorly in recent decades, but most have outperformed the historical growth record of the United States, Germany, England, and France.
   (ii) In nearly all the developing countries, life expectancy today is better than in the United States in 1910.
   (iii) In less than 30 years, the achievement of most developing countries in terms of lower infant mortality rates is far better than the historical record in Massachusetts between 1850 and 1910.
   (iv) On balance, the evidence suggests that the advantages of "backwardness" outweigh the disadvantages.

Exercise 3

a. By draining surplus from the colonies, the capitalist powers could offset the historical tendency of profits to decline and provide higher living standards to home-country workers. Both of these effects serve to delay or prevent the crises that would otherwise serve as catalysts for the overthrow of the capitalist system, according to Marxian analysis.

b. According to modern theories of imperialism, "neocolonial" powers drain surplus from the LDCs through profits of multinational enterprises that operate in or export to the LDCs, through heavy debt service payments, through paying low prices for LDC primary products, and through influencing LDC consumption patterns in a manner which increases the demand for imported goods.

c. (i) Local elites may form alliances with the capitalist powers in return for sharing in the appropriated surplus, as well as for military equipment and political support to maintain themselves in power.
   (ii) The alliances may stifle development by facilitating the drain of surplus to the imperialist center, by distorting the LDC economy in the direction of increased inequality and luxury consumption, and by consolidating the power of the indigenous elites, to the detriment of effective development policy.

d. The answer is specific to each individual, but a good answer should include some explanation, as well as discussion of both the "agree" and "disagree" positions.

Exercise 4

a. A Mexican trader can buy a ton of popcorn for $200, ship it to the United States where it sells for $300, and earn a profit of $100 per ton. Similarly, a trader can buy steel in the United States for $300 per ton, ship it to Mexico where local steel is priced at $500, and earn a profit of as much as $200 per ton.

b. (i) Increase.
   (ii) Popcorn consumers are hurt, when the price of popcorn increases.
   (iii) Decrease.
   (iv) Steel producers and steel workers are hurt as competition from imports depresses the price of steel, and imports displace (higher cost) domestic output.

c. (i) $500,000
   (ii) 2500; $750,000
   (iii) 2500
   (iv) 2500

d. (i) The business people who control the export revenues might use the earnings to buy luxury consumption goods rather than steel for development purposes.
   (ii) Popcorn consumers and steel producers may have enough political influence to block a move to free trade.

Exercise 1

a. (i)   1.8.
    (ii) 1,800,000/1,200 = 1,500.
    (iii) 1,500 × 16 = 24,000.
    (iv) 300.
    (v)   1.62.
          1,620,000/1,200 = 1,350.
    (vi) 1,350 × 20 = 27,000.

b. (i)   24,000.
    (ii) 300 workers.
    (iii) 1,350; 27,000.
    (iv) See line S_1S_1 in Figure 3–2a.

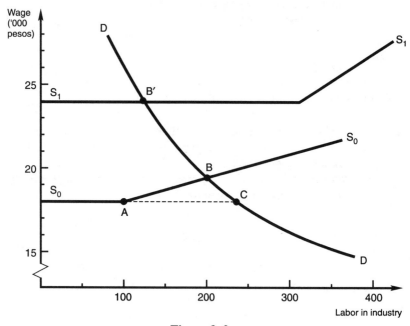

Figure 3–2a

c. (i) See point B' in Figure 3–2a.

> Job creation: less.
> Output: less.
> Real wage cost to employers: higher
> Real standard of living per worker: lower (because higher food prices outweigh the higher peso wage).
> Profits for reinvestment: less.

(ii) Food supplies are more scarce relative to the number of mouths to feed, so food prices rise relative to other prices. This means that the terms of trade between industry and agriculture become less favorable to industry. Urban workers must be paid more (relative to price of manufactured goods) to attract labor, since workers have the alternative of going back to the farm and consuming their share of banana output. The higher wage cost reduces employment, output, and profits for reinvestment.

d. (i) *In Figure 3–1*: Each point on the agricultural production function shifts vertically upward by 50 percent. *In Figure 3–2*: The rise in food supplies, relative to the number of mouths to feed, will cause banana prices to decline. This reduces the peso wage required to attract any given labor supply to industry. The labor supply curve shifts downward, perhaps even below S_0S_0.

(ii) By shifting industry's labor supply curve downward, the increase in agricultural productivity will generate more jobs, more output, and higher profits for reinvestment and growth. Although the nominal wage is lower, it buys more food than before. So real standards of living improve for urban workers.

Exercise 2

a. (i) $22,050 million.
   (ii) $10,710 million.
   (iii) $32,760 million.
   (iv) See Table 3–1a.

Table 3–1a
GNP for the United States and India

	United States			India		
	Quantity	Price ($)	Value of output (million $)	Quantity	Price (Rs)	Value of output (million Rs)
Steel (millions of tons)	105	210 per ton	22,050	12	6,100 per ton	73,200
Retail services (millions of person-years)	2.1	5,100 per person-year	10,710	5	32,000 per person-year	160,000
Total GNP (in local currency)			32,760			233,200

b. (i) Rs233,200 million.
   233,200/30 = $7,773 million.
   (ii) 32,760/7,773 = 4.21.

c. (i) $2,520 million.
   (ii) $25,500 million.
   (iii) $28,020 million.
   (iv) 32,760/28,020 = 1.17.
   (v) The exchange-rate method grossly understates the dollar value of India's nontraded services. Nontraded goods and services do not enter the market for foreign exchange, so there is no reason to expect that one obtains a proper dollar valuation simply by multiplying the rupee value times the exchange rate. If the exchange rate is distorted, then converting the rupee value to dollars using the prevailing exchange rate does not provide a proper dollar valuation even for traded goods like steel.

d. (i) Rs233,200 million
   (ii) Rs72,000 million
   (iii) Rs150,000 million
   (iv) Rs222,000 million
   (v) 32.1%

Exercise 3

a. (i) $g = s/k$, so $s = 20\%$.
   (ii) $g = 27/2.5 = 10.8\%$.
   (iii) The ICOR is likely to rise; this would indicate lower productivity. The reason is the law of diminishing returns. Presuming that investments with the highest productivity are undertaken first, more rapid accumulation of new capital stock will generally entail somewhat lower marginal productivity and produce smaller increments in real GDP.

b. (i) The prevailing saving rate and ICOR will yield a growth rate of just $g = s/k = 14/5 = 2.8$ percent.
   (ii) $g = 4$ percent could be achieved if the ICOR declined to 3.5.
   (iii) The economy needs more-efficient investment. The government should promote less capital-intensive industries, encourage more labor-intensive production processes within each industry, and dismantle controls that reduce efficiency in production and investment.

c. *[More difficult]* The arithmetic gives $k = s/g = -38.3$. This means that each $1 of incremental capital stock was associated with a *decline* in output of $38.3. Unless investment took the form of tools of destruction which were used locally, it is silly to interpret the number mechanically. What we see here is that the rate of investment was quite adequate, but this capital accumulation was more than offset by growing inefficiency. Output dropped despite the additional capital stock, not because of it.

Exercise 4

a. (i)   200; $K/Q = 2$.
   (ii) 300; ICOR $= 2$ because the change in capital is 200 and the change in output is 100.
   (iii) 300; $K/Q = 2$.
   (iv) Yes. As many as 30 workers could be withdrawn from soup production with no loss of output. The marginal product of labor is zero here.

b. (i)   200; $K/Q = 2$.
   (ii) 300; ICOR $= 2$ as in a(ii).
   (iii) 360 since the point is approximately 3/5 of the way between the isoquants for $Q = 300$ and $Q = 400$; $K/Q = 1.67$.
   (iv) No. The marginal product of labor is not zero with the neoclassical production function. If labor is withdrawn, production will drop.
   (v)   (Change in K)/(change in Q) $= 200/160 = 1.25$. The ICOR has changed because production is less capital-intensive now. Less extra capital is needed per extra unit of output, so investment productivity is higher. With a neoclassical production function there is not a fixed-coefficient relationship between inputs and outputs.

c. See Figure 3–5a.
   The shape of the production function shows that the increments in output decline (slightly) as successive increments in labor are added to the fixed stock of capital. This is what is meant by diminishing returns to labor.

d. *[Optional]* To the right of $L = 90$ the production function is flat, with $Q = 300$. In this range the marginal product of labor is zero. To the left of $L = 90$ the production function is a straight line from the origin to the point $L = 90$, $Q = 300$. In this range, each additional worker adds 3.33 units of output, so the marginal product of labor is 3.33.

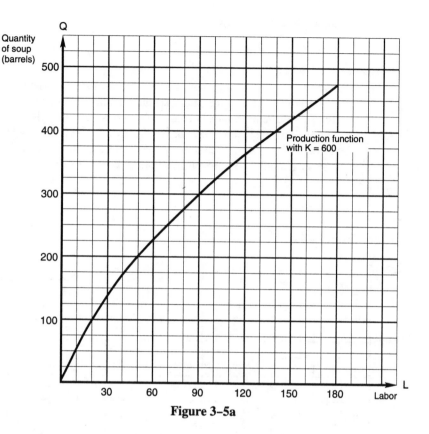

Figure 3–5a

Exercise 5

a. (i) $g = 0 + (.45)(4) + (.55)(2.7) = 3.285\%$.
   (ii) $a = 4.5 - 3.285 = 1.215\%$.
   (iii) The residual incorporates all the changes that increase the
productivity of the available factors of production. Examples
include technological change, improvements in managerial
efficiency, and improvements in the quality of the workforce.

b. (i) $1 = a + (.4)(5) + (.6)(3)$, so $a = -2.8\%$.
   (ii) Clearly, productivity and efficiency are declining, not increasing.
If productivity gains were zero ($a = 0$), the economy would be
growing by 3.8 percent per annum.

c.   (i)   Using the sources-of-growth equation,

$$8.4\% = 1.2\% + .67 \times g_K + .33 \times 2.6\%, \quad \text{so} \quad g_K = 9.5\%.$$

    (ii) $(.67 \times 9.5)/8.4 = .758 = 75.8\%$.

  (iii)   Fully three-fourths of Singapore's growth performance can be attributed to capital accumulation (keeping in mind that the data include investments in human capital as a component of capital accumulation). Just under one-third of the growth rate is explained by growth of the labor force. Barely one-seventh of GDP growth can be attributable to improvements in total factor productivity.

Exercise 6

a. See Figure 3–6a.

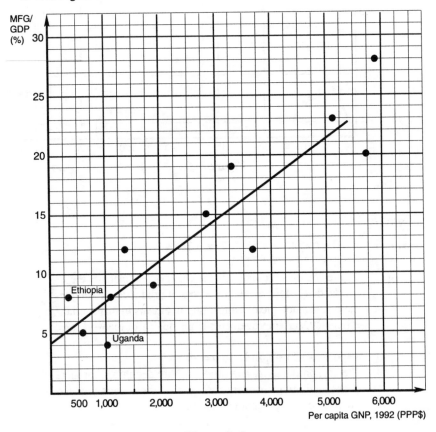

Figure 3–6a

b. Many differences in economic structure, natural resource wealth, history, and policy can account for such deviations. Uganda could have below-average manufacturing output because it has chosen policies that emphasize agriculture, in which it may have a comparative advantage. On the other hand, the relatively high share of manufacturing in Ethiopia, given the income level, could reflect a poor resource base for nonmanufactured products, a distorted price system that overvalues manufactured output, or even a year of drought, which reduced output from agriculture. In fact both these countries have been wrecked by civil wars; this could distort the structure of their economies. In general, one must be careful about interpreting positive deviations as "good," or negative deviations as "bad." Still, significant deviations do raise provocative questions about differences in development paths.

CHAPTER 4   Development and Human Welfare

Exercise 1

a. 10.9%
    25.7%
    43.7%
    65.7%
    100.0%

b. See Lorenz curve for Hungary in Figure 4–2a.

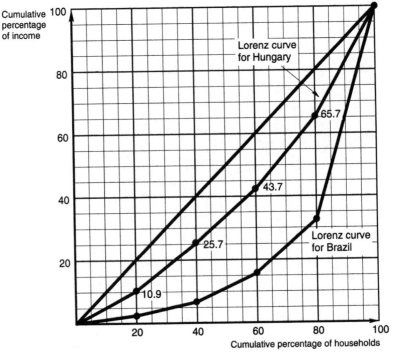

Figure 4–2a

c. Area A = 0.11.
   Gini = 0.11/0.50 = 0.22.

d. The Lorenz curve for Hungary lies uniformly nearer the diagonal; this indicates that Hungary has a more equal size distribution of income.

e. Hungary has a substantially lower Gini concentration ratio; this indicates that the size distribution of income is much more equal, which is just what the Lorenz curves show.

Exercise 2

a. (i) 8.1%
       19.4%
       48.4%
   (ii) As explained in the textbook, household surveys generally produce income statistics that understate incomes. Many households are either reluctant to divulge accurate information on income, or they may not be well informed about their total income.

b. (i) A: 500/2 = 250 rupees.
        B: 700/3 = 233 rupees.
        C: 900/4 = 225 rupees.
        D: 1,100/5 = 220 rupees.
        E: 3,000/6 = 500 rupees.
   (ii) Household D
        Household C
        Household E
   (iii) Quite so. For example, household D is the poorest in terms of per capita income, but the second "richest" in total income.

c. (i)   Households A, B, C, and D.
   (ii) 14.
   (iii) 14/20 = 70%.
   (iv) 9/20 = 45%; only households C and D are at or below the revised poverty line.

d. *Observed* differences in household income are totally due to the fact that the household heads are at different ages. Every household is exactly the same in terms of its lifetime income path. In a fundamental sense, there is complete equality in Pauvritania.

Exercise 3

a. 40%, 20%. (There is perfect equality.)

b. 200/600 = 33%; 200/600 = 33%.

c. (i) 29%, 29%.
   (ii) 40%, 20%. Perfect equality again.
   (iii) The *share* of income accruing to the poorest 40 percent dropped as the first factories opened, but then returned to its initial level once all the workers had modern-sector jobs. The declining income share of the poorest 40 percent occurred because other workers became better-off, not because the poorest farmers became poorer. While income inequality worsened at first, the extent of poverty declined throughout the process.

d. (i) 200/900 = 22%; 400/900 = 44%.
   (ii) 600/2000 = 30%; 600/2000 = 30%.
   (iii) During the early stages of development, wages are stagnant and the lion's share of the growing value-added accrues to capitalists, who own the means of production. As labor markets tighten up, real wages rise and the share of income accruing to owners of capital declines. These dynamics cause income inequality to rise during the early stages of development and then decline after the turning point is achieved.

Exercise 4

a. (i) See the plot of points in Figure 4–4a.
   (ii) The data clearly reveal a tendency for HDI to rise with per capita income. (The corresponding regression equation has $R^2 = .80$. But

there are still notable departures from the underlying pattern. Country-specific characteristics such as government policy, patterns of asset ownership, and development strategies clearly influence observed performance in terms of the HDI.

(iii) See the Pattern Line in Figure 4–4a.

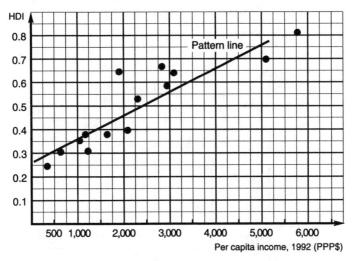

Figure 4–4a

b. (i) Tanzania: Gini = 0.572.
   Kenya: Gini = 0.551.
   Colombia: Gini = 0.474.
   Peru: Gini = 0.443.

(ii) The facts do *not* bear out the hypothesis. Of the four countries with the highest Gini ratios, only Kenya has an HDI value that is well below the Pattern Line. Peru's HDI is actually above the line.

(iii) Bangladesh: Gini = 0.280.
   Sri Lanka: Gini = 0.294.
   Pakistan: Gini = 0.301.
   India: Gini = 0.311.

(iv) Again, the facts do not bear out the hypothesis. Of the four countries with the lowest Gini ratios, only Sri Lanka has an HDI value which is well above the pattern line. In fact, Pakistan's HDI is far below the pattern line, despite the low Gini ratio.

(v) One must conclude that income inequality does not explain much of the variation in HDI performance. Determinants of the HDI are much more complex and country specific.

c. (i) See Figure 4–5a.

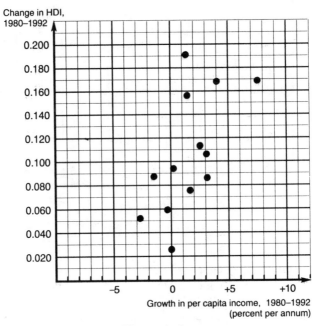

Figure 4–5a

(ii) The wide spread of data points indicates that factors other than economic growth strongly affect changes in the HDI. For example, health and education policies are likely to explain some of the differences. Nonetheless, there is a positive relationship between growth and human development. (This is not surprising since an adjusted index of per capita income is a component of the HDI.)

Exercise 5 [Advanced]

a. (i) See column 3 in Table 4–3a.

Table 4–3a

Measures of Inequality and Income

	Gini ratio (1)	GDP per capita 1992 (PPP$) (2)	Log Y (3)	$(\text{Log } Y)^2$ (4)	Predicted Gini (5)
Ethiopia	0.312	340	5.829	33.977	0.35
Tanzania	0.572	630	6.446	41.547	0.39
India	0.311	1,010	6.918	47.855	0.42
Bangladesh	0.280	1,210	7.098	50.387	0.42
Kenya	0.551	1,230	7.115	50.620	0.42
Ghana	0.358	1,640	7.402	54.796	0.43
China	0.351	1,910	7.555	57.076	0.43
Pakistan	0.301	2,130	7.664	58.735	0.43
Bolivia	0.411	2,270	7.728	59.715	0.43
Sri Lanka	0.294	2,810	7.941	63.059	0.43
Indonesia	0.322	2,970	7.996	63.941	0.42
Peru	0.443	3,080	8.033	64.524	0.42
Tunisia	0.391	5,130	8.543	72.980	0.41
Colombia	0.474	5,760	8.659	74.973	0.40

(ii) See column 4 in Table 4–3a.
(iii) See column 5 in Table 4–3a.

b. (i) See the solid line in Figure 4–6a.

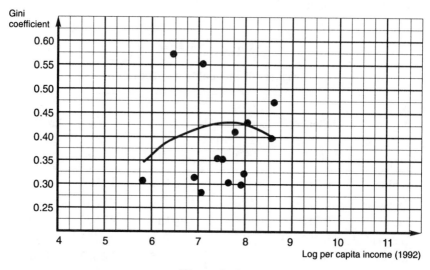

Figure 4–6a

(ii) The statistical relationship produces a curve with the basic properties of an inverted U, but without much downward bend. As per capita GDP begins to rise, predicted inequality increases initially; as per capita GDP reaches about $2,000 (log = 7.6), predicted inequality flattens out and then declines slightly. The result is consistent with Kuznets' inverted-U hypothesis, but the empirical association between inequality and per capita income is rather weak.

c. (i) See the scatter plot of data points in Figure 4–6a.
(ii) Many of the data points are not close to the regression line.
(iii) The Gini ratio is within 0.05 of the predicted value on the regression line for 4 of the 14 countries: Ethiopia, Bolivia, Peru, and Tunisia. Inequality is much worse than the predicted value in Tanzania, Kenya, and Colombia. In the other 7 countries, income inequality is less than the predicted value.

Exercise 1

   a. $P^E = \$1.00$.
      $Q^E = 370$ bouquets per week (approximately).

   b.   (i)   See Line S' in Figure 5–2a.

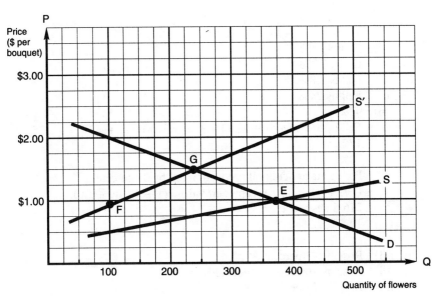

Figure 5–2a

      (ii) $P' = \$1.50$.
           $Q' = 240$ bouquets per week (approximately).
     (iii)   Consumers are hurt. They end up paying a higher price, and the quantity consumed declines.

   c.   (i)   Traders can procure flowers across the border at a price far below P', smuggle the contraband into Gardenia, and sell the flowers at a price near P'. The result is high profits from the sale of smuggled flowers.
      (ii) $0.50 per bouquet.
           $0.90 per bouquet.
           $90.00 for 100 bouquets.

d. The more flowers that are smuggled, the more consumers are drawn away from the official market. The infant domestic industry will lose sales to the parallel market. This loss of sales may kill off the domestic industry, or it may slow down the learning process required to make domestic production competitive. Then again, competition in the parallel market might force domestic producers to "grow up" more quickly!

e. Bribery of officials—or officials seeking out bribes—can be expected as a consequence of the high profits from smuggling.

Exercise 2

a. (i)   Cedi 36,957.
          Cedi 26,723.
          Fell by 28%.
   (ii)   Fell by 24%.
   (iii) 43%.
          Fell by 56%. Derivation: $(1 + \text{real growth}) = (1 + .43)/(1 + 2.25)$.
   (iv)   17%.
          70%.
          Per capita agricultural production fell by 31 percent.
          Derivation: $(1 + \text{per capita growth}) = (1 + .17)/(1 + .70)$.
   (v)   216 times higher.
   (vi)   19.8%, 3.8%.

b. (i)   Rose by 11 percent.
   (ii)   Rose by 100 percent (doubled).
   (iii) Rose by 26 percent.
   (iv)   Rose by 125 percent.
          Rose by 60 percent.
   (v)   688 percent.
   (vi)   12.8 percent.

c. (i)   1.2% per annum.
   (ii)   Fell, 1.6% per annum.
   (iii) Fallen, 13.5%.
   (iv)   Instead of *rising* to Cedi 29,656 in 1992, from Cedi 26,723 in 1983, per capita real GDP would *decline* 13.5 percent to Cedi 23,112. Per capita real GDP was 28.3 percent higher in 1993 than what would have been the case had the prereform trend continued.
   (v)   To the extent that the outcome *without* reforms would have been even worse than we have allowed for, the benefits from the reform program would be greater than the 28.3 percent improvement calculated above.

Exercise 3

a. (i)   The market works through supply and demand. The market prices for maize and rye reflect a balance between consumer preferences and resource costs of production. Farmers choose the allocation of cropland between maize and rye to maximize their utility from earning cash to purchase nonfood consumer goods, as opposed to consuming their own maize.

   (ii)   With income shifted from maize eaters to bread eaters, the demand curve for maize shifts to the left and the demand curve for bread (and therefore rye) shifts to the right. This change in market conditions will result in more allocation of land to bread (and rye) and less allocation of land to maize.

b. (i)   Too much. The share of national income going to bread eaters is deemed "too high," so the market overvalues rye relative to maize. In terms of national goals, the market equilibrium allocates too much land to rye and too little land to maize.

   (ii)   Since bread output is now below the optimal amount, so is demand for rye. Farmers, therefore, will produce less rye and more maize than is warranted on grounds of economic efficiency.

  (iii)   Too much. At the market equilibrium, the marginal *social* cost of bread—inclusive of the externality costs—exceeds the value of bread to consumers. The social optimum entails less bread being produced and consumed, and hence less rye. Therefore, the social optimum would allocate less land to rye production.

c. (i)   Although the farmers have more maize to eat, their cash incomes drop: they are selling less, at an unchanged price. The net effect is unambiguously to reduce farmers' welfare. Under the market system, the farmers were choosing between maize and rye production to maximize their utility. The fact that they chose to produce more rye prior to the imposition of controls shows that they valued extra income more than extra maize!

   (ii)   Yes. At the controlled level of output, there are buyers who would willingly pay more than the controlled prices for bread and rye. This gap between the controlled price and the price that buyers are willing to pay creates economic rent opportunities, which induce parallel market trades and payoffs to officials to "look the other way."

  (iii)   In the short run farmers produce less rye and more maize. But the extra maize supplies reduce the value of maize and therefore reduce the incentive for investment and productivity enhancements in farming. Thus, total farm output may grow more slowly due to the controls.

Exercise 4

a.   (i)   Businesses have a strong incentive to stockpile inventories of imported goods in anticipation of the sharp rise in import prices that could come at any time.

   (ii)   No contest. Savers prefer to place their funds in foreign bank accounts and then repatriate the savings *after* the anticipated devaluation (if conditions then seem more stable). Via capital flight they expect large gains from speculating against their own currency.

  (iii)   The two answers above show that macroeconomic instability can distort market allocations of scarce foreign exchange and domestic savings. Much of the available foreign exchange is used to buy idle inventories, and much of the available savings is unavailable to the domestic economy.

b.   The licensing requirements undercut the vital flexibility advantage of the market. Normally, the market will induce automatic resource reallocations in response to changing economic conditions. But not in Bejeebers.

c.   (i)   The monopolist charges a higher price than the competitive one, and produces less than the competitive output. Also, the price exceeds the marginal cost of production, so the allocation of resources to textile production falls short of the efficient outcome.

   (ii)   Yes. Even though there is still just one domestic producer, allowing imports introduces effective competition. The monopolist cannot charge a price higher than the price of imports, and she has to match cost-reducing innovations elsewhere in order to stay in business.

d.   (i)   Dune buggies. Because the price of dune buggies is unusually low relative to the price of sedans.

   (ii)   Yes, but sedans only. While the cost of local assembly is double the world price, imported sedans cost triple the world price due to the tariff. So local assemblers can thrive. For dune buggies, however, the cost of local assembly is higher than the local price of imported dune buggies, which bear no tariff.

  (iii)   First, the relative price distortion induces many people to drive imported dune buggies when they would have preferred imported sedans, in the absence of the tariffs. Second, the tariff structure also distorts capital investment and employment patterns by encouraging the highly inefficient local assembly of sedans.

e.   The steel company can sustain excessive operating costs, poor product quality, and bad customer services. The company may then lose money, but the managers are not accountable to operate at a profit. Under such circumstances, the market does not automatically compel efficiency.

CHAPTER 6   Planning Models

Exercise 1

a.   (i)   See Table 6–3a.

Table 6–3a
1995 Interindustry Flow Matrix for Duahla

	Agriculture (1)	Manufacturing (2)	Total intermediate use	Final use	Total use
	Using sectors		Total		
1. Agriculture	50	20	**70**	930	1,000
2. Manufacturing	50	**100**	**150**	250	**400**
3. Total purchases	**100**	120	220		
4. Value-added	900	**280**	GNP = **1,180**		
5. Total output	**1,000**	400			**1,400**

(ii) $900/1,180 = .76 = 76\%$.
$100/1,000 = .10 = 10\%$.
$120/400 = .30 = 30\%$.

b.   See Table 6–4a.

Table 6–4a
1995 Input-Output Coefficients with Matrix for Duahla

	X_1 Agriculture (1)	X_2 Manufacturing (2)
	Using sectors	
1. Agriculture (X_1)	.05	.05
2. Manufacturing (X_2)	.05	.25
3. Total purchases	.10	.30
4. Value-added	.90	.70
5. Total output	1.00	1.00

c. $X_1 = .05X_1 + .05X_2 + 1,500.$
$X_2 = .05X_1 + .25X_2 + 500.$

193

d. Solving the second equation for X_2 gives $X_2 = .0667 X_1 + 666.67$. Plugging this expression for X_2 into the first equation and solving gives

$X_1 = 1,619.70$, compared with $X_1 = 1,000$ in 1990, and
$X_2 = 774.70$, compared with $X_2 = 400$ in 1990.

e. (i) I in agriculture $= (1,619.7 - 1,000) \times 2 = \$1,239.40$.
    I in industry $= (774.7 - 400) \times 7$ $= 2,622.90$.
    Total I over five years $= 3,862.30$.
  (ii) Annual I requirement $= 772.50$/year.
 (iii) The annual investment requirement amounts to 65 percent of initial GNP—a figure quite incompatible with the resources available to a poor country. Hence, the plan is inconsistent. Target outputs must be scaled back.

f. (i) A SAM would add rows and columns showing receipts and expenditures for each factor of production and for major institutions, including the government and various categories of households. The SAM can incorporate rows and columns showing savings and investment flows through the financial markets, as well as receipts and outlays from the balance-of-payments accounts.
  (ii) Any three:

SAMs provide a consistent framework to organize a more comprehensive set of economic accounts.

SAMs provide a more complete statistical picture of economic flows.

SAMs highlight data weaknesses requiring research.

SAMs can be converted into a more comprehensive economic models for determining the effects of various interventions or shocks.

Exercise 2

a. (i) See point 1 in Figure 6–2a. This target is not consistent. The point lies outside the country's production possibilities frontier. It is not achievable given the country's resource constraints.
  (ii) See point 2 in Figure 6–2a. This target is consistent. The point lies inside the country's PPF, so the combination of production levels is achievable. (Point 2 cannot be optimal, though, since it lies well inside the PPF.)

(iii) See point 3 in Figure 6–2a. This target is consistent. The point lies
       on the country's PPF, so the combination of production levels is
       achievable. (It is not optimal, however, as you will see momentarily.)

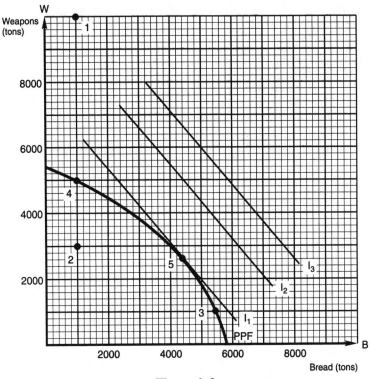

Figure 6–2a

b. See point 4 in Figure 6–2a. At this point the economy produces exactly
    1000 loaves of bread and otherwise maximizes the output of weapons.

c. (i) See the community indifference curves labeled I_1, I_2, and I_3 in
         Figure 6–2a.
    (ii) See point 5 in Figure 6–2a.

Exercise 3

a. Equation 6–4 states that the amount of new production capacity (this year's Y capacity over and above last year's) is proportional to last year's investment. The constant of proportionality ($1/k = 0.2$) is the reciprocal of the ICOR. This equation is a transformation of the Harrod-Domar model to a year-by-year format, with an ICOR value of $k = 5$.

b.　(i)　$Y_1 = 100 + .2(20) = \$104$.
　　(ii)　$I_1 = S_1 + F_1$
　　　　　$= .15(104) + 8 = \$23.60$.
　　(iii)　$Y_2 = 104 + .2(23.60) = \$108.72$.
　　(iv)　$g = (108.7/104) - 1 = .045 = 4.5\%$.
　　(v)　Higher domestic saving rate s.
　　　　　Higher investment productivity (lower ICOR k).
　　　　　Higher inflow of foreign saving F.

c.　(i)　$M_1 = 20 + 8 = \$28$.
　　(ii)　$I_1 = 28 - 10 = \$18$.
　　(iii)　$Y_2 = Y_1 + .2(18) = \$107.6$.
　　　　　$g = (107.6/104) - 1 = .035 = 3.5\%$.
　　(iv)　Higher export earnings.
　　　　　Higher inflow of foreign saving F.
　　　　　Reduced reliance on *imported* capital goods; the I term in Equation 6–7 has an implied coefficient of 1.0, which could be reduced to the extent that investment can make use of domestically produced capital goods.
　　(v)　In this case, boosting the domestic saving rate will *not* generate more rapid growth, since saving is not the binding constraint.

Exercise 4

a.　(i)　PV $= 600/1.12 = \$535.71$.
　　(ii)　PV $= 1,500/(1.09)^2 = \$1,262.52$.
b.　(i)　NPV $= -1,000 + 600/(1.10) + 600/(1.10)^2 = \$41.32$.
　　(ii)　NPV $= -\$24.57$.
　　(iii)　This investment is worthwhile if the appropriate discount rate is 10 percent, but not if it is 15 percent.
　　(iv)　IRR $= 13\%$.
　　(v)　Less.

d.　(i)　See Table 6–5a.

Table 6–5a
Two Proposed Investment Projects for Galaxia

Project A: Space Probe

Year	Costs ($)	Benefits ($)	Net benefits ($)	Discount factor at 5%	Present value ($)
0	100	0	−100	1.0000	−100.00
1	50	0	−50	0.9524	−47.62
2	5	10	5	0.9070	4.54
3	5	10	5	0.8638	4.32
4	5	155	150	0.8227	123.41
5	5	155	150	0.7835	117.53

NPV = 102.18

Project B: Irrigation Channel

Year	Costs ($)	Benefits ($)	Net benefits ($)	Discount factor at 5%	Present value ($)
0	100	0	−100	1.0000	−100.00
1	50	0	−50	0.9524	−47.62
2	5	125	120	0.9070	108.84
3	5	125	120	0.8638	103.66
4	5	10	5	0.8227	4.11
5	5	10	5	0.7835	3.92

NPV = 72.91

(ii)　Project A.

d.　(i)　NPV for project A = $23.93.
　　　　NPV for project B = $31.51.
　　(ii)　Project B.

(iii)   The present value of any future payment declines when a higher discount rate is used, and more remote payments decline more strongly (since they are discounted more years). The NPV of both projects declines when $r = .15$ is used, but the NPV for project A declines relatively more because the bulk of its benefits occur in later years.

e. Applying shadow prices reduced the net benefits of project A relative to project B. This result occurs because the scarcity cost of imports to project A is higher with shadow pricing, while the opportunity cost of using unskilled labor in project B is lower. On both counts, shadow pricing enhances the attractiveness of project B.

Exercise 5 [Optional]

a.   (i) $2X_C + 2X_T = 100$.
      (ii) See line L in Figure 6–3a and the shading bounded by line L.

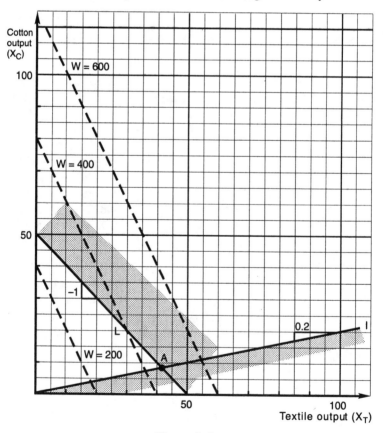

Figure 6–3a

b. (i) $X_C = .2X_T$.
    (ii) See line I in Figure 6–3a and the shading bounded by line I.

c. (i) $W = 5FC + 11FT$.
    (ii) $FC = X_C - .2X_T$.
    (iii) $W = 5X_C + 10X_T$.
    (iv) See lines $W = 200$, $W = 400$, and $W = 600$ in Figure 6–3a.

d. See point A in Figure 6–3a. The production point that maximizes social welfare entails the highest feasible level of textile output, which is approximately 42 units judging from the graph. Cotton is produced only to the extent of the input requirement of the textile industry; no extra is produced as a final product.

CHAPTER 7   Sustainable Development

Exercise 1

a.   (i)   See answers in Table 7–1a.

Table 7–1a
Demographic Data

Year	Production (metric tons)	Resource rent ($600 per m.ton)	Present value ($r = 12\%$)
1995	140,000	$84 million	$ 84.0 million
1996	90,000	$54	$ 48.2
1997	90,000	$54	$ 43.0
1998	90,000	$54	$ 38.4
1999	90,000	$54	$ 34.3
Total	500,000		$247.9 million

(ii) $247.9 million
$84 million
$84 million

(iii) Falls.
$84 + 54/(1.15) + 54/(1.15)^2 + 54/(1.15)^3 + 54/(1.15)^4 = \$238.2$ million.

(iv)   The discount rate reflects the real rate of return on alternative investments. When this rate rises, then revenue accruing in the future has less present value; less money *today* will generate a comparable sum in the future. Thus, a higher discount rate reduces the present value of a given cash flow in the future.

b.   (i) $2,750 in 1996
$3,025 in 1997
$3,328 in 1998
$3,660 in 1999

(ii) $850 in 1996
$1,125 in 1997
$1,428 in 1998
$1,760 in 1999

(iii) $84 + 76.5/(1.12) + 101.3/(1.12)^2 + 128.5/(1.12)^3 + 158.4/(1.12)^4 = \$425.2$ million.

c.   (i) $600.
    (ii) $850/1.12 = $759.
    (iii) Vice versa. Zambia should produce less in 1995 and more in 1996. The forgone resource rent from reducing output by 1 ton in 1995 is more than offset by the discounted value of the resource rent from an extra ton the following year. Even after applying the 12 percent discount to the net earnings in 1999, there is a gain from deferring production.
    (iv)   The condition for optimality is $600 = (P1996 − $1,900)/1.12. Solving gives P1996 = $2,572.

d.   (i) $1,000.
    (ii) $140 + 90/(1.12) + 90/(1.12)^2 + 90/(1.12)^3 + 90/(1.12)^4 = 413.4 million.
    (iii) The government's valuation is $247.9 million, so the asking price is $347.9 million. MMC accepts this, since it values the resource at $413.4 million under its management. The government comes out ahead by $100 million, while MMC clears $65.5 million in present value of resource rents. In this example the reduced costs under private management generate extra resource rents, which permit both parties to gain from the transaction.

Exercise 2

a.   (i)   The ecological factor is that families have to go farther to gather firewood as nearby supplies are depleted, so the payoff per unit of effort declines. The economic factor is that wood is allocated to the highest-value uses when the supplies are low; as supplies rise the firewood gets allocated to lower-value uses.
    (ii)   Excessive harvesting will reduce the woodlands' natural rate of regeneration, and so cause a decline in the sustainable harvest. Also, if the market is flooded with firewood, the price may decline, reflecting low value at the margin.
    (iii) Quite simply, this point represents extinction of the woodlands due to overharvesting. This can occur if the deforestation causes severe soil erosion or if cutting down too many trees leads to an invasion of nonwoody plants, like the *alang-alang* in Indonesia. Madagascar, in fact, has suffered badly from massive deforestation.

b. (i) See point E_1 in Figure 7–1a.

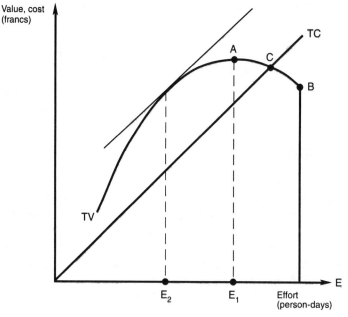

Figure 7–1a

(ii) The two are identical. Since the marginal cost is zero in this case, net benefits rise whenever the marginal benefit is greater than zero. So the efficient harvest coincides with the peak of the *TV* curve.

c. (i) See point E_2 in Figure 7–1a. This outcome is determined by finding the point on line *TV* where its slope (tangent) is equal to the slope of line *TC*.

(ii) Point E_2 lies to the left of maximum *TV*. Moving beyond E_2 entails marginal costs of the effort exceeds the value of the marginal harvest of firewood. In this case it is *not* efficient to push effort all the way to the peak of the *TV* curve.

d. (i) The gathering of firewood creates a negative externality. My decision to put in an extra day of gathering reduces the amount that you will gather! The total harvest value rises by less than my gain. So my *private* assessment may show marginal benefits in excess of the marginal cost, even though the community's marginal benefit is insufficient to justify any extra gathering.

(ii) Similar logic applies beyond point E_1. My decision to gather more firewood may not only crowd you out, but it may deplete the sustainable harvest absolutely. Yet an extra effort can be worth the cost if I get a sufficiently large share of the shrinking pie. Another factor is population growth. Additional families gain from harvesting firewood as long as there is any net benefit at all to share with other members of the community—out to point C in Figure 7–1

(iii) As just explained, it may be fully rational for additional families to push the total effort out to point C. Even a minor drought (which *shifts* line *TV* to the left) could then push the woodland over the edge into extinction. Also, government subsidies for competing land uses could induce individuals to cut woodlands to extinction.

(iv) No. With open access the free market leads to an inefficient over-exploitation of common resources, in some cases unsustainably.

Exercise 3

a. (i) See the line labeled SMC in Figure 7–2a.

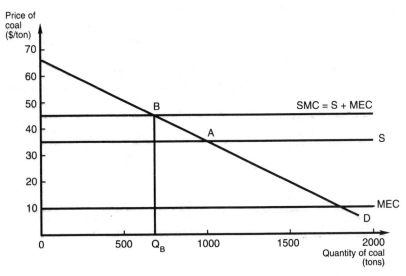

Figure 7–2a

(ii) See point B and output level Q_B in Figure 7–2a.
(iii) $35
      $35
      $10
      $10

      (iv) The net benefit would be zero, because the marginal benefit to coal users equals the marginal social cost.

      (v) Yes. Each ton produced still generates $10 worth of pollution.

b.   (i) $10.

    (ii) The tax-inclusive price paid per ton by the power company now includes the actual cost of having the coal supplied *plus* an additional amount, via the tax, which equals the external cost per ton from pollution. The power company's internal decision on buying coal now takes into account the marginal *social* cost.

c.   (i) No. Coal can now be brought to the market and used for a social marginal cost of just $30. The optimal output of coal is now higher than it was when the SMC was $35.

    (ii) No! The power company still has to pay $35 per ton of coal as long as the $10 tax is in place. The tax becomes an impediment to the adoption of the new technology and reduction of pollution.

   (iii) Yes! Now the tax bill depends on the amount of pollution produced. The power company can spend $5 to save $10 in tax by adopting the new pollution-control equipment.

d.   (i) The cost of losing valuable forests is not borne by the cattle ranchers, so clearing the land creates an external diseconomy; the optimal market outcome would involve *less* ranching. The subsidy to ranchers accelerates the rate of deforestation, and moves the economy further from the optimal market outcome.

    (ii) The diverted water reduces water flow in the river, and so imposes an external cost on those living downstream. This is an external diseconomy. (In fact the irrigation reduced the water flow so much that it killed off a large fishing industry in the Aral Sea.) To correct for the externality, the irrigation water would be taxed, not subsidized. The government policy moves the market further from the efficient outcome.

   (iii) Vehicle use creates external costs in the form of air pollution and traffic congestion. By raising the price of gasoline, the government in this case is moving the market closer to the efficient outcome.

Exercise 4

a.   (i)   See line MEC in Figure 7–3a.
    (ii)   M$410.
    (iii) M$21,000.

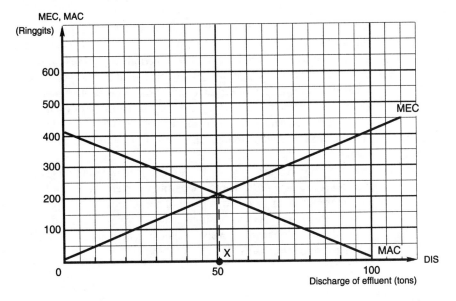

Figure 7–3a

b.   (i)   0
        100
    (ii)   See line MAC in Figure 7–3a.
    (iii) M$410.
    (iv) M$21,000.
    (v)   In this simple example, the cost of zero abatement is exactly the
        same as the cost of full abatement. (So no one can accuse the
        author of biasing the numbers!)

c.   (i)   See point X in Figure 7–3a.
    (ii)   50.

d. (i) M$5,500, M$5,500, M$11,000.
   (ii) 45, 55, M$4,500, M$6,600, M$11,100.
   In this case the combined cost is higher than at point X.
   (iii) 45, 55, M$4,500, M$6,600, M$11,100.
   Again, the combined cost is higher than at point X.
   (iv) The combined cost is minimized at point X, where MEC = MAC.

e. (i) The permits allow discharges up to point X, which is exactly the optimum.
   (ii) There is surely room for a deal. You sell permits at a price that is above M$150 but less than M$210. For each permit sold, you have to clean up an extra ton of effluent; this costs you M$150, which is more than covered by income from selling the permit. For each permit bought, I get to reduce my abatement effort by 1 ton; this saves me M$210, which more than covers the cost of the extra permit.
   (iii) Our transaction has *no effect* on the total amount of pollution. The total cost to society *falls*; due to the permit transfer, a less costly abatement activity is adopted in place of a more costly activity.
   (iv) Yes! As shown by the example immediately above, anyone who can find or develop less-expensive abatement methods can convert the innovation into profits.

Exercise 5

a. 10% per year; $3,000.

b. (i) $800.
   (ii) 5%.
   (iii) 5% × 800 = $40.
   400 – 40 = $360.
   360/400 = 90%.
   (iv) Depletion amounts to 10 percent of GNP, on top of 10 percent depreciation of made capital. So ANNP is 80 percent of GNP = $320 per capita.
   (v) 20% (which is a stiff requirement).

c.   (i)   See line 2 in Table 7–2a.

Table 7–2a
Gross and Net Domestic Product in Indonesia, 1982–1984
(billions of constant 1973 rupiah)

	1982	1983	1984
1. GDP	12,325	12,842	13,520
2. Growth rate of GDP	**4.2%**	**5.3%**	
3. *Less* depreiation	–616	–642	–676
4. Net domestic product (NDP)	**11,709**	**12,200**	**12,844**
5. *Less* net change in natural resources:			
a. Petroleum	–1,158	–1,825	–1,765
b. Forests	–551	–974	–493
c. Soils	–55	–71	–76
d. Total depletion	**–1,764**	**–2,870**	**–2,334**
6. *Adjusted* net domestic product (ANDP)	**9,945**	**9,330**	**10,510**
7. Growth rate of ANDP	**–6.2%**	**12.6%**	
8. Gross domestic investment (GDI)	2,783	3,776	3,551
9. Net Domestic Investment (NDI)	**2,167**	**3,134**	**2,875**
10. *Adjusted* net domestic investment (ANDI)	**403**	**264**	**541**
11. GDI as % of GDP	**22.6%**	**29.4%**	**26.3%**
12. ANDI as % of ANDP (net investment rate)	**4.1%**	**2.8%**	**5.1%**

(ii)   See line 3.
(iii) See line 5d.
(iv)   See line 6.
(v)   See line 7.

(vi) The ANDP growth rate is quite different from the GDP growth
       rate. For 1982–83, GDP growth is positive whereas ANDP growth
       is negative. The ANDP figure is a better measure of *sustainable*
       growth, because the economy must replace depreciation of made
       capital and depletion of natural capital in order to sustain produc-
       tion capacity. Output obtained from depleting natural capital
       cannot be sustained indefinitely.
d.   (i)   See line 9 and 10 in Table 7–2a.
     (ii) See lines 11 and 12.
     (iii) Based on the GDI figures, it appears that Indonesia's investment
           rate was quite high. But after taking into account depreciation and
           depletion, net capital accumulation was no more than 4 percent of
           net output.

Exercise 6

a.   (i) $3 million.
     (ii) 9% × $20 million = $1.8 million.
     (iii) 2.05 × 1.8 = B3.69 million.

b.   (i) $1.8 million, B3.69 million.
     (ii) 3.69 – 2.0 = B1.69 million.
     (iii) $20 million × 2.05 = B41 million.

c. If the ICO grants $3 million to the government of Bolivia, to place in dollar
    investments to generate an annual income for conservation, the yield would
    be far less than the benefit to Bolivia of having $20 million of debt for-
    given. Hence, the debt-for-nature swap generates much more annual
    funding for national parks in Bolvia. Also, the swap hands the respon-
    sibility for funding over to Bolivia; the forests become an activity of
    Bolivian nationals, not a hand-me-down from international conservationists.

CHAPTER 8   **Population**

Exercise 1

a.

Table 8–2a
Demographic Data

Group	Income range, 1992 (PPP\$)	PPP\$, 1992	CBR (per 1000) 1970	CBR (per 1000) 1992	CDR (per 1000) 1970	CDR (per 1000) 1992	Rate of natural increase (%) 1970	Rate of natural increase (%) 1992
1	Less than \$1,000	485	46	48	21	17	**2.5**	**3.1**
2	\$1,000–\$2,000	1378	44	32	18	11	**2.6**	**2.1**
3	\$2,000–\$3,000	2527	43	32	16	9	**2.7**	**2.3**
4	\$3,000–\$4,000	3340	43	28	16	8	**2.7**	**2.0**
5	\$4,000–\$5,000	No large-country observations in this income range						
6	\$5,000–\$6,000	5515	40	27	12	7	**2.8**	**2.0**
7	Over \$6,000	7828	34	24	9	6	**2.5**	**1.8**

b.   (i)   See lines CBR70 and CDR70 in Figure 8–1a.

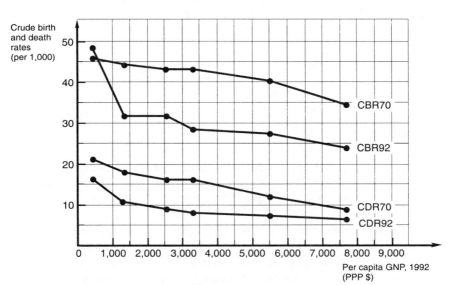

Figure 8–1a

(ii) Yes. The graph shows both the CBR and CDR declining as per capita income rises. It shows that the death rate declines faster at early stages of development, and so causes the rate of natural increase to rise. At later stages, the birth rate falls at a faster rate, and so leads to a reduction in the rate of natural increase.

c. (i) See lines CBR92 and CDR92 in Figure 8–1a.
   (ii) The graph for 1992 shows that the CBR and CDR again decline as per capita income rises. But this time the sharpest drop in birth rates occurs between group I and group II. The graph corresponds to a demographic transition in which all but the poorest countries already have reached the stage of declining crude birth rates.
   (iii) Between 1970 and 1992 all groups except the poorest had declining birth rates. Every group had declining death rates. The poorest countries were still back at the first stage of the transition, at which death rates are dropping but not birth rates, so population growth is accelerating. All other groups reached the stage at which birth rates are falling much faster than death rates, so population growth is slowing down.

d. (i) Per capita income would have to rise to between $2,900 and $3,000. (The exact point is $2,934.)
   (ii) Per capita income would have to rise above $5,515.
   (iii) At 2 percent per year growth ($r = .02$), the move from $500 to $5,515 would take 120 years! Proof: $5,515 = 500 \, e^{rt} \Rightarrow 5515/500 = e^{rt} \Rightarrow \ln 11.03 = rt \Rightarrow 2.40 = .02t$. Therefore $t = 120$.

Exercise 2

d. (i) –
   (ii) –
   (iii) –
   (iv) –
   (v) +
   (vi) 0 (In Becker's model individual decisions are based on private benefits and costs; social costs do not enter the decision, and preferences are fixed.)

b. Such programs can (1) help couples avoid having more children than they desire; (2) enable couples to improve the spacing of births and thereby improve the health of the mother and children, while slowing the arrival of each new generation; and (3) educate couples about the health effects of having fewer, better-spaced births, and thereby alter their perceptions of the costs and benefits of larger families.

c. Points 1 and 2 in part b are legitimate motives for government action, entirely consistent with abiding by individual preferences. An additional motive for intervention is based on the external diseconomies from individual decisions to have more children. Where external diseconomies are significant, decisions based on self-interest cause overexploitation of common resources at the expense of social welfare.

d. Becker contends that desired family size declines with income because of the opportunity cost of parents' time, which children consume voraciously. Becker also argues that both the quality and quantity of children are desired goods. As parents' income rises, child quality becomes much more achievable, so utility maximizing parents make a trade off in this direction. Easterlin adds that development, urbanization, and modernization also alter preferences in the direction of fewer children and more consumption of other kinds of goods and services.

Exercise 3

a. (i) See Table 8–3a.

Table 8–3a
Demographic Worksheet for Fecund, 1995–2000

Year	Number of children*	Number of middle-age adults	Number of older adults	Total population	Rate of pop. growth (%)	Number of births	Number of infant deaths
	(1)	(2)	(3)	(4)	(5)	(6)	(7)
1995	100	100	100	300	0	200	100
1996	100	100	100	300	0	200	100
1997	**100**	**100**	**100**	**300**	**0**	**200**	**40**
1998	**160**	100	**100**	**360**	20	**200**	**40**
1999	**160**	**160**	**100**	420	16.7	**200**	**40**
2000	**160**	**160**	**160**	480	14.3		

*Columns 1 to 4 refer to population at the beginning of the year, column 5 is the growth rate relative to the previous year, and columns 6 and 7 refer to births and deaths occurring during the year.

(ii) Population growth rate = 0 percent.

b. (i) See Table 8–3a.
(ii) Population growth rate = 20 percent.
(iii) See Table 8–3a.
(iv) Population growth rate = 16.7 percent.

c. (i) See Table 8–3a.
(ii) Even though fertility has dropped to the replacement level in 1999, the population continues to increase because of age-structure

effects. The baby-boom generation just reached childbearing age in 1999, so the number of babies born stays high. (Note that the population will stabilize after the year 2000 at 480 people.)

d. As shown for Fecund, the age structure is the cause of the demographic momentum. Declining mortality rates and high birth rates have created very young populations. Therefore the number of adults entering child-bearing age will be rising for two decades, and so may the number of children born, even with falling age-specific fertility rates. This demographic momentum can echo for several generations.

Exercise 4

a. (i) Rise, 20 percent.
   (ii) 1996: 2.0
        1997: 2.0
        1998: 2.6

b. (i) Decrease: There are more people but not more workers.
   (ii) Decrease: With a higher dependency rate, each worker has more mouths to feed; this is likely to increase consumption and reduce saving.
   (iii) Decrease: With more children, but no corresponding increase in GNP, government revenues, and fundings for education, will probably not keep pace with the school-age population.
   (iv) Decrease: Lower savings in 1998 implies less capital formation and therefore less capital per worker in 1999 compared to what would have been the case without the population bulge.
   (v) Ambiguous: Compared to the case without the spurt of population growth, there is now less capital in 1999, but also more labor. These two factors have opposite effects on total GNP. What is *un*ambiguous is that incomes will be lower in per capita terms.

c. (i) No one will advocate reversing the decline in the infant mortality rate as a solution! But the government could adopt family planning programs and mother-and-infant health programs to reduce fertility rates more quickly.
   (ii) The government can adopt measures that alter the incentives to have children, such as better opportunities for education and employment, especially for women, and social security schemes, to name just two.
   (iii) Even if the government could not alter fertility rates, it could miti-gate the adverse economic effects by adopting policies to enhance saving and to increase the efficiency and productivity of labor and capital. Population growth is not the sole determinant, nor even the most important determinant, of economic development.

Exercise 5

a. See the last two columns of Table 8–4a.

Table 8–4a
Population and Per Capita Income

Labor force	GNP ($ millions)	Population (millions)	Per capita income ($)
10	10,000	20	500
20	28,000	40	700
30	48,000	60	800
40	72,000	80	900
50	98,000	100	980
60	118,000	120	983
70	134,000	140	957
80	148,000	160	925

b. See curve *PP* and points POP* and PCI* on Figure 8–2a.

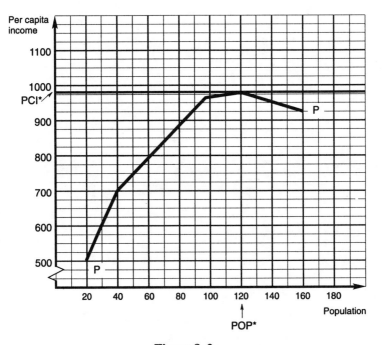

Figure 8–2a

c. Yes! There may still be strong reasons for the government to be concerned about reducing the rate of population growth. First, the *rate of increase* of the population may be too fast. Rapid growth may lead to changes in the age structure, in savings rates, in capital deepening, and so on, that cause living standards now and in the future to be lower than they otherwise could be. Second, due to demographic momentum, it may be necessary to slow down the rate of population growth now in order to avoid greatly overshooting the optimum population.

d.	POP	PCI	
(i)	+	+	
(ii)	–	+	(Because optimum population occurs with a smaller population.)
(iii)	+	+	
(iv)	–	+	(Assuming diminishing marginal productivity of labor sets in earlier.)

CHAPTER 9   Labor's Role

Exercise 1

a.   (i) $w/r = 1.0$.
    (ii)   Slope $= -1.0$.
    (iii)   See line B_0 on Figure 9–2a.

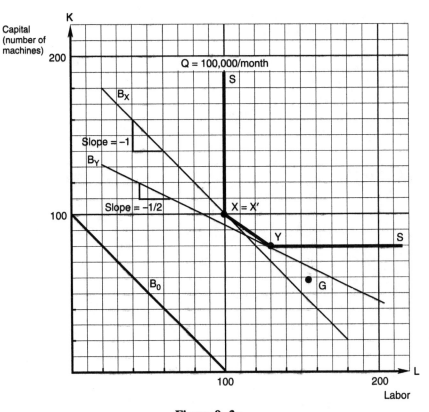

Figure 9–2a

b.   (i)   See point X on Figure 9–2a.
    (ii)   See line B_X on Figure 9–2a.
    (iii) $L = 100$, $K = 100$.
    (iv) $K/L = 1.0$.

c. (i) High.

    (ii) The three policies can include, *inter alia*:

        Minimum wage

        Interest rate controls or subsidies

        Investment tax breaks if linked to capital costs

        Exchange controls that lower the cost of imported capital goods

d. (i) $w/r = 0.5$.

    (ii) See point Y on Figure 9–2a.

    (iii) See line B_Y on Figure 9–2a.

    (iv) $L = 130$, $K = 80$, and $K/L = 80/130 = 0.615$.

e. (i) 50%.

    (ii) 38.5%.

    (iii) $\sigma = 38.5/50 = 0.77$.

    (iv) 20%, 30%.

Exercise 2

a. (i) $L = 100$, $K = 100$.

    (ii) $C_P = \$80,000$.

    (iii) $L = 130$, $K = 80$.

    (iv) $C_P' = \$87,000$.

    (v) Increase.

b. (i) $K/L = 0.333$.

    (ii) $C_C = \$80,000$.

    (iii) $C_C' = \$75,000$.

    (iv) Decline.

c. (i) Cotton.

    (ii) Cotton.

    (iii) Cotton, polyester.

    (iv) Rise, fall.

    (v) The cotton shirts, which are more labor-intensive, gain market share at the expense of the less-labor-intensive polyester shirts. In addition, the decline in the cost of producing cotton shirts reduces shirt prices; this boosts sales, production, and employment. Both of these market adjustments promote employment in the industry. (In addition, Exercise 1 showed that the polyester-shirt industry converts to a more labor-intensive production process.)

d. (i) Yes. Point G lies below line B_Y. It involves lower costs to produce the same output, so it is a more profitable and more competitive production process.

(ii) Point *G*. An appropriate technology is one that entails lower resource costs, relative to the country's factor endowments. As long as factor prices reflect the opportunity costs of labor and capital, then the most appropriate technology is that which minimizes the cost of production. This technology economizes on the use of scarce factors, and it takes best advantage of the more abundant factor.

Exercise 3

a. (i) See the horizontal line at $w_F' = \$300$, and points L_s' and L_d' are shown in panel F of Figure 9–3a.

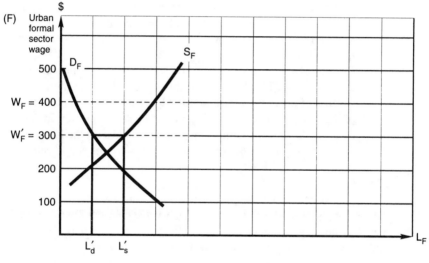

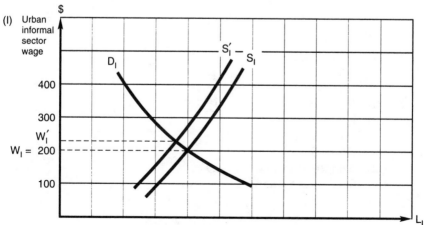

Figure 9–3a

      (ii)   The queue shrinks. There are now fewer workers seeking urban formal-sector positions and more such jobs are available.

  b. (i)   The supply curve in panel I shifts to the left. As more workers are absorbed in formal-sector jobs, there is a decrease in the labor supply to the informal sector. See curve S_I' in panel I of Figure 9–3a.

      (ii) The informal-sector wage will rise. See W_I' in panel I of Figure 9–3a.

  c. (i)   Migration would occur if the increase in the informal-sector wage results in a higher *expected* urban wage.

      (ii) If migration occurs, it shifts outward the supply curves for both the urban labor markets. This causes a decline in the equilibrium wage rate in the informal sector and a lengthening of the queue for jobs in the formal sector (where a minimum wage policy remains in effect).

      (iii) The rural-labor supply curve would shift to the left to the extent of the migration. This effect is probably minuscule in the short run because of the large size of the rural labor force relative to the size of the adjustments taking place in the urban labor market. In the long run, however, continued migration should shift the labor supply curve in the rural sector enough to boost the equilibrium rural wage significantly.

  d. Formal-sector businesses might choose to pay wages above the market-clearing equilibrium level due to *efficiency wage* considerations. Better pay may promote healthier and more efficient workers; it may also induce less turnover, less absenteeism, and less shirking.

Exercise 4

  a. (i) $4/10 = 0.4$.
      (ii) $(15\%)(0.4) = 6\%$.

  b. (i)   6% of 150 = 9; 2% of 1000 = 20.
      (ii) $\eta = 0.4$.
          $g(V_i) = 15\%$.
          $S_i = 0.15$.
      (iii) $\Delta E_i = (0.4)(15\%)(0.15) = 0.9\%$.
      (iv) $0.9/2.0 = .45 = 45\%$.

c. (i)   33.3% [Derivation: Solve $(0.4)g(V_i)(0.15) = 2$ percent].
    (ii) 0.89 [Derivation: Solve $(\eta)(15$ percent$)(0.15) = 2$ percent].
    (iii) A higher employment elasticity would be encouraged by policies
          that provide incentives for more-labor-intensive industrial growth.
          These include policies that raise the effective cost of capital, elimi-
          nate artificial increases in the industrial real wage, promote adoption
          of more appropriate technologies, or develop small-scale industry.

d. (i) $\Delta E_i = (0.4)(15\%)(0.35) = 2.1\%$.
    (ii) 21.
    (iii) The reason is simple: compared to Kita, Chikita already has more
          than twice as many workers in industry; so an identical rate of
          growth in the industrial sector involves a larger number of new
          jobs in Chikita *relative to* the labor force. Both countries experi-
          ence 15 percent industrial-sector growth; both countries have an
          employment elasticity of 0.4, but Chikita starts with a higher *share*
          of the labor force already working in industry.

e. Indirect job creation arises from interindustry linkage effects, since the
    growth of industrial output requires increased production of inputs from
    other sectors. Secondary job creation arises from consumption effects.
    As more people are hired in industry, consumption demand increases for
    the products of other sectors. Both these channels generate additional
    nonindustrial jobs. Therefore, the employment effect computed in part d
    understates the total amount of job creation attributable to industrial
    growth.

Exercise 5

a. .667 (the probability level for which $p(W_u) = W_r$).

b. (i) $p = 150/165 = .909$.
    (ii) $w_u^* = (0.909)(1,500) = 1,364$ rupiah.
    (iii) $M - (0.1)(1,364 - 1,000) = 36.4$, which rounds to 36 migrants per
          year.

c. (i) $p = 9/15 = .60$.
    (ii) $w_u^* = (0.6)(1,500) = 900$ rupiah.
    (iii) There will be no rural-to-urban migration, but rather reverse
          migration, since $W_r > W_u^*$ for the urban unemployed.

CHAPTER 10   **Education**

Exercise 1

a. See curves *A*, *B*, and *C* in Figure 10–2a.

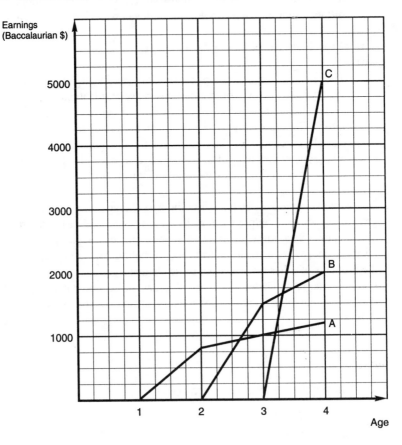

Figure 10–2a

b.   (i)   Age 2: 0 – 800 = –$800.
Age 3: 1,500 – 1,000 = +$500.
Age 4: 2,000 – 1,200 = +$800.

(ii)   No! With *r* = 40 percent = 0.40, the net present value of the incremental earnings from attending secondary school will be

$$-800 + 500/(1.4) + 800/(1.4)^2 = -\$35,$$

even if the explicit costs of secondary school, for the family, are
zero (which they aren't). In present-value terms, the forgone
earnings outweigh the net future benefits.

c. (i) Age 3: $(0 - 1,500) - 500 = -\$2,000$.
         Age 4: $(5,000 - 2,000) = +\$3,000$.
    (ii) $V' = -2,000 + 3,000/(1 + r)$.
    (iii) Private rate of return = 50 percent. (You invest $2,000 and get
         back $3,000 one year later.)

d. (i) Age 3: –$2,500 (i.e., $1,000 of explicit costs plus $1,500 of
         forgone earnings).
         Age 4: +$3,000.
    (ii) $V' = -2,500 + 3,000/(1 + r)$.
    (iii) 20%.

Exercise 2

a. (i) $2,500.
    (ii) Private rate of return = 25 percent, from $PV = -2,000 + 2,500/(1 + r)$
         $= 0$.
    (iii) Social rate of return = 0 percent, from $PV = -2,500 + 2,500/(1 + r)$
         $= 0$.

b. (i) Age 3: –$2,100.
         Age 4: +$2,100
    (ii) Age 3: –$2,600.
         Age 4: +$2,100
    (iii) Private rate of return = 0 percent.
         Social rate of return = –19.2 percent.

c. (i) The private rate of return ranges from 0 to 50 percent, while the
         social rate of return ranges from 20 to –20 percent, depending on
         how one analyzes the available data. The highest returns are de-
         rived by assuming that current earnings differentials will continue
         and that the differentials are *caused* entirely by getting a college
         education. These assumptions may not be valid. Therefore, results
         of the cost-benefit analysis cannot be applied mechanically to
         validate investments in higher education in Baccalauria.

Exercise 3

a.   (i)   800/700 = 1.14.
     (ii) 200/300 = 0.67.
     (iii) Manufacturing, by far.
     (iv) (1.14)(800) = 912 workers in agriculture.
           (0.67)(538) = 360 workers in manufacturing.

b.   (i)   In agriculture: (1.14)(.95) = 1.08.
           In manufacturing: (.67)(.85) = 0.57.
           (note: Answers may differ slightly depending on rounding.)
     (ii) Agriculture: (1.08)(800) = 864.
           Manufacturing: (0.57)(538) = 307.
     (iii) 864 + 307 = 1,171.

c.   (i)   0 percent in agriculture, 25 percent in manufacturing.
     (ii) In agriculture: 0.
           In manufacturing: (.25)(307) = 77.
           Total = 77.
     (iii) 77.

d.   (i) $50 + 5 \times 4 = 70$.
     (ii) 77.
     (iii) 7.
     (iv) This calculation suggests a need for additional investment in voca-
           tional education. With present capacity only 20 skilled workers
           will be trained over the next five years, but the plan requires train-
           ing 27 skilled workers. Filling this gap requires a 35 percent
           increase in vocational training capacity.

e.   (i)   Rise.
     (ii) 70.
     (iii) 77; 7/77 = .091 = 9.1%.

f. Many weaknesses can be cited to answer this question. Possibilities
   include:

      Projected GNP growth may be wrong.

      Projected output structure may be inaccurate due to changing
      input/output coefficients.

      Vocational training skills may not fit employers' needs.

      Some of the apparently required jobs may yield benefits that are
      smaller than training costs.

      Jobs now filled by unskilled workers may come to require skills
      (educational deepening).

Exercise 1

a. See Table 11–2a.

Table 11–2a
1995 National Food Balance Sheet for Sucrose

	Coconuts	Sugar
Sources (million kg)		
Production	**350**	140
Imports	0	**30**
Exports	150	0
Total domestic supply	500	170
Uses (million kg)		
Accumulation of stocks	**20**	20
Waste	40	**40**
Processed as nonfood product	40	10
Food consumption	**400**	**100**
Per capita kg/year consumed	400	100
Calories/kg	1500	**3511**
Per capita calories/day	**1644**	962
Total per capita calories/day = **2606**		

b. (i) 2606.
    (ii) 2606/2400 = 1.086 = 108.6%.

c. (i) 400 kg/year; 250 kg/year.
    (ii) See Table 11–3a, column 1.

d. (i) See Table 11–3a, column 2.
    (ii) See Table 11–3a, column 3.
    (iii) 2811, 1989.

Table 11–3a
Nutrition Analysis by Class, Sucrose, 1991

	Per capita kg/year consumed (1)	Calories/kg (2)	Per capita calories/day (3)
A. Landowners			
Coconuts	450	1500	1849
Sugar	100	3511	962
			Sum = 2811
B. Landless laborers			
Coconuts	250	1500	1027
Sugar	100	3511	962
			Sum = 1989

e. The malnutrition problem has *not* been solved. The food balance sheet shows a national average figure for calorie supplies as a percentage of requirements, but this average mixes well-fed landowners and poorly fed landless workers. For the latter group, the daily food supply provides only 1989 calories per capita, which is just 83 percent of requirements. There is ample food for all, but it is not evenly distributed.

f. (i) $500 - 20 - 80 - 40 = 360$ kg/year per capita.
   (ii) 90 kg/year. Derived from: $(\frac{3}{4} \times 450) + \frac{1}{4} \times X = 360$.
   (iii) 1332 calories/day, 55.5 percent of the daily requirement.

Exercise 2

a. (i) See the data plot and the line LIFE in Figure 11–1a.
   (ii) The best-fit line clearly slopes upward; this indicates a positive relationship between per capita income and life expectancy even among low-income countries. Looking at the data plot more closely, one sees no discernible upward trend at income levels below $1,000 (PPP). Beyond this point life expectancy does tend to rise, but still with a lot of variance around the underlying trend. (Note: The regression equation has $R^2 = .54$ and the coefficient of per capita income is statistically significant.)

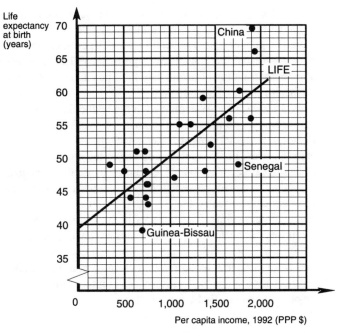

Figure 11–1a

b. (i)   China.
    (ii) Senegal and Guinea-Bissau.
    (iii) Life expectancy does not depend solely on per capita income.
          Policies relating to health and nutrition matter greatly and differ
          widely from country to country. The same goes for the distribution
          of income, farm land, and food entitlements. With effective policies,
          a few countries like China managed to deliver excellent health
          outcomes despite being very poor.

c. (i)   Yes. The data reveal a clear inverse relationship. Life expectancy
          rises as infant mortality rates fall. This is no surprise since the
          computation of life expectancy takes the infant mortality rate
          directly into account. (A graph of the data points shows a very
          good fit between these two variables. The correlation coefficient
          works out to be –.75 and it is statistically significant.)
    (ii) No, surprisingly. One might be able to imagine an inverse relation-
          ship from a graph of the data, but there is more noise than trend.
          (The correlation coefficient is –.3 and it is not statistically signifi-
          cant.) In low-income countries, infant mortality rates do not seem
          to be strongly affected by the prevalence of low-weight births,
          indicating prenatal malnutrition.

(iii) Yes. Although there is a lot of variance in the relationship, one can see a definite association: infant mortality rates tend to drop where there is a greater access to health care. (The correlation coefficient here is –.49 and it is statistically significant.) The data confirm that a better distribution of health care facilities makes a difference in the health status of the population.

(iv) This is no surprise. As explained in the textbook, health outcomes for the masses do not depend so much on the availability of *doctors*, whose services are often concentrated in the major urban areas anyway. For low-income countries the most effective form of health care depends on nurses and other auxiliary medical personnel to deliver preventative care and basic primary treatment throughout the countryside.

(v) Again, no big surprise. As you saw in the Worked Exercise and in Exercise 1, the calorie supply statistics are national averages which say very little about the nutrition status of the poor. Also, nearly all these low-income countries show poor performance in terms of food supplies; so differences in infant mortality rates may be determined mostly by other factors.

Exercise 3

a. (i) $-24,575$ francs $= -1,000,000 + (600,000/1.15) + (600,000/1.3225)$.
   (ii) $41,322$ francs $= -1,000,000 + (600,000/1.10) + (600,000/1.21)$.
   (iii) IRR $= 13\%$.

b. (i) 300,567 francs.
   (ii) 388,430 francs.

c. Basically, every figure on the benefits side is a very rough guesstimate. It is quite difficult to measure the effects of a particular health project on worker productivity or on work time. The estimated value of improved health as an end in itself is even more imprecise. In addition, the benefits from malaria control may be undermined by other environmental and medical problems that remain unresolved. Yet malaria control may be a necessary component of a package of improvements that, taken together, generate major benefits. All these considerations make it very difficult to estimate the rate of return of the project.

Exercise 4

a. (i) At $P = 15$: 10 kg/person $\times$ 100 people $= 1000$ kg.
   (ii) At $P = 10$: $15 \times 100 = 1500$ kg.

    (iii) At $P = 5$: $30 \times 100 = 3000$ kg.

    (iv) $P^* = 7.5$ shillings/kg.

b. (i) 3000 kg.

    (ii) 1000 kg.

    (iii) 4000 kg; 1000 kg.

c. (i) $P^* = 7.5$ shillings/kg.

    (ii) 2000 kg.

        5000 kg.

        7000 kg.

    (iii) See point X in Figure 11–2a.

    (iv) $7.5 \times 7,000 = 52,500$ shillings.

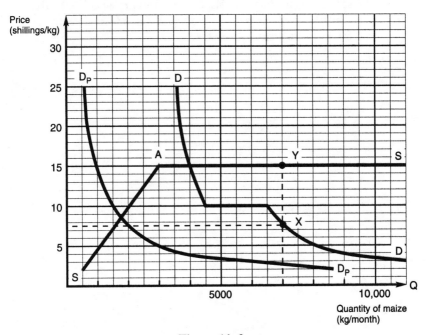

Figure 11–2a

d. (i) 15 shillings/kg.

    (ii) See point Y in Figure 11–2a.

    (iii) $15 \times 7,000 = 105,000$ shillings.

    (iv) 52,500 shillings (cost = 105,000 shillings, revenue = 52,500 shillings).

e. (i) 10 kg.

    (ii) 10 kg.

    (iii)   1000 kg/month.
    (iv)   15 shillings.
    (v) $15 \times 1,000 = 15,000$ shillings.

f.   (i)   52,500 shillings/month.
         15,000 shillingss/month.
   (ii)   4000 kg/month.
         2000 kg/month (1000 kg at the market equilibrium plus 1000 kg
         of government procurement).
   (iii) Policy 2 accomplishes the same objective at a far lower cost, in
         terms of both government budget outlays and foreign exchange
         costs. One basic reason is that policy 2 does not subsidize the
         nonpoor and does not invite costly leakage of maize to wasteful
         uses such as feeding animals. Policy 2 is far more cost-effective
         (unless there are enormous offsetting differences in administrative
         costs or the degree of corruption).

CHAPTER 12   Capital and Saving

Exercise 1

a. See Table 12–2a.

Table 12–2a
GDP and Investment Projections to 2005, Country B

	2000	2001	2002	2003	2004	2005
Y_t	1,276.3	**1,340.1**	**1,407.1**	**1,477.4**	**1,551.3**	**1,628.8**
I	191.4	201.0	211.0	221.6	232.6	244.3
ICOR	3.0	3.0	3.0	3.0	3.0	3.0
$\Rightarrow Y_{t+1}$	**1,340.1**	**1,407.1**	**1,477.4**	**1,551.3**	**1,628.8**	

b. (i) 1.63.
   (ii) 1.34.
   (iii) (1.63/1.34) – 1 = 0.22 = 22%. Since the two countries have identical initial characteristics and identical investment levels each year, the entire difference is attributable to the lower ICOR in country B, reflecting more efficient use of scarce capital.

c. See Table 12–3a.

Table 12–3a
GDP and Investment Projections to 2005, Country B

	2000	2001	2002	2003	2004	2005
Y_t	1,276.3	**1,340.1**	**1,410.3**	1,487.5	**1,572.4**	**1,665.8**
I	191.4	**210.5**	**231.6**	**254.8**	**280.2**	308.3
ICOR	3.0	3.0	3.0	3.0	3.0	3.0
$\Rightarrow Y_{t+2}$	**1,340.1**	**1,410.3**	**1,487.5**	**1,572.4**	**1,665.8**	

d. (i) 1.67
   (ii) 25%

e. (i) $g(Y) = 6.7\%$. (Derivation: $(1 + g)^5 = 1665.8/1207.3$).)
   (ii) $I/Y = 26.8\%$.
   (iii) $I/Y = 18.5\%$ (since $I = 308.3$ and $Y = 1,665.8$).

Exercise 2

a. (i) See Figure 12–2a.

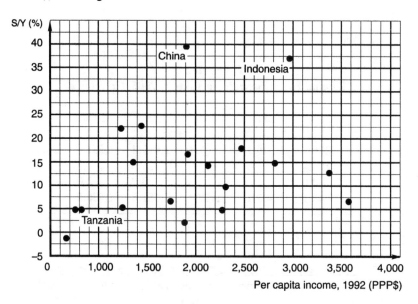

Figure 12–2a

(ii) There is a very weak positive relationship between per capita income and savings across countries, but there is also a considerable amount of variance; this indicates that individual country characteristics are more important than per capita income in determining saving ratios. (If you compute the regression line, you will find that the effect of per capita income on S/Y is statistically significant, but the simple regression has an R^2 of just .09.)

b. (ii) China (39 percent) and Indonesia (37 percent).
    (ii) China had by far the fastest growth rate; Indonesia was also among the leaders in terms of growth performance.

c. (ii) Tanzania (42 percent) and China (36 percent).
    (ii) For Tanzania, the investment ratio is far higher than the savings ratio, which is just 5 percent. The difference is due to inflows of

foreign saving, primarily foreign aid. For China, the relationship is reversed: the investment ratio is less than the savings ratio. This indicates that China experienced a net *outflow* of financial resources. Domestic savings amounting to 3 percent of GDP were invested outside China.

d.   (i)   See the 19 data points plotted on Figure 12–3a.

 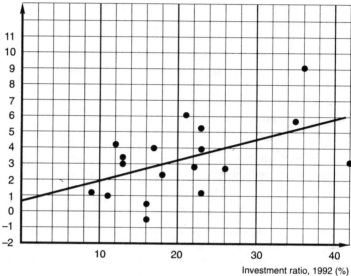

Figure 12–3a

(ii)   See the straight line drawn in Figure 12–3a. There is a clear positive correlation between the investment ratio and GDP growth, but again growth rates for individual countries are often well above and well below the average pattern. Still, the strong positive link between investment and growth justifies the considerable attention paid to sources and uses of capital investment.

(iii)   Below the best-fit line. For any given investment rate, a country with a high ICOR will not achieve as rapid a growth rate as a country with an average ICOR (i.e., a country on the best-fit line). Remember: $g = (I/Y)/\text{ICOR}$, so growth is *inversely* related to the ICOR value.

232 / CHAPTER 12

Exercise 3

a. See Table 12–5a for answers to i, ii, iii, and iv.

Table 12–5a
(billions of baht, at constant 1987 prices)

	1980	1990
Government budget		
Revenue	122.0	337.2
Current expenditure	120.5	206.2
Capital expenditure	42.1	49.6
Gross domestic product	829.3	1,790.1
Gross domestic savings	166.9	603.4
Gross domestic investment	219.1	738.2
Government savings (S_g)	**1.5**	**131.0**
Private savings (S_p)	**165.4**	**472.4**
Foreign savings (S_f)	**52.2**	**134.8**
Private-sector income (Y_{priv})	**707.3**	**1,452.9**

b. (i) $MPS_g = 129.5/215.2 = .602 = 60.2\%.$
$MPS_{priv} = 307.0/745.6 = .412 = 41.2\%.$
   (ii) Rise, 1.9 billion baht. (Government saving will rise by 6.0 while private saving declines by 4.1.)

c. (i) 14.7%, 18.8%.
   (ii) No. Over this period the government achieved a very high MPS, which indicates that a large share of additional tax revenue was saved for use in capital projects. In this case the Please effect is not borne out. (Even in Thailand, however, the Please effect *did* apply during some earlier periods.)

d. (i) Simple. Governments can and do borrow to finance capital expenditures they cannot cover out of current revenue. If the borrowing comes from domestic sources, then the government is absorbing part of private-sector savings and crowding out private investment. If the borrowed funds originate from abroad, then the country is incurring foreign debt.

(ii) The effect is the opposite of part i: the government makes net repayments of debt.

Exercise 4

a. (i)

Y^d	S	S/Y^d
200	0	0
300	50	16.7%
400	100	25.0%

(ii) No. This savings function implies that S/Y^d will increase steadily as incomes rise; in practice the ratio remains roughly constant over time.

b. (i)

Y^d	S	S/Y^d
200	0	0
300	50	16.7%
400	100	25.0%

(ii) 66.8, 16.7%.
(iii) 16.7%, 25.0%, 16.7%.

c. (i) Yes. The example shows that S/Y^d is stable at 16.7% after allowing for the adjustment in household perceptions of permanent income.

(ii) Yes. Since the high-income group includes a disproportionately large number of households with positive transitory incomes, this group will save more on average. The opposite holds for low-income households.

(iii) In this case, saving rates should be high in good years when export prices are high and income includes a large, positive transitory element. In contrast, saving rates should be low in bad years when export prices are low and income includes a large, negative transitory component.

CHAPTER 13   Fiscal Policy

Exercise 1

a. (i)   See column 3 of Table 13–1a.

Table 13–1a
Tariff Revenues in Buibui

Price (Sh) (1)	Quantity (2)	Tariff (Sh per T-Shirt) (3)	Tariff revenue* (4)
50	1,000	0	0
55	751	5	3,755
60	579	10	5,790
65	455	15	6,825
70	364	20	7,280
75	296	25	7,400
80	244	30	7,320
85	204	35	7,140
90	171	40	6,840

*Ignoring domestic supply response.

(ii) See column 4 of Table 13–1a.

b. (i) $t^* = $ Sh25. $P^* = $ Sh75.
   (ii) When the tariff is raised beyond Sh25 per T-shirt, the decline in
        the volume of imports is proportionately larger than the increase
        in the tariff per unit of imports. So total tariff revenues drop. The
        decline in the volume of imports is a result of the price-elastic
        demand conditions and the fact that the domestic price increases
        with the tariff.

c. (i) $Q_s = 140$.
   (ii) $Q_m = 296 - 140 = 156$.
   (iii) Revenue $= 156 \times 25 = $ Sh3,900.

     (iv) The revenue calculation in Table 13–1 considered only the decline in the quantity demanded as a result of the increased domestic price. Here we also consider the fact that at the higher price, a large fraction of the demand will be satisfied by domestic production of T-shirts; this will further reduce imports and tariff revenues.

     (v) $t' = $ Sh20.

d.   (i) With a tax of Sh25 per shirt, the market price is Sh75 and the quantity demanded is 296 shirts. Tax revenue = $25 \times 296 = $ Sh7,400.

    (ii) With a tax of Sh40 per shirt, the market price is Sh90 and the quantity demanded is 171 shirts. Tax revenue = $40 \times 171 = $ Sh6,840.

e.   (i) The two taxes generate identical revenue for tax rates below Sh25, but for higher tax rates the excise tax generates more revenue. The reason is that the tax base is broader. With the excise, the full market volume is subject to tax regardless of whether supplies are produced locally or imported.

    (ii) The excise tax is more neutral since it applies the same tax rate to all the T-shirts regardless of origin. The import duty artificially alters the relative prices of imports versus locally produced goods. This may sound great, but see parts iv and v.

   (iii) No. The basic supply cost of imported shirts is lower than for domestically produced shirts; because the excise tax applies equally to both, domestic producers gain no advantage and cannot compete profitably against (less-costly) imports.

   (iv) The excise tax is superior in terms of efficient resource allocation. It does not induce scarce domestic resources into inefficient production of a low-priority product that can be obtained at less cost from other sources. This point is fundamental and not widely understood.

    (v) On this criterion the tariff comes out on top. Because they are generally channeled through a small number of ports of entry, imports can be monitored and assessed with relative ease. Domestic producers involved in silk-screening may be widely dispersed and small in scale; this makes it difficult and costly for the government to monitor sales and assess the tax.

Exercise 2

a. (i) See line *G/Y* in Figure 13–2a.

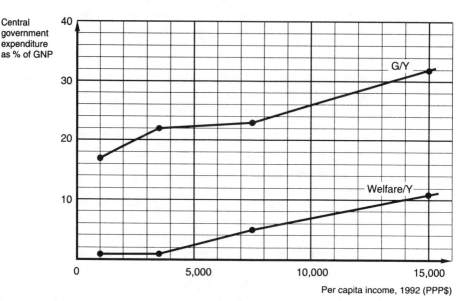

Figure 13–2a

(ii) Yes. Although there is a great deal of variation from country to country, the averages by income group show that more developed countries still tend to channel a larger share of income to the government sector, in accordance with Wagner's law.

(iii) See line WELFARE/*Y* in Figure 13–2a.

(iv) The graph tells us that high-income countries devote a larger share of GDP to welfare and social security spending. The reason is certainly *not* that poverty is more widespread in high-income countries. Rather, it is that taxpayers in high-income countries are more able and willing to bear these transfers.

b. (i) See the data plot and line *TR* in Figure 13–3a.

(ii) Yes. The *TR* line clearly slopes upward, indicating that higher levels of per capita income are associated with higher tax ratios.

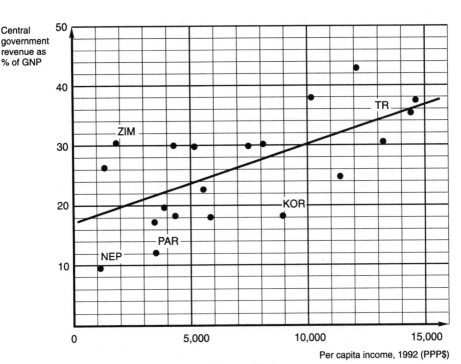

Central government revenue as % of GNP

Per capita income, 1992 (PPP$)

Figure 13–3a

c. (i) See the point labeled ZIM.
   (ii) From Table 13–2, one can see that Zimbabwe has a relatively high export share of GDP. The large volume of trade is convenient to tax. Also, Zimbabwe's exports include a reasonably large share of fuels and minerals, which again are easy sources of revenue. In short, Zimbabwe's tax capacity is relatively high for a country at its level of income.
   (iii) See points NEP (for Nepal), PAR (Paraguay), and KOR (Korea).
   (iv) Quite so. In all three of these countries, international trade accounts for a relatively low share of total GDP, and easy-to-tax exports of fuels and minerals are negligible. These countries have below-average tax capacity, given their levels of income.

d.   (i) $12.13 + 0.0014 \times 1,360 + 0.0817 \times 27 + 0.12 \times 16 = 18.2\%$.
    (ii)   Kenya's actual tax ratio, 26.2 percent, is much higher than the estimated tax capacity. This doesn't necessarily indicate good economic policy. While the government is very effective at generating tax revenue, it is also squeezing hard on a poor economy and introducing a lot of tax-induced distortions. Economic growth might well improve if more resources were left to the private sector

e.   (i)   For Korea the index of tax capacity is 27.4 percent, while the actual tax ratio is just 18.2 percent. The Korean government is taxing rather lightly.
    (ii)   Yes. Compared to the international average tax ratio for a country in its income range, Korea had plenty of room to boost tax collections by another 1 percent of GDP. (But would higher taxation be desirable? And would the taxpayers accept higher taxes?)
    (iii)   No. First, extra tax revenue might be used for recurrent expenditure rather than be saved for capital projects. Secondly, a higher tax bite would diminish disposable income and reduce private-sector saving; total domestic saving could even drop (which is the Please effect).

Exercise 3

a.   (i) $10\% \times \$1,500 = \$150$.
    (ii) $10\% \times \$700 = \$70$.

b.   (i)   Firm a, $100;
        Firm 2, $200;
        Firm 3, $400;
        Total value-added = $1,500.
    (ii)   Firm 1, $10;
        Firm 2, $20;
        Firm 4, $80;
        Total value-added tax = $150, 10%.

c.   Firms 1, 2, and 3 pay $10, $20, and $40, respectively, while firm 4 pays $0. Total tax collected is $70.

d. $150 again! Firm 2 pays $30 because it cannot claim credit for VAT that was paid on purchases of cotton.

e. Firm 3 sells $350 worth of shorts locally and exports $350 worth. The firm owes $35 of VAT on its local sales and zero on its export sales. It claims a credit of $30 for VAT paid on its purchased inputs. So its net VAT payment is $5.

Exercise 4

a.   (i)   See curve $S'S'$ in Figure 13–4a.

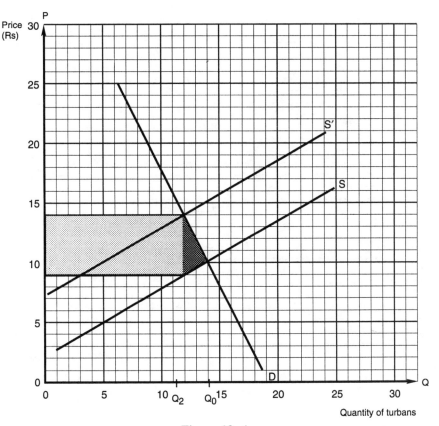

Figure 13–4a

(ii) $P_1 = $ Rs14.

(iii)   If the price were to increase from Rs10 to Rs15 following imposition of the tax, the quantity demanded would fall short of the quantity supplied. Market forces would cause the price to decline to the equilibrium level of Rs14.

b. (i)   Rs9.
    (ii) Rs4; Rs1.
    (iii) 80%; 20%.

c. (i)   See curve $S'S'$ in Figure 13–5a.
    (ii) $P_1 = $ Rs12.

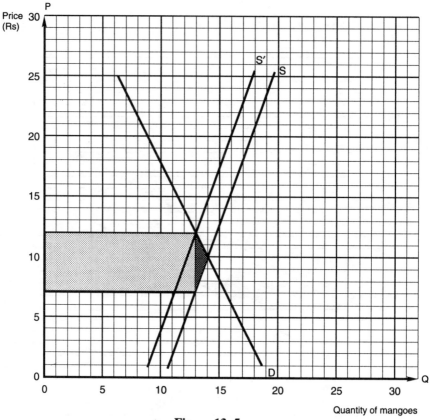

Figure 13–5a

d. (i)   Rs7.
    (ii) Rs2; Rs3.
    (iii) 40%; 60%.

e. (i)   Declined.
    (ii) Decline.
    (iii) Supply; left.
    (iv) Higher.
    (v)   Larger.

Exercise 5

a. See the heavily shaded triangle in Figure 13–4a.

b. See the heavily shaded triangle in Figure 13–5a.

c. (i) The tax revenue is shown by the lightly shaded rectangle in Figure 13–4a.

   (ii) Consumers and producers suffer a welfare loss in the turban market equal to the area of the shaded rectangle plus the shaded triangle, but the amount indicated by the rectangle is simply a transfer to the government, not a net loss to society. Presumably the government uses these funds to supply valuable public services. Hence the net cost to the economy—the excess burden—is just the area of the triangle.

d. (i) The excess burden is *smaller* in the market for mangoes. The area of a triangle is (1/2) × (base) × (perpendicular height). Look at the triangles in Figures 13–4a and 13–5a sideways; they have the same base because the tax is the same in both cases. However, the height of the triangle in Figure 13–4a is higher, so it has a larger area, which represents a greater excess burden.

   (ii) For a given tax and a given elasticity of demand, the excess burden is greater the smaller the price elasticity of supply. The smaller supply elasticity results in a smaller decline in output, and therefore a smaller loss of social welfare due to the tax.

CHAPTER 14   Financial Policy

Exercise 1

a. (i), (ii), and (iii): see columns 3, 4, and 5 in Table 14–1a.

Table 14–1a
Real versus Nominal Interest Rates, 1995
(% per annum)

Country	Nominal interest rate (1)	Inflation rate (2)	Real interest rate (3)	Approximate real interest rate (4)	Inflation tax rate (5)
Malaysia	5.9	3.8	**2.0**	**2.1**	**3.7**
S. Korea	14.7	5.1	**9.1**	**9.6**	**4.9**
Turkey	75.6	82.4	**–3.7**	**–6.8**	**45.2**
Venezuela	17.5	71.2	**–31.4**	**–53.7**	**41.6**
Russia	242.4	205.2	**12.2**	**37.2**	**67.2**

b. Borrowers. Suppose the nominal interest rate is 10 percent while the inflation rate is 30 percent. If I borrow $100, then at the end of one year I am obliged to pay back $110. In terms of real purchasing power I pay back less than I originally borrowed. The lender would have to receive $130 at the end of the year just to break even.

c. (i) $1.48/2.12 - 1 = -0.301 = -30.1\%$.
   (ii) $48\%(1 - .10) = 43.2\%$.
   (iii) $1.432/2.12 - 1 = -.325 = -32.5\%$.
   (iv) The supply of deposits to the banks is greatly constrained. Holding deposit accounts is a losing proposition, so no one will hold more than the minimum necessary amount in this form.

d. (i) $1.68/2.12 - 1 = -.208 = -20.8\%$.
   (ii) $68\%(1 - .35) = 44.2\%$.
   (iii) $1.442/2.12 - 1 = -.320 = -32.0\%$.
   (iv) The demand for loans is virtually unlimited! Getting a loan is like a gift from the bank—at the expense of the depositors.

e. (i)   There is huge excess demand for funds.
    (ii) The market's price-rationing mechanism breaks down completely. Banks have to allocate scarce financial resources using some arbitrary rationing or screening device that may bear no relation to productivity in using the resources.
    (iii) There is plenty of opportunity for the informal financial market to flourish, since there are lots of unsatisfied borrowers and lots of savers who would hold financial assets if the yield were attractive.

Exercise 2

a. (i)   35%
    (ii) 30
    (iii) $30; $70

b. 70 percent of Family B's savings is held in an unproductive form. Total economic returns would be larger if the savings were channeled into productive investments by more capable farmers such as Family A. In addition, much of the $30 that Family B has invested in hens would be more productive if it were used instead by Family A.

c. (i) $20.
    (ii) They will invest $20 in hens and place the remainder of their savings in bank deposits.
    (iii) $80.
    (iv) The marginal rate of return on direct investment in hens exceeds the interest rate on bank deposits.
    (v)   After investing all $100 of their savings in hens, the rate of return in further investments exceeds 15 percent. A profit can be earned on further investments, after paying interest on the loan.
    (vi) $80, so that their total investment would be $180.

d. The funds Family B held in unproductive form are now channeled via the banks to productive investments handled by Family A. Also, $10 of the money that Family B previously invested will now flow to Family A with whom the resources yield a higher return.

e. (i)   Family B won't put any money in the bank. It can now obtain a far higher *real* return on jewelry than on bank deposits, since the real interest rate on bank deposits is negative.

(ii) Yes! The value of jewelry appreciates at a rate that exceeds the interest cost of a loan. You can obtain a loan, invest in totally unproductive jewelry, then sell the jewelry to pay off the loan and pocket a nice profit.

(iii) The advantages of intermediation are lost because less savings will flow to bank deposits. To the extent that banks have funds to lend, many borrowers will allocate loan funds to unproductive uses, which are profitable only because of inflation.

Exercise 3

a. (i) $M/Y = 300/1{,}000 = 0.3$.
   (ii) $g_M = 6\% \times 1.5 = 9\%$.
   (iii) $300\,(1.09) = \$327$.
   (iv) The elasticity exceeds unity because of financial deepening and monetization. The demand for money increases more rapidly than income because a larger share of economic activity takes place using money, and an increasingly large share of savings is held in the form of liquid financial assets.

b. (i) $g_M = 9\% + 10\% = 19\%$.
   (ii) $300\,(1.19) = \$357$.
   (iii) $25\% - 9\% = 16\%$.

Exercise 4

a. (i) $357.
   (ii) $\Delta DC = \$57$.
   (iii) $7.
   (iv) $37.
   (v) $57.

b. (i) $BD = 0.05\,(1{,}000) = \$50$.
   (ii) $7.
   (iii) $257.
   (iv) $257/250 - 1 = 0.028 = 2.8\%$.
   (v) Decline; 6.5 percent (because $1.028/1.10 - 1 = -0.065$).
   (vi) No. It would be very difficult to sustain $g_Y = 6$ percent when credit to the private sector is shrinking by more than 6 percent in real terms.

c. (i) 10%; 250 (0.10) = $275.
    (ii) 57 – 25 = $32; 3.2%.

d. Even though ΔDC is exactly $57, money supply growth will now be
    too rapid to achieve the 10 percent inflation target. Specifically, ΔM =
    $\Delta DC + \Delta IR = 57 + 24 = 81, which exceeds the money supply target.
    Therefore, $g_M = 81/300 = 27$ percent, and inflation jumps to $27 - 9 = 18$
    percent.

Exercise 5

a. (i) See column 6 in Table 14–2a.
    (ii) See Figure 14–2a.

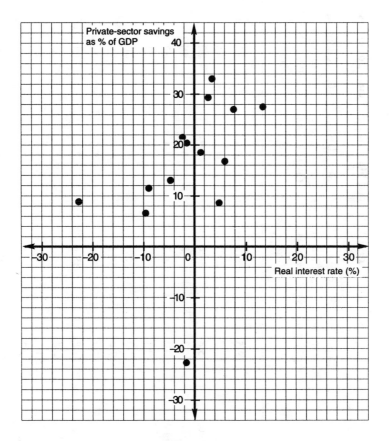

Figure 14–2a

Table 14–2a

1992 Financial Statistics, Selected Countries

Country	Deposit interest rates (avg % p.a.) (1)	Inflation (% p.a.) (2)	Real deposit interest rate (avg % p.a.) (3)	Gross domestic savings (% GDP) (4)	Government savings (% GDP) (5)	Private-sector savings (% GDP) (6)
Nepal	8.5	20.4	–9.9	12	5.4	**6.6**
Kenya	13.7	25.1	–9.1	15	3.1	**11.9**
Zimbabwe	3.8	34.6	–22.9	10	0.7	**9.3**
Philippines	14.3	7.8	6.0	18	1.6	**16.4**
Indonesia	20.4	6.2	13.4	37	9.2	**27.8**
Paraguay	20.1	14.7	4.7	13	4.6	**8.4**
Jordan	3.3	5.3	–1.9	–18	4.9	**–22.9**
Ecuador	47.4	50.3	–1.9	25	4.5	**20.5**
Tunisia	7.4	5.8	1.5	21	2.8	**18.2**
Costa Rica	15.8	18.6	–2.4	23	1.2	**21.8**
Thailand	12.3	4.1	7.9	35	8.0	**27.0**
Uruguay	54.5	62.3	–4.8	13	0.0	**13.0**
Malaysia	7.2	4.4	2.7	35	5.6	**29.4**
S. Korea	10.0	6.3	3.5	36	2.9	**33.1**

(iii) There is a hint of a positive relationship, since the countries with the highest real interest rates (Indonesia and Thailand) are also in the top rank in terms of private savings. But there is a great deal of variation in saving rates, unrelated to the real interest rate. (For your information, a regression of (S_p/Y) on r yields a small positive slope, but the R^2 is only .16 and the coefficient of r is not statistically significant.)

(iv) It means that consumption exceeds income. Some source of foreign savings is footing the bill. (Refer back to Chapter 12.)

b. (i) See Figure 14–3a.

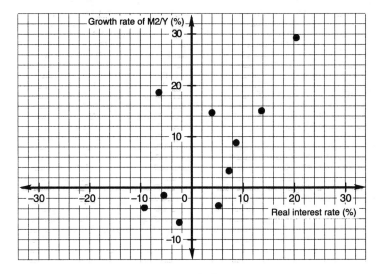

Figure 14–3a

(ii) The relationship is far from perfect, but one can discern a fairly clear pattern associating higher real interest rates with more rapid growth of M2/Y. Financial deepening and monetization take place more rapidly when monetary assets bear a higher real rate of return.

Exercise 6

a. (i) Fall.
   (ii) $100.
   (iii) Pesos.
   (iv) 100 (20) = 2,000.

b. (i)   Rise.
   (ii) Selling.
   (iii) Decline.
   (iv) Decline; 50(20) = 1,000.

c. (i)   Rise
   (ii)   Reduce
   (iii) Exceed
   (iv)   Buy
   (v)   Increase
   (vi)   Increase
   (vii) Increase

CHAPTER 15   Foreign Capital and Debt

Exercise 1

a. (i)   The ratio of debt to GDP in Indonesia doubled, from 28 percent to 59 percent. In Nigeria the ratio rose far more dramatically, from 9 percent in 1980 to 119 percent in 1989; this represented a 12.8-fold increase in debt relative to GDP. Notice, however, that the change in this ratio was not due solely to accumulation of debt; between 1980 and 1989 the denominator rose 58 percent in Indonesia, while it *fell* 12.7 percent in Nigeria. Taking this into account, Indonesia's debt more than tripled, while Nigeria's debt rose 11.5-fold.

   (ii) The debt-service ratio (DSR) measures interest costs and repayment of principal as a fraction of export earnings. In the case of Indonesia the DSR rose faster than D/Y because:

   The average interest rate on debt rose (line 7).

   Principal repayments also rose from 7 percent of exports in 1980 to 20 percent in 1989 (subtract line 6 from line 5).

   Exports did not grow as quickly as GDP (compare line 17 with line 18).

   (iii) The slower rise in the DSR *cannot* be explained by rapid export growth or lower interest rates, since the facts show otherwise. Therefore, the explanation must be that Nigeria managed to reschedule a large portion of its accumulating debt burden, and so defer repayments to the future.

   (iv) At the beginning of the decade it was no contest. Indonesia had more debt and a larger debt-service burden relative to both GDP and exports. At the end of the decade Nigeria had a much larger debt load, although its debt-service burden was lower as a result of rescheduling—which defers payments but does not make them go away. Overall, Indonesia was in a better position to work itself out of its debt problem.

b. (i)   Declined by 33.8 percent, rose by 42.5 percent.
   (ii) −4.5%, +4.0%.

c. (i)   Because Nigeria's exports were less diversified. At the start of the decade oil accounted for 93 percent of Nigeria's export earnings, compared to just 72 percent in Indonesia. Then, during the decade, Indonesia did a much better job of promoting nonfuel exports. As a result, Indonesia was much less vulnerable to the 1986 plunge in world oil prices.

(ii) The low interest rate can only be explained by a high proportion of concessional loans in Indonesia's debt portfolio at the beginning of the decade. The large increase in interest rates is an indication that much of the new debt incurred during the decade was obtained on more commercial terms. Instead of depending mostly on soft loans, Indonesia had to resort increasingly to loans at market-based interest rates.

(iii) There are two possible reasons. First, like Indonesia, Nigeria might have lost access to concessional loans and faced more market-determined interest costs. Second, unlike Indonesia, Nigeria's credit ratings surely deteriorated due to poor macroeconomic management. The higher riskiness of lending to Nigeria would also increase the interest costs of the country's external debt.

(iv) There is no direct evidence of the recession which bottomed out in 1982, but the sluggish growth of GNP and exports for the decade as a whole reflect the lingering effects of this recession.

d. (i) In 1989, the domestic savings ratio was 21 percent in Nigeria and 37 percent in Indonesia. During the decade Nigeria's ratio dropped considerably, while Indonesia's ratio held steady. In 1989 the government deficit was 10.5 percent of GDP in Nigeria compared to 2.1 percent in Indonesia. Considering the saving rates and government deficits, Nigeria had just 10 percent of GDP available to finance private investment and debt repayment, compared to an extraordinary 35 percent in Indonesia.

(ii) Indonesia. Its exports grew 2.4 percent per year during the 1980s, while Nigeria's exports *fell* by 2.3 percent per year. The best evidence that Indonesia successfully promoted its exports is seen in its more diverse export base; between 1980 and 1989 nonoil earnings rose from less than 30 percent of total exports to nearly 60 percent (line 9), whereas Nigeria failed completely to diversify its export base.

(iii) Indonesia was able to reduce food imports because the growth of agricultural output, at 3.2 percent per annum, outpaced the population growth rate of 1.9 percent. In the early 1970s Indonesia was the world's biggest food importer; by the mid-1980s it was nearly self-sufficient in food. In contrast, agricultural output per capita fell by 1.8 percent per year during the 1980s in Nigeria (from lines 19 and 16), for an overall drop of 15 percent for the decade. Obviously Nigeria grew more dependent on food imports, but without much spare foreign exchange to afford them.

(iv) Indonesia had a lower ICOR than Nigeria during 1965 to 1980 (2.6 versus 5.1). During the 1980s Indonesia's ICOR rose to 5.5, but Nigeria's investment was so unproductive that economic growth was negative despite significant amounts of investment.

This could be due to Nigeria's increasingly shallow financial markets (see Chapter 14); while the ratio of M3 to GDP rose from 13 to 30 percent in Indonesia, it fell from 22 to 18 percent in Nigeria. Another possible explanation is that productive private investment suffered from far more crowding out in Nigeria (see i).

(v) While Nigeria's population growth was accelerating, Indonesia's was declining, due partly to effective family planning programs. Nigeria's faster population growth certainly worsened its performance in terms of per capita income growth during the 1980s.

(vi) Although Indonesia's foreign debt rose quite a bit between 1980 and 1989, so did its GDP (up 58 percent) and exports (up 24 percent). This is why the ratios of debt to GDP and debt to exports did not increase dramatically. Compare this to Nigeria, where debt expanded nearly as much, but GDP fell by 13 percent and exports dropped by 19 percent.

e. (i) This is an opinion question, but the evidence is fairly clear-cut. Indonesia used much of the borrowed funds for productive investment; under such conditions, foreign borrowing promotes economic development.

(ii) Another opinion question. A strong case can be made that Nigeria would have been better-off if it had not borrowed at all. The bulk of the funds appear to have been spent on ill-conceived projects (e.g., poorly planned steel mills) or on consumption. The availability of foreign funds also served to postpone essential macroeconomic adjustments, and so left the country in a deep hole.

(iii) To avoid foreign borrowing altogether, a country must eliminate its savings-investment gap and its import-export gap. The first adjustment entails boosting domestic saving rates and/or cutting investment (though adverse effects of the latter can be offset by improving the efficiency of capital formation). The second adjustment entails boosting exports and/or cutting imports.

Exercise 2

a. (i) $g = 20/5 = 4\%$.
   (ii) $s = 40\%$; $g = 40/5 = 8\%$.

b. (i) See point X' in Figure 15–1a.
   (ii) See point Y' in Figure 15–1a.
   (iii) See line AA in Figure 15–1a.
   (iv) See point E in Figure 15–1a.
   (v) $C = \$90$; $I = \$30$.

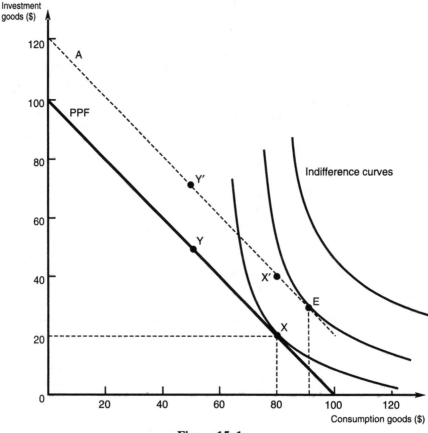

Figure 15–1a

c. (i) $30; $10.
(ii) 30%; 10%.
(iii) $g = 30/5 = 6\%$.

d. (i) $g = 30/4 = 7.5\%$.
(ii) Yes. If aid is channeled into particularly capital-intensive projects (e.g., hydroelectric power stations, tarred roads, ports), then the ICOR could rise with the aid inflow. Without knowing the social profitability of such investments, one cannot say whether they should or should not be undertaken.

e. (i)   Aid inflows would probably be used for different projects than inflows due to commercial borrowing or foreign direct investment. Without more information one cannot predict which would lead to higher economic growth.

(ii) In the future, nonaid sources of foreign savings would require much larger repayments. These repayments are negative foreign savings, which *reduce* total savings and investment in the future. This is why it is so important for foreign savings to be used productively—to enable the country to service the loans (or equity) in the future.

Exercise 3

a. (i) See Figure 15–2a. The line BIG is fitted through the points for large countries, which are represented by bullets.

   (ii) See Figure 15–2a. The line NOTSOBIG is fitted through the points for small countries, which are represented by squares.

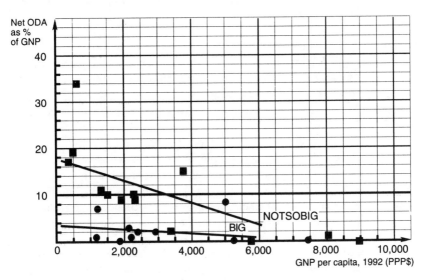

Figure 15–2a

(iii) Yes, both contentions are supported. The line for large countries is below the line for small countries; this indicates a lower aid ratio for large countries. And both lines slope down to the right; this shows that as GNP per capita rises, aid falls as a share of GNP.

b. (i) Although there are some exceptions, the data clearly show that FDI tends to rise with per capita income. This holds for both groups of countries in Table 15–2.

   (ii) The huge flow of FDI to China suggests that larger countries are more attractive destinations for foreign investment. Yes, this seems to hold generally, because the FDI figures tend to be much greater for very large countries than for smaller countries at any income level.

(iii)   South Korea's negative figure means that the country has become a net supplier of foreign investment, unlike all the other countries in the table which are net recipients. Investments abroad from South Korean companies exceeded investments in Korea from foreign companies by $497 million in 1992.

c. (i)   See line 2 in Table 15–3a.
   (ii)   See line 4 in Table 15–3a.
   (iii) The record is mixed. In Kenya the net resource flow declined modestly, in Senegal it held steady, but in Zambia it rose quite a lot. Zambia received much greater foreign savings inflows in 1990 than in 1980.
   (iv)   See line 6 in Table 15–3a.
   (v)   Again the record is mixed. In Kenya, the net resource flow per capita fell by more than one-third, in Senegal it fell by about one-fifth, but in Zambia the net resource flow per capita was nearly twice as high in 1990 as in 1980.
   (vi)   In constant-price terms, the decline in foreign savings per capita was severe in both Kenya (60 percent) and Senegal (50 percent). Even after adjusting for inflation, Zambia still had a higher level of net resource flows per capita in 1990, but not much.

d. (i)   Net income payments in 1990 were –$310.4 million for Kenya, –$235.8 million for Senegal, and an enormous –$437.0 million for Zambia. These income payments absorbed 32 percent of Kenya's net resource inflows, 46 percent of Senegal's inflows, and 45 percent of Zambia's inflows.
   (ii)   For 1980, not really; for 1990, not really. The net resource transfer was positive. Hence, inflows of foreign savings more than covered the debt-service payments for these countries. One might say that the countries suffered in the sense that they had to divert the inflows of capital to pay debt service, when the funds could have been used instead for investment or consumption. But the reality is that gross resource inflows would not have been so large if the countries had less debt service to pay. The donors, in effect, were providing foreign aid to pay themselves back!

Table 15-3a
Foreign Saving and Balance of Payments for Three African Countries
(millions of U.S.$)

	Kenya 1980	Kenya 1990	Senegal 1980	Senegal 1990	Zambia 1980	Zambia 1990
1 Trade in goods and nonfactor services						
a Exports ($ millions)	2,007.3	1,910.7	806.8	1,474.7	1,609.0	1,361.0
b Imports ($ millions)	(2,846.4)	(2,562.3)	(1,214.7)	(1,749.1)	(1,765.0)	(1,897.0)
2 *Net resource transfer ($ millions)*	**839.1**	**651.6**	**407.9**	**274.4**	**156.0**	**536.0**
3 Income payments						
a Earned ($ millions)	53.9	23.9	23.7	22.8	16.0	2.0
b Paid ($ millions)	(248.2)	(334.3)	(122.3)	(258.6)	(221.0)	(439.0)
4 *Net resource flow ($ millions)*	**1,033.4**	**962.0**	**506.5**	**510.2**	**361.0**	**973.0**
5 Population (millions)	16.7	24.9	5.7	7.3	5.6	8.1
6 *Net resource flow per capita ($)*	**61.9**	**38.6**	**88.9**	**69.9**	**64.5**	**120.1**

(iii)   Much of the inflow had to be in the form of foreign aid, since these African countries were not popular destinations for direct foreign investment and the international banks certainly were not willing lenders following the onset of the debt crisis. A sizable amount of the apparent inflow could have come in the form of a build-up of unpaid interest on old commercial debts, since this enters the balance of payments accounts as if it were new lending.

(iv)   Apart from statistical discrepancies, the gap between domestic savings and investment equals the gap between exports and imports. In 1980 all three countries depended heavily on foreign savings to supplement domestic savings as a source of funds for investment. In 1990 Kenya and Senegal, but not Zambia, had reduced the size of their savings-investment gap, as indicated by the decline in net resource transfers.

Exercise 4

a.   (i)   The values of G_d are:
           Jamaica   12.4%
           Madagascar   4.5%
           Zambia   12.3%

   (ii)   The ratio of debt to GDP would be climbing by 13.1 percent per year, which is quite unsustainable. The calculation is $1.21/1.07 - 1 = .131$.

   (iii)   India required some combination of lower interest rates on external debt, smaller trade deficits, and faster growth of export earnings, or an arrangement to restructure its debt.

b.   (i)   The values of G_d are:
           Jamaica   10.1%
           Madagascar   3.9%
           Zambia   11.6%

   (ii)   Some combination of lower interest rates on its debt, higher domestic savings, lower domestic investment, and faster growth of GDP, or an arrangement to restructure its debt.

c.   (i)   The required values of g_e (export growth) are:
           Jamaica   12.4%
           Madagascar   4.5%
           Zambia   12.3%

    (ii)   Madagascar can plausibly increase exports at a pace that stabilizes the ratio of foreign debt to exports, but the required export-growth rates for Jamaica, Zambia, and India are implausibly large. (Even if dollar inflation soared, the interest rates would rise in tandem so that would not bail them out.) These countries have to adjust their macroeconomic policies.

d.   (i)   The required values of g_y (GNP growth) are:

Jamaica	10.1%
Madagascar	3.9%
Zambia	11.6%

    (ii)   Only the figure for Madagascar is plausible as a sustainable growth rate.

e. Madagascar is in good shape, as long as it can continue to obtain such low interest rates (soft loans). Jamaica, Zambia, and India need to adjust to avert imminent debt crises.

Exercise 5

d.   (i)   The calculation for the first figure is

$$2\% + 0.3(10\%) + 0.6(2\%) + 0.1(1\%) = 6.3\%$$

        The other answers are calculated in the same way, giving: 6.9 percent, 6.6 percent, and 7.2 percent.

    (ii)   0.3 percentage points.

b.   (i)   The units are percentage-point changes in the growth rates.

dg_K	dg_Y
1.00	0.30
1.33	0.40
1.00	0.40
1.25	0.38

    (ii)   The first figure, 0.30, means that the extra investment made possible by foreign aid would increase GDP growth by 0.3 percentage points, for example, from 6.3 to 6.6 percent.

(iii) First, the additional investment could unlock other resources that were previously underutilized, such as labor or land resources. If so, it is incorrect to hold g_L and g_T constant. The simple Harrod-Domar model then gives a better answer. Using the first line of the table as an example and assuming that the ICOR equals K/Y, foreign investment amounting to 4 percent of GDP would boost growth by $4/3 = 1.33$ percentage points, not 0.30. Also, foreign aid could improve the project selection process, enhance efficiency, and reduce the capital-output ratio.

(iv) If the aid is used for consumption rather than investment, then it might make virtually no contribution to economic growth. And if it is invested in inappropriate capital-intensive projects, the effect on economic growth may be smaller than indicated, because investment productivity might decline.

CHAPTER 16 Agriculture

Exercise 1

a. (i) See Table 16–2a.

Table 16–2a*

Chemical fertilizer (F) (kg) (1)	Labor (L) (kg) (2)	Rice output (Q) (3)	Production cost (C) (Rs) (4)	Value of output (V) (Rs) (5)	Net income (Y) (Rs) (6)	Incremental cost (ΔC) (Rs) (7)	Incremental output value (ΔV) (Rs) (8)
0	4	800	**800**	1,600	**800**		
						350	**1,400**
50	5	1500	**1,150**	**3,000**	1,850		
						350	**1,200**
100	6	2100	**1,500**	**4,200**	2,700		
						350	**1,000**
150	7	2600	**1,850**	**5,200**	3,350		
						350	800
200	8	3000	2,200	**6,000**	3,800		
						350	600
250	9	3300	**2,550**	**6,600**	4,050		
						350	400
300	10	3500	**2,900**	**7,000**	4,100		
						350	200
350	11	3600	**3,250**	**7,200**	3,950		
						150	0
400	11	3600	**3,400**	**7,200**	3,800		

*Assumes P_R = Rs2, P_L = Rs200, and P_F = Rs3.

    (ii) No shift in the production function in Figure 16–1, since none of the technical relationships has changed. In Figure 16–2, no shift in *MC* since costs have not changed, but *MR* will shift up to the level Rs2/kg.

    (iii) Q' = 3500 kg.
           F' = 300 kg.
           Y' = Rs4,100.

b. (i) 500 kg; 17% (3500/3000 – 1).
   (ii) Rs3,300; 413% (4100/800 – 1).
   (iii) 1500 kg; 2000 kg; 33 percent.
   (iv) As farmers increase output, the demand for farm labor increases from $L = 8$ to $L = 10$ per farm (in the example). Hence, the demand curve for farm labor shifts to the right. At the same time, the labor supply curve will shift to the left because higher rice prices increase the cost of living; this implies that higher wages are needed to attract a given supply of labor. Both of these labor market adjustments cause P_L to increase.
   (v) The increase in P_L will increase the farmer's production costs. Depending on the magnitude of the wage increase, MC might shift upward enough to reduce the optimal output level. At a minimum, the increase in P_L would reduce the extent to which the farmer's income increases. In effect, a portion of the gains would be shared by rural farm workers

c. (i) See Table 16–3a.

Table 16–3a*

(F) (kg) (1)	(L) (2)	(Q) (kg) (3)	(C) (Rs) (4)	(V) (Rs) (5)	(Y) (Rs) (6)
0	4	800	800	800	0
50	5	1500	1,075	1,500	425
100	6	2100	1,350	2,100	750
150	7	2600	1,625	2,600	975
200	8	3000	1,900	3,000	1,100
250	9	3300	2,175	3,300	1,125
300	10	3500	2,450	3,500	1,050
350	11	3600	2,725	3,600	875
400	11	3600	2,800	3,600	800

*Assumes P_R = Rs1, P_L = RS200, and P_F =Rs1.5.

   (ii) $Q'' = 3300$ kg.
        $F'' = 250$ kg.
        $Y'' = $ Rs1,125.
   (iii) Again, no shift in the production function in Figure 16–1, because there is no change in the technical relationship between inputs and outputs. The MR line in Figure 16–2 remains horizontal at Rs1 per kg. The MC line, however, shifts downward, and the condition

$MC = MR$ would now be satisfied at $Q'' = 3300$ kg. (Graphing the new MC curve in Figure 16–2 gets a bet messy.)

Exercise 2

a. (i) See columns 2 and 3 of Table 16–4a.

Table 16–4a*

(F) (kg) (1)	(L) (2)	(Q) (kg) (3)	(C) (Rs) (4)	(V) (Rs) (5)	(Y) (Rs) (6)
0	8	1600	1,600	1,600	0
50	10	3000	2,150	3,000	850
100	12	4200	2,700	4,200	1,500
150	14	5200	3,250	5,200	1,950
200	16	6000	3,800	6,000	2,200
250	18	6600	4,350	6,600	2,250
300	20	7000	4,900	7,000	2,100
350	22	7200	5,450	7,200	1,750
400	22	7200	5,600	7,200	1,600

*Assumes $P_R =$ Rs1, $P_L =$ RS200, and $P_F =$ Rs3, but with high-yielding variety of rice.

(ii) See columns 4, 5, and 6 of Table 16–4a.
(iii) $Q^* = 6600$ kg.
$F^* = 250$ kg.
$Y^* =$ Rs2,250.

b. (i) $(2,250 + 2,250 + 2,250 - 2,000)/4 =$ Rs1,188.
(ii) Not necessarily. Although the farmer's *average* income would increase using the new variety of rice, the associated risk may well outweigh the gain. Poor peasant farmers would not eagerly adopt a technology if they knew that there were a 1 in 4 chance of suffering substantial losses.

c. (i) Lacking rural credit to carry them from planting to harvest, small farmers in some poor countries cannot afford to buy the fertilizer needed for using modern seed varieties.
(ii) Increased food output cannot be translated into cash income if farmers cannot inexpensively get their products to market. Reliable

marketing and transportation services are essential conditions for
inducing farmers to switch to modern seed varieties.

(iii) Quite simply, farmers won't use the new rice seeds if they don't
learn how. Extension workers help to introduce new varieties
and to train farmers in proper techniques for planting, weeding,
watering, and applying fertilizer to the new varieties.

Exercise 3

a. (i) See the "Sharecrop farmer" column in Table 16–5a.

Table 16–5a

Rice output (Q) (kg)	Net income retained by:	
	Sharecrop farmer (Rs)	Tenant farmer (Rs)
800	−200	−400
1500	−25	−50
2100	75	200
2600	100	350
3000	50	400
3300	−75	350
3500	−275	200
3600	−550	−50

(ii) $F = 150$ kg.
$Q = 2600$ kg.

(iii) Compared to the situation shown in Figure 16–2, the sharecropper
faces the same *MC* curve, but *retained* marginal revenue is lower
by 25 percent. Hence, the *MR* curve is lower, and $MC = MR$ at a
lower output level.

(iv) The independent proprietor is more efficient, because marginal
revenue in the eyes of the sharecropper understates the marginal

benefits to the economy of additional production. Output $Q^* = 3000$ is the best balance between marginal social benefits and marginal social costs.

b. (i) See the "tenant farmer" column in table 16–5a.
   (ii) $F = 200$ kg.
        $Q = 3000$ kg.
   (iii) The rental payment increases total expenses for the farmer and thereby reduces income. But this is a fixed payment that does not distort either *marginal* costs or marginal revenues. In this case the income-maximizing output is the efficient output.

c. Compared with Figure 16–2, the MC and MR curves shift down by identical amounts. Hence, the level of output at which $MC = MR$ is unaffected. Under this contract the sharecropper operates efficiently.

Exercise 4

a. (i) $Q_1 = 300$ million kg.
   (ii) $P_2 = $ N$0.40.
   (iii) $Q_2 = 150$ million kg.
   (iv) 150 million kg.

b. (i) $Q_m = 150$ million kg.
        US$75 million (= N$150 million).
   (ii) $S_0 = $ N$0.20.
        N$30 million (= 150 million × 0.20).

c. (i) $P_3 = $ N$1.00.
       $P_4 = $ N$1.40.
   (ii) $S_1 = $ N$0.60.
        N$180 million (= 300 million × 0.60).
   (iii) The farm price policy has a much higher *budgetary* cost: N$180 million versus N$30 million for the imports.
   (iv) Although less costly to the government, the import policy imposes a heavy burden on domestic farmers by reducing farm-gate prices. This discourages grain production and impairs incentives for investment and innovation in agriculture. (The imports also are a drain on foreign exchange.)

Exercise 5

a. (i) 6 hectares; 4 workers.
   (ii) See line $C = \$1,200$ in Figure 16–4a.

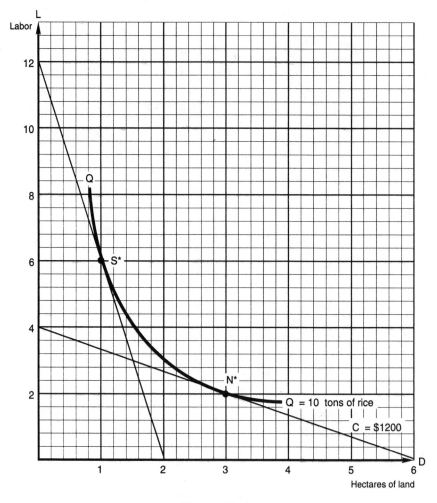

Figure 16–4a

   (iii) See point N^* in Figure 16–4a.
   (iv) $D = 3$; $L = 2$.
   (v) 3.33; 5.

b. (i)   See the isocost line for South Nasi in Figure 16–4a.
    (ii) See point S^* in Figure 16–4a.
    (iii) $D = 1; L = 6.$
    (iv) 10; 1.67.

c. (i)   South.
    (ii) North.
    (iii) Nothing! The differences in factor productivity do not imply dif-
          ferent degrees of efficiency. Rather they are the result of efficient
          responses to different factor endowments. In North Nasi, where
          land is relatively abundant, it is efficient to use lots of land per
          unit of rice. In South Nasi, where land is relatively scarce, it is
          efficient to produce rice using a technique that economizes on
          land. The same goes for differences in labor productivity.

CHAPTER 17   **Primary Exports**

Exercise 1

a.   (i) $M = 40$.
            $B = 20$.
    (ii)   Slope $= -1$.
   (iii)   1 ton.
            1 ton.
   (iv)   1 ton.
            $P_M/P_B = 1$.

b.   (i)   1/3 ton.
            3 tons.
   (ii)   See line TT in Figure 17–2a.

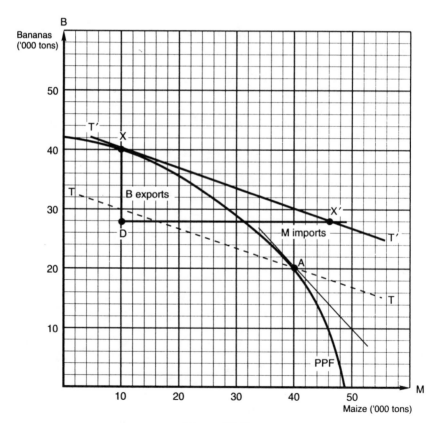

Figure 17–2a

     (iii) Slope = –1/3.
     (iv) 1 ton.
      (v) $6,000.
          3 tons.
     (vi) 3 tons.
          Bananas.

c.   (i) See point X and line $T'T'$ in Figure 17–2a.
    (ii) $M = 10$.
        $B = 40$.
   (iii) 10.
        30.
   (iv) See point X' in Figure 17–2a.
    (v) See Figure 17–2a: the trade triangle involves exporting XD of
         bananas and importing DX' of maize.

d. Yes. Free trade means that maize producers will face lower relative prices,
    and banana consumers will pay a higher relative price. The net gain is not
    evenly distributed, so some groups may be harmed, on balance.

e.   (i) Bananas; maize
    (ii) A decline in the terms of trade means that line $T'T$ would be steeper.
         Point X, the optimal production point, would slide to the south-
         east, and point X' would lie closer to A. The trade triangle would
         shrink as would the gains from trade. Overall, the optimum would
         involve allocating fewer resources to banana production for export.

Exercise 2

a. Colombia: $T_n = P_x/P_m = 69/113 = .61$
                       = 61 expressed as an index number.
    Malawi: $T_n = 61$.

b.   (i) Colombia: $T_i = P_xQ_x/P_m = 110$.
         Malawi: $T_i = 73$.
    (ii) The income terms of trade are higher because export volumes
         increased; this offsets at least partly the effect of lower export
         prices and higher import prices.
   (iii) Colombia's export volume rose more than enough to offset the
         declining net barter terms of trade; as a result, the country's
         overall import capacity increased.

c. (i) Colombia: $T_s = (P_x/P_m)Z_x = 100$.
       Malawi: $T_s = 64$.

   (ii) The numbers show that the import capacity earned per unit of
        labor in the export sector held steady in Colombia, while it fell by
        36 percent in Malawi. Since both countries suffered the same de-
        cline in net barter terms of trade, the difference must be due to low
        productivity growth in Malawi. In general a value for T_s below
        100 means that the capacity to buy imports fell *per unit of factor
        input* in the export industry—taking into account productivity
        changes as well as price changes for exports and imports.

d. Obviously, both countries would have been better off without the decline
    in net barter terms of trade. But only Malawi ended up with a reduced
    capacity to purchase imports. Colombia avoided this adverse outcome
    by expanding export output and by increasing productivity in the export
    sector. Nonetheless, even Colombia lost ground in terms of import
    capacity *relative to* GDP: the income terms of trade rose just 10 percent
    while GDP rose 40 percent.

e. (i) For Colombia: RER = 201.
       For Malawi: RER = 133.

   (ii) Colombia. Both countries' currencies depreciated in real terms,
        since more local currency was needed at the end of the decade to
        buy a unit of foreign exchange, after adjusting for inflation. But
        the depreciation was much larger in Colombia. Since a real
        depreciation makes exports more profitable, exchange-rate policy
        in Colombia was indeed more conducive to export growth.

Exercise 3

a. (i) R will increase, as P and Q both rise.
   (ii) R will remain unchanged; Q goes up, but then P goes down in
        equal proportion (since the price elasticity of demand is unity).

b. (i) When demand is unstable, the price of copper is also unstable: P
        rises and falls as D shifts to the right and to the left.
   (ii) When supply is unstable, the price of copper is unstable: P rises
        when S shifts to the left, and P falls when S shifts to the right.
  (iii) Revenues are even more unstable than prices since fluctuations in
        Q reinforce the changes in P that occur when the demand curve
        shifts back and forth.

    (iv)   The picture is quite different when the supply curve is the source of instability. As the *S* curve shifts back and forth, total export revenues ($P \times Q$) remain stable here, because the price elasticity of demand is unity.

    (v)   If demand were inelastic, export revenues still rise and fall in tandem with demand shifts. But the effect of *supply* shifts would be different. With inelastic demand, the price changes are proportionately larger than the output changes. Therefore, $P \times Q$ *falls* when *S* shifts to the right, and it rises when *S* shifts to the left. In short, export revenues fall when supply goes up and they rise when supply goes down!

c.   (i)   Buy; sell.

    (ii) See line *D'* in Figure 17–3a.

         The Fund must sell the amount *EF* in Figure 17–3a.

    (iii) See line *D"* in Figure 17–3a.

         The Fund must buy the amount *EG* in Figure 17–3a.

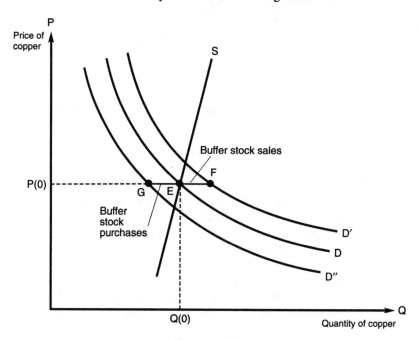

Figure 17–3a

(iv) See line S' in Figure 17–4a.
   The Fund must buy the amount EF in Figure 17–4a.
(v) See line S" in Figure 17–4a.
   The Fund must sell the amount EG in Figure 17–4a.

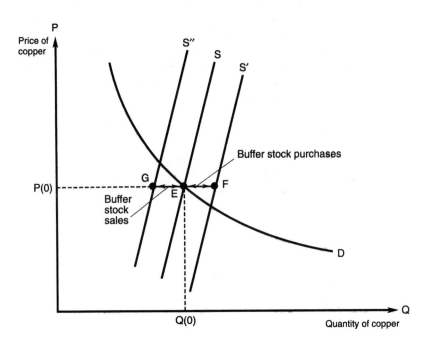

Figure 17–4a

d. (i) No. Export earnings are destabilized, since export volume fluctuates while the price remains stable.
   (ii) Yes. Export earnings are stabilized, because both P and Q are held stable by Fund operations.

e. (i) See lines S' and D' in Figure 17–5a.
   (ii) To maintain P(0), the Fund would have to purchase amount XY each period. It will eventually run out of funds and collapse.

(iii) This time demand shifts out more than supply, so to maintain $P(0)$, the Fund has to sell copper every period. Eventually the buffer stock copper reserves will be exhausted, at which time the operation will collapse.

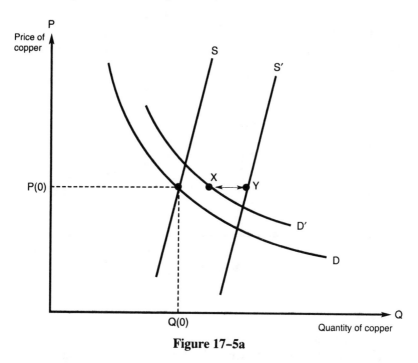

Figure 17–5a

f. (i) See line C in Figure 17–6a.
  (ii) See price level $P(C)$ in Figure 17–6a.
  (iii) No. With unitary price elasticity of demand, the percentage increase in price is offset by an equal percentage decline in volume. Sales revenues do not increase unless demand is price inelastic.
  (iv) Any individual exporter can undercut the cartel price by a small amount and greatly increase sales volume; this would boost export earnings.

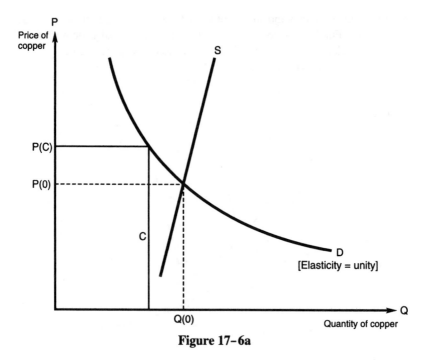

Figure 17–6a

Exercise 4

a. (i) Sh5; Sh2.
   (ii) With the sharp decline in shilling revenues per box of marbles, marble output and exports both fell. Many producers went out of business because they could not earn a profit exporting at the lower shilling price of marbles.

b. (i) Sh200; Sh80.
   (ii) With competing imports now selling at a much lower shilling price, domestic rice producers faced a severe profit squeeze. Consequently, domestic rice output dropped dramatically.
   (iii) The fall in employment in the marble and rice industries greatly outweighed the extra jobs generated by the diamond mines. With a net decline in the demand for labor, employment fell and real wages fell.

c. (i) When the central bank converts dollars into shillings and the shillings are spent by government, the money supply increases. Because of the large magnitude of royalty revenues in Bounty, the money supply increased very quickly.

   (ii) The increase in demand for services and the increase in the money supply caused a large increase in the price of nontradables.

d. (i) The real exchange rate fell from 100 to 73, so the Bountian shilling *appreciated* by 27 percent.

   (ii) With a fixed nominal exchange rate and a 2 percent rise in world prices for tradables, the shilling price facing producers of tradables rose by 2 percent, while the domestic cost of nontradable inputs (such as labor) climbed by 40 percent. This accentuated the profit squeeze on marble and rice producers.

e. Very simply, the government may be encouraged by the rapid growth of revenues to embark on ambitious debt-financed spending programs, based on the *prospect* of continued revenue growth from diamond royalties in future years. This would leave the government highly vulnerable to any downturn in diamond prices or production.

f. (i) To offset the adverse consequences on employment (in marbles and rice) and inflation (in nontradables), the government must avert the large appreciation of the shilling and the surge in the domestic money supply. To avert the appreciation, the government must use or hold most of the foreign exchange earnings externally, for imports or for foreign investments. To avert an inflationary rise in the money supply, the government must run a very conservative budget program, probably requiring surpluses during the boom period.

   (ii) A large portion of the earnings bonanza should be held in financial assets (abroad) and used only to the extent that highly productive capital investments can be undertaken, consistent with a noninflationary budget program.

CHAPTER 18   Industry

Exercise 1

a. (i) $L_{b3} = \sum\limits_{i=1}^{3} a_{i3}.$

    (ii) 0.75.

    (iii) Service.

b. (i) Each unit of services (S) output creates an *indirect* requirement for
0.54 – 0.25 = 0.29 units of manufactured goods (M) in addition to
the 0.25 units required as direct inputs into S. The indirect requirement occurs because, to produce the required direct inputs, the M,
S, and agriculture sectors in turn generate secondary requirements
for inputs of M goods. And so on.

    (ii) To get 1 unit of S output requires 1 unit of S production *plus* in-
direct requirements for inputs of intermediate S goods. Therefore,
the total requirement for S goods must exceed unity. More generally,
for every sector i, $r_{ii} \geq 1$.

    (iii) 0.61 + 0.54 + 1.20 = 2.35.

    (iv) Manufacturing.

    (v) S has the largest direct backward-linkage index, but M has the
largest total backward-linkage index. This can be due to only one
thing: the indirect linkages are stronger for the M sector. Why?
Because more of the M sector's direct linkages involve M and S
inputs, which in turn create large secondary linkage effects.

c. (i) $250.

    (ii) $X_{11} = \$20.$
       $X_{12} = \$40.$
       $X_{13} = \$30.$

    (iii) 20 + 40 + 30 = $90.

    (iv) 90/250 = 0.36.

    (v) 30/80 = 0.375.

    (vi) Manufacturing.

d. (i) It doesn't mean much! If production in manufacturing increases by
1 unit, then there will be enough M around to satisfy the direct input

requirements of 0.55 units of additional production in sectors A, M, and S combined—assuming that the structure of demand for M products has not changed. The number does *not* mean that an extra unit of M output *will* stimulate 0.55 units of added production, spread through the economy in fixed proportions!

(ii) At best, the index of forward linkages is a secondary consideration in determining whether industry or any particular industrial activity is a suitable leading sector. It says that M is a potential bottleneck, because of large interindustry requirements for M inputs, and that extra capacity in M *permits* additional expansion without running up against M-input constraints (which could be relieved by imports, anyway).

Exercise 2

a. (i) $10/80 = 0.125$.
   $20/40 = 0.50$.
   $50/20 = 2.50$.

   (ii) $2.50/0.50 = 5$.
   $2.50/0.125 = 20$.

   (iii) This range is not unrealistic. The text cites a study of the weaving industry in which the K/L value for T_3 is 22 times higher than that of T_1. The range of K/L values for T_3 relative to T_2 is lower in this exercise (2.50) than the corresponding ratio for industries such as spinning (7.3), brickmaking (13.8), and sugar processing (7.8), as reported in the text.

b. See points T_1, T_2, and T_3 in Figure 18–1a and the isoquant formed by connecting these points.

c. (i) Modern: T_3.
         Informal: T_1.
   (ii) Appropriate: T_2.
   (iii) See line B_m in Figure 18–1a.
   (iv) See line B_i in Figure 18–1a.
   (v)   See line B_s in Figure 18–1a.

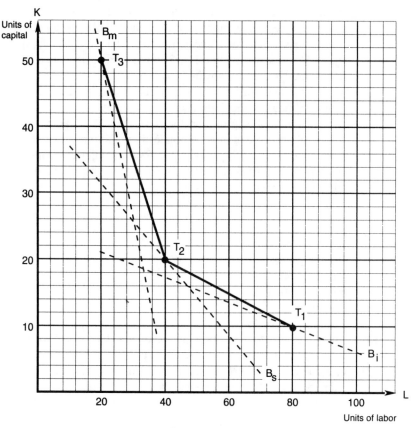

Figure 18–1a

d. (i) 50 thousand.
   10 thousand.
 (ii) 20 thousand.
   80 thousand.
 (iii) Modern: 50,000(F175) + 20,000(F100) = F10.75 million.
   Informal: 10,000(F175) + 80,000(F100) – F9.75 million.
   Appropriate: 20,000(F175) + 40,000(F100) = F7.50 million.
 (iv) 50/10 = 5 times as much capital.
   Only 20/80 = .25 = 25% as many jobs.
   10.75/9.75 – 1 = .103 = 10.3% higher opportunity cost.

e. (i) Modern: 50,000(F100) + 20,000(F200) = F9 million.
   Informal: 10,000(F500) + 80,000(F100) = F13 million.
 (ii) Modern, informal, informal.
 (iii) Certainly not! The distorted factor prices permit high-cost, capital-intensive producers to thrive, but low-cost, labor-intensive pro-

ducers will go out of business. The government of Couteau might point with pride at its modern knife industry, but the cost is very high, in terms of inefficient use of scarce resources and forgone job creation.

Exercise 3

a. (i) The question calls for two reasons for scale economies. Plausible answers include:

>   Technical efficiencies in use of larger kilns, since capacity increases with the cube of the radius whereas cost increases with the square of the radius

>   Greater efficiency in handling inventories of raw materials and finished products

>   Greater specialization of labor in larger production units

>   Discounts on input costs for producers who operate on a larger scale

(ii)   400 thousand tons.

(iii) $125/100 - 1 = 0.25 = 25\%$ higher cost.

(iv) $200/100 - 1 = 1.00 = 100\%$ higher cost.

b. (i) 20%.

(ii)   The domestic market can support no more than five production units, each operating at the MES. Thus, the brick industry is likely to be a monopoly or an oligopoly, not a competitive industry.

(iii)   Including exports there can be as many as 20 producers, each operating at the MES. There is much more scope for competition.

c. (i) 20

(ii)   70.

(iii)   About 225.

(iv)   Domestic demand amounts to just one-third of the minimum efficient scale for producing clay presses in Amigo. Producing at this low level of capacity entails a cost of about P350,000 per press—more than twice the cost per press at an efficient scale of production.

d. (i) Without a doubt, the clay press industry would be dominated by a monopoly supplier. Demand is too low to support multiple production units.

(ii)   Protecting the inefficient clay press producers will hurt the brickmakers, as the cost of their main equipment would more than double. This will reduce domestic sales, export potential, and profitability in the brickmaking industry.

CHAPTER 19   Trade and Industrialization

Exercise 1

a. (i)   Ksh600.
    (ii) See line P_W in Figure 19–3a.

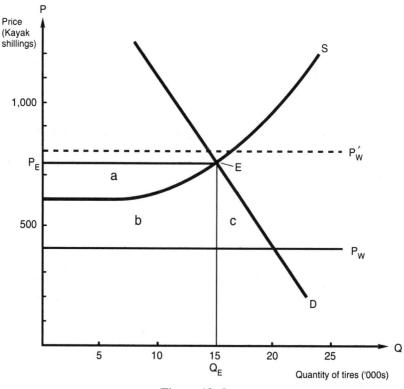

Figure 19–3a

(iii) 20 thousand tires.
      Ksh400.
      $20,000 \times 400 = $ Ksh8 million.
(iv) 100%.
(v) $800,000.

b. (i)   Ksh800.
    (ii) See line P'_W in Figure 19–3a.

(iii)   See point E in Figure 19–3a.
(iv)   15 thousand tires; see Q_E in Figure 19–3a.
        Ksh750; see P_E in Figure 19–3a.
(v)   15,000 × 750 = Ksh11.25 million.
        0%.
(vi)   Ksh0 (because no tires are imported now).
(vii) $0 (ditto).
(viii) 15 thousand tires.

c. Using labels a, b, and c as shown in Figure 19–3a:
   (i)   Lost consumer surplus = area $a + b + c$.
   (ii) Producers' surplus = area a.
   (iii) Deadweight loss = area $b + c$.

d. (i) If costs rise 50 percent, curve S shifts vertically upward by 50
        percent. The supply curve now lies wholly above line P'_W because
        domestic output is more expensive than imports, despite the high
        tariff! With such inefficiency, domestic producers cannot compete.
        Domestic output drops to zero and imports rise to just over 14,000
        tires, which is the quantity demanded at the tariff-ridden market
        equilibrium price of Ksh800 (where D and P'_W intersect).
   (ii) If demand rises 50 percent, curve D shifts to the right by 50 per-
        cent. The market price rises to Ksh800, but no higher, since imports
        can always be obtained at this price (which includes the tariff).
        At Ksh800 per tire, domestic demand is just under 22,000 tires.
        Domestic supply equals 17,000 tires (where P'_W intersects S),
        and imports account for the remainder.

e. Successful import substitution means that the protected infant industry
   grows up and can compete with imports without continued protection. In
   the figure, this requires that S shift down enough (through increased efficiency) so that at least a significant portion of the curve lies below P_W.
   Otherwise, the import substitution policy is unsuccessful: high-cost
   domestic production depends on continued protection: this perpetuates
   the welfare losses and inefficiencies.

f. (i) Point E again, where $Q = 15,000$ tires and $P = $ Ksh750.
   (ii) The market outcomes are identical; both the tariff and the quota
        eliminate tire imports entirely in this case, so the domestic
        supply and demand curves determine the same outcome either
        way.

g. (i)   If costs rise 50 percent, imports are still stuck at zero because of the quota. The intersection of the new S with D will be at approximately $Q = 12,000$ and $P = $ Ksh 975. Domestic consumers end up with fewer tires at a much higher price.

  (ii) Again, imports are not permitted in to restrain the price. The new D will intersect S at approximately $Q = 19,000$ and $P = $ Ksh 900. Compared to the case with a 100 percent tariff, consumers end up with a higher price and lower quantity as a result of the quota.

  (iii) This is a recipe for monopolistic supply conditions. The domestic producer can take advantage of this market power to restrict output and raise the price—generating higher profits at the expense of consumers.

Exercise 2

a. (i)   Rs90,000.
  (ii) $V_w = \$1,000$
        $= $ Rs10,000.

b. (i) $P_d = $ Rs125,000.
  (ii) $C_d = $ Rs90,000.
  (iii) $V_d = $ Rs35,000.
  (iv) $(35,000 - 10,000)/10,000 = 2.50 = 250\%$.
  (v)   ERP $= 250\%$.

c. (i)   ERP $= 25\%$.
  (ii) 25%.

Exercise 3

a. (i) $R = 100$ pesos/\$.
  (ii) 100 pesos per pound.
  (iii) 500,000 pesos.
  (iv) 2,000 pesos.

b. (i)   50 pesos
  (ii) 250,000 pesos
  (iii) 1,000 pesos

c. (i)   Over
  (ii) Less profitable
        Less expensive

    (iii) $70 million

           $20 million

    (iv) $50 million

d. (i) Zero.

    (ii) 50%.

    (iii) 50%.

    (iv) Behind the wall of protection created by foreign exchange controls, capital and labor resources will be drawn into manufacturing blue jeans. These resources will be drawn away from coffee production (which is now less profitable) and from machinery production (because the overvalued exchange rate makes it cheaper to buy imported machinery).

    (v) By reducing the cost of machinery, the government's trade policy encourages the use of more capital-intensive production techniques, which hampers job growth and the long-term prospects for improving workers' real incomes.

e. (i) See line D' in Figure 19–4a.

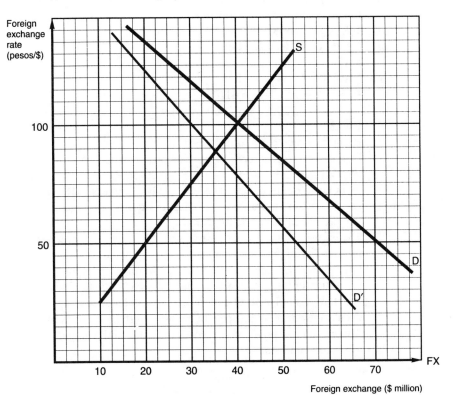

Figure 19–4a

(ii) The tariff reduces the demand for foreign exchange; this causes the market-equilibrium exchange rate to decline by about 12 percent, to around P88 per dollar.

(iii) At an exchange rate of P88 per dollar, coffee producers will earn P88 per pound of exports. The domestic price of imported machines will be P440,000.

(iv) Compared to the free-trade situation, coffee exports have become less profitable. By causing a decline (appreciation) in the equilibrium exchange rate, the tariff on blue-jean imports hurts the export industry.

Exercise 4

a. (i) $VA_b = 400 - 160 = Kw240.$
   $VA_c = 400 - 120 - 60 = Kw220.$
   (ii) Beef: $1 - 160/400 = 0.60.$
   (iii) Copper: $1 - 120/400 - 60/400 = 0.55.$

b. (i) $ERS = [.50/(1 - .60 - .20)] = .50/.20 = 2.50 = 250\%$
   (all other terms equal zero here).
   (ii) $1.25 \times \$10 \times 40Kw/\$ = Kw500.$
   (iii) $VA_b = 500 - 160 = Kw340.$
   Kw240.
   (iv) $340/240 - 1 = .417 = 41.7\%.$
   $ERS = .25/.60 = .417 = 41.7\%.$
   (v) $VA_c = 400 - 120(1.333) - 60 = Kw180.$
   Kw220.
   (vi) By increasing the cost of intermediate inputs, the tariff on imported shovels reduces the profitability of exporting copper. $ERS = [-(.3)(.3333)/.55] = -.182 = -18.2$ percent. Because of the input tariff, domestic value-added must be compressed 18.2 percent (compared to free trade), so copper exports can remain competitive in the world market.
   (vii) The trade policies distort the structure of industry. They reduce the profitability of producing copper for export, while enhancing the returns on producing beef exports and aspirin as an import substitute for the local market. The key point is that the ERS structure can induce beef exports and aspirin production to expand even if they have no prospect of becoming efficient and even if the resource cost of production exceeds the value of the output, assessed at undistorted prices.

c.   (i) $ERS_a = .10/.20 = .50 = 50\%$.
$ERS_b = .10/.60 = .167 = 16.7\%$.
$ERS_c = .10/.55 = .182 = 18.2\%$.

(ii)   The structure of protection becomes far less distortionary after the reforms. The strong bias in favor of aspirin production is smaller now, while the bias against copper production has been transformed into positive, though moderate, protection. Resources will shift away from aspirin production back to copper. When the tariffs and subsidies are uniform at 10 percent, the ERS values differ from sector to sector because the uniform *nominal* protection rate applies to different amounts of domestic value-added. The aspirin industry has the lowest amount of domestic value-added, so it still gets the highest *effective* subsidy.

Exercise 5

a.   (i)   See the column labeled "1996" in Table 19–1a.

Table 19–1a
Pampa's Wheat and Clothing Industries

Wheat	1995	1996	1996*
1. World price ($ per bushel)	4	4.40	4.40
2. Exchange rate (P/$)	20	**20**	**23**
3. Exporter receives (P per bushel)	80	**88**	**101.2**
4. Export tax rate (%)	10	**10**	**10**
5. Net revenue per bushel, after tax (P)	72	**79.2**	**91.08**
6. Domestic production cost per bushel (P)	64	80	80
7. Exporter's profits per bushel (P)	12	**−0.8**	**11.08**

Clothing	1995	1996	1996*
8. World price ($ per unit)	50	55	55
9. Exchange rate (P/$)	20	**20**	**23**
10. Border price (P per unit)	1,000	**1,100**	**1,265**
11. Tariff rate (%)	25	**25**	**25**
12. Domestic price[†] (P per unit)	1,250	**1,375**	**1,581.25**
13. Domestic production cost per unit (P)	1,100	1,375	1,375
14. Domestic producer's profits per unit (P)	150	**0**	**206.25**

*P = pesos.

[†]Domestic price = (import price)(1 + tariff rate).

(ii)   See the column labeled "1996" in Table 19–2a.

Table 19–2a
Index Numbers for Wheat Exports

	1995	1996	1996a	1996b
1. R_o	100	100	115	100
2. N_e	1.00	1.00	1.00	1.136
3. P_w	100	110	110	110
4. P_d	100	125	125	125
5. $REER_e$	100	88	101.2	100

(iii)   The decline in the real effective exchange rate facing wheat exporters reduces profitability in the industry. The reason is that
domestic production costs rose more rapidly than revenues from
selling wheat to the world market. Indeed, you can see in Table
19–1a that profits from wheat exports are negative in 1996. If
nothing is done, exports will drop sharply.

b.   (i) $REER_m = 88$.
[$REER_m = REER_e$ because N_m and N_e remain fixed (so far), while
exportables and importables are affected equally here by changes
in P_w and P_d.]
(ii)   The decline in $REER_m$ reduces profitability for domestic clothing
producers. Domestic production costs rose faster than the price of
imported clothing. The bottom figure in column 1996 of Table
19–1a shows that domestic producers just break even, despite the
25 percent tariff in their favor.

c.   (i)   See the columns labeled "1996a" in tables 19–1a and 19–2a.
(ii) $REER_m = 101.2$. (Again, $REER_e = REER_m$ because there are still
no changes in N_e or N_m.)
(iii)   Both $REER_e$ and $REER_m$ are slightly higher than in 1995 and much
higher than without the 1996 devaluation. Production of both goods
becomes profitable again.

Note an important nuance: profits in the domestic clothing industry soar, while profits in wheat production are still slightly lower
than in 1995. This occurs because the 25 percent protective tariff
and the 10 percent export tax apply to the *peso* price of competing
imports and the *peso* price of exports. These peso prices both rise
with devaluation. The devaluation accentuates the prevailing trade
policy distortions and draws resources toward clothing production,
even though the REER is identical for both sectors.

d. (i) $N_e = 1.136$.
    (ii) $t_e = -0.0224 = -2.24\%$ (a subsidy of 2.24%).
        [Derivation: $1.136 = (1 - t_e)/(1 - 0.1)$.]

e. (i) $N_m = 1.136$.
    (ii) $t_m = 0.42 = 42\%$ (a tariff of 42%).
        [Derivation: $1.136 = (1 + t_m)/(1 + 0.25)$.]

Exercise 6

a. Slope $= -1$.
    1 ton.

b. (i) 2 tons.
    (ii) A half ton.
    (iii) 1/2.
    (iv) See point *B* in Figure 19–5a.

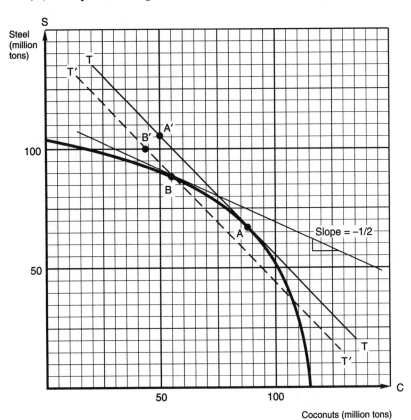

Figure 19–5a

c. (i) See lint $T'T'$ in Figure 19–5a.
   (ii) See point B' in Figure 19–5a.

d. (i) See the curve PPF_{95} in Figure 19–6a.
   (ii) See point B_{95} in Figure 19–6a.
   (iii) See line $T_{95}T_{95}$; its slope equals -1.0.
   (iv) See the consumption point B'_{95} which lies along $T_{95}T_{95}$ to the northwest of the production point B_{95}.

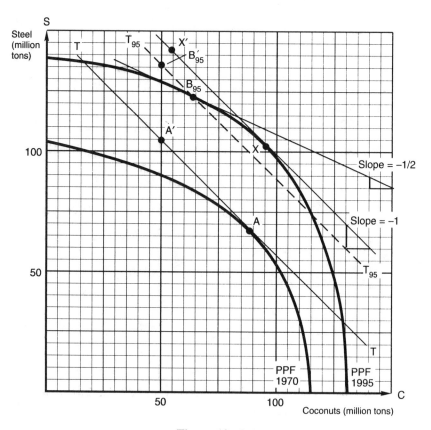

Figure 19–6a

e. (i) If the tariff were eliminated, then the relative domestic prices would adjust to world prices and resources would get reallocated from steel to coconut production. Optimal production would be at point X in Figure 19–6a, and the country could trade to a point like X'. This outcome is unambiguously preferred to the best point achievable on line $T_{95}T_{95}$. Conclusion: Anglia is bette- off dropping the tariff on steel imports in 1995. Let the infant industry grow up!

(ii) In an unsuccessful case, the import substitution policy would greatly retard economic growth; the PPF would not shift out enough to provide higher standards of living over the quarter-century when the policies are in place.

(iii) Import substitution often ends up with disappointing results due to the distortions engendered by the protective policies that are used to implement the strategy. Highly protective tariffs, quantitative restrictions, and overvalued exchange rates frequently combine to create stagnation in agriculture; high-cost, noncompetitive manufacturing; retarded backward linkages; heavily politicized bureaucratic controls; wasteful rent-seeking activities; a bias to capital-intensive production; and poor export performance, combined, ironically, with a high degree of dependence on imported intermediate goods and capital goods. Once domestic production has grown enough to supply the limited domestic market for consumer goods, further growth becomes very difficult.

Exercise 7

a. (i) See answers in the left-hand side of Table 19–3a.

(ii) Gaskets: domestic production in Tanya
Pumps: imports from countries other than Kenzania
Tractors: domestic production in Tanya

Table 19–3a
Acquisition Costs for Tanya

Source of supply	Prior to customs union			After customs union		
	Gaskets	Pumps	Tractors	Gaskets	Pumps	Tractors
A. Imports from Kenzania						
1. Price of imports (Ksh)	18	6,000	100,000	18	6,000	100,000
2. Price of imports (Tsh)	18	6,000	100,000	18	6,000	100,000
3. Tariff charged (Tsh)	7.2	2,400	40,000	0	0	0
4. Domestic price (= 2 + 3) (Tsh)	25.2	8,400	140,000	18	6,000	100,000
B. Imports from other countries						
1. Price of imports ($)	2	500	8,000	2	500	8,000
2. Price of imports (Tsh)	20	5,000	80,000	20	5,000	80,000
3. Tariff charged (Tsh)	8	2,000	32,000	8	2,000	32,000
4. Domestic price (= 2 + 3) (Tsh)	28	7,000	112,000	28	7,000	112,000
C. Production in Tanya						
1. Domestic production price (Tsh)	24	8,000	95,000	24	8,000	95,000

b. (i) See the answers in the right half of Table 19–3a.

(ii) Gaskets: imports from Kenzania replace higher-cost domestic production in Tanya.
Pumps: imports from Kenzania replace *lower*-cost imports from other countries due to Kenzania's new tariff advantage.
Tractors: Tanyan producers now export to the Kenzanian market.

c. (i) Tanya benefits from trade creation in that it gets gaskets at a lower resource cost through imports (from Kenzania). Also, its tractor industry gains because it penetrates the export market to Kenzania (where production costs are higher). These gains from trade arise with the (partial) elimination of tariffs.

(ii) Tanya loses from trade diversion because the country now obtains pumps (from Kenzania) at a *higher* foreign exchange cost. The switch to a high-cost source occurs because of the tariff differential.

CHAPTER 20   Managing an Open Economy

Exercise 1

a. (i)   Referring to the market for tradables:
    Event 1: The demand curve shifts to the left; this results in an external surplus.
    Event 2: The supply curve shifts to the right; this results in an external surplus.
    Event 3: The supply curve shifts to the left; this results in an external deficit.
    Event 4: Neither curve shifts, but there is movement along both the curves in response to the rise in the real exchange rate; the rise in the relative price of tradables leads to an external surplus.

  (ii)   Referring to the market for tradables:
    Event 1: The demand curve shifts to the left; this results in higher unemployment and slack economic conditions.
    Event 2: Some of the added purchasing power is likely to spill over into higher demand for nontradables; then the demand curve will shift to the right, and so causes inflationary pressures.
    Event 3: The decline in exporters' incomes would cause domestic demand for nontradables to shift to the left, and so causes slack economic conditions.
    Event 4: Neither curve shifts, but there is movement along the two curves in response to the rise in the real exchange rate; the relative price of domestic goods falls, and this induces a greater volume of demand and smaller quantity supplied. The resulting excess domestic demand is inflationary.

b. (i)   There is excess demand for tradables; this signifies an external deficit.
  (ii)   There is excess supply of nontradables; this indicates that unemployment will be high and resources will be idle.
  (iii)   Referring to the market for tradables:
    Event 1: The increase in demand worsens the external deficit.
    Event 2: The leftward shift in supply worsens the external deficit.
    Event 3: The increase in supply eases the external deficit.
    Event 4: The appreciation reduces the relative price of tradables, and so stimulates demand and reduces supply; this makes the external deficit worse.

(iv) Referring to the market for nontradables:

Event 1: The demand curve shifts to the right; this reduces the contractionary imbalance.

Event 2: If the loss of foreign support feeds through to a cut in government spending on nontradables, then the demand curve will shift to the left, and so worsen the economic downturn.

Event 3: Incomes will rise, and so shift demand to the right; this puts the economy closer to internal balance.

Event 4: The appreciation increases the relative price of nontradables; this reduces the quantity demanded and increases production incentives. The result is an increase in the excess supply condition.

c. (i) The *EB* line has a positive slope because external balance can only be preserved if a rise in absorption is accompanied by an increase in the real exchange rate. Then the rise in demand for tradables due to higher absorption is offset by an improvement in the trade balance due to an increase in the relative price of tradables, which reduces demand and augments supply.

(ii) The *IB* line has a negative slope because internal balance can only be preserved if a rise in absorption is accompanied by a decline in the real exchange rate. Then the rise in demand for nontradables due to higher absorption is offset by the effects of having a higher relative price for nontradables; this relative-price change induces a switch in the composition of demand toward fewer nontradables, while providing an incentive for shifting production to supply more nontradables.

d. (i) Referring to the external balance:

Event 1: No shift, but the economy moves off the *EB* line toward the west. The result is an external surplus.

Event 2: *EB* shifts to the right. At the initial real exchange rate, the market for nontradables could now accommodate greater absorption. The initial impact is an external surplus.

Event 3: *EB* shifts to the left. At the initial real exchange rate, the market for nontradables can no longer accommodate the same level of absorption. This creates an external deficit.

Event 4: No shift, but the economy moves off the *EB* line toward the north. The result is an external surplus.

    (ii)   Referring to the internal balance:

           Event 1:   No shift, but the economy moves off the *IB* line toward the west. The result is a recession.

           Event 2:   The inflow of foreign exchange does not boost the supply of nontradables (at least not in the short run), yet it may add to absorption and boost demand. There is no shift in the *IB* line, but the economy may move to the east from point 1 and cause inflationary pressures.

           Event 3:   The drop in incomes will reduce absorption. This does not shift the *IB* line, but it moves the economy off the line toward the west and cause a recession.

           Event 4:   No shift. The economy moves off the *IB* line toward the north, which is in the inflationary zone. The rise in the relative price of tradables induces a switch of expenditures into nontradables; this is inflationary.

e.   (i)   At point 2 there is an external surplus. An obvious clue: higher absorption would be consistent with external balance.

    (ii)   At point 2 the domestic economy suffers from inflationary pressures. Clue: lower absorption is needed to achieve internal balance.

    (iii)   Referring to the external balance:

           Event 1:   The economy moves east toward *EB*; the external surplus declines.

           Event 2:   The *EB* line shifts left; the external surplus declines and may even turn into a deficit.

           Event 3:   The *EB* line shifts right; the external surplus gets bigger.

           Event 4:   The economy moves south toward *EB* (which does not shift); the external surplus declines.

    (iv)   Referring to the internal balance:

           Event 1:   The economy moves east and gets farther from *IB*; the inflationary condition worsens.

           Event 2:   The *IB* line does not move, but if the cutoff of financing reduces absorption, then the economy moves west, closer to the *IB* line; domestic inflationary pressures abate.

           Event 3:   Higher incomes are likely to increase absorption and moves the economy east, away from *IB*; inflationary pressures worsen.

           Event 4:   The economy moves south and gets closer to *IB* (which does not shift); inflationary pressures ease.

Exercise 2

a. (i) The *EB* line shifts to the right; export earnings now purchase a much greater supply of tradables, so a higher level of absorption is now compatible with external balance.

   (ii) See line *EB2* in Figure 20–5a.

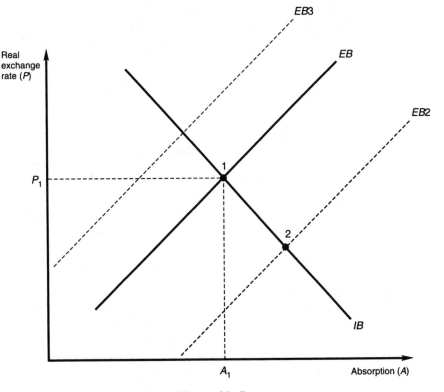

Figure 20–5a

   (iii) At point 1 there is still an internal balance, since nothing has happened to shift line *IB*. But the economy is now operating well to the left of the new *EB* line. There is a large external surplus, indicating that the economy is accumulating foreign exchange reserves.

   (iv) See point 2 in Figure 20–5a. The economy needs an increase in absorption together with an appreciation of the real exchange rate—if the boom were permanent!

(v)   If the real exchange rate did not change, then the increase in absorption would, indeed, cause inflation. But appreciation of the exchange rate shifts more resources into production of nontradables, and also directly reduces inflationary pressures by making tradables cheaper. The combination of adjustments to move the economy to point 2 leaves the economy in a condition of internal balance.

(vi) The real exchange rate equals P_T/P_N, where $P_T = e \times P_T^*$. If the official exchange rate e, cannot be changed, then P_T is fixed, since the world market price is exogenous. Therefore, a rise in P_N is the only way to reduce the real exchange rate to P_2. In this case, the adjustment *process* necessitates some domestic inflation in response to the rise in absorption. Still, once point 2 is achieved, there is no further inflationary pressure.

b.   (i)   See line *EB3* in Figure 20–5a.

(ii) Point 2 is nowhere near *EB3*; Antiquity faces a large trade deficit. There is no internal imbalance since point 2 is on the *IB* line. The overall macroeconomic situation, however, is unsustainable.

(iii) With absorption fixed, a large real depreciation can restore external balance, but the economy would then be way off the *IB* line in the inflation zone. The depreciation would increase domestic prices of tradables and induce a consumption switch toward nontradables; this would result in excess demand in that market.

(iv) With a fixed real exchange rate, a decline in absorption can restore external balance, but the economy would then be way off the *IB* line in the high unemployment zone. In this case external balance is restored by contracting the whole economy. Clearly, the only way to achieve overall macroeconomic balance is by using an appropriate combination of changes in A and P.

c.   (i)   This adverse change in the terms of foreign financing worsens the external balance and shifts the *EB* line even further to the left. The magnitude of the required adjustment in A and P rises.

(ii) The new inflow of foreign financing shifts the *EB* line back to the right; this reduces the magnitude of the external imbalance, as well as the magnitude of the required adjustments.

Exercise 3

a. (i)   Brazil: point 4
    (ii) Chile: point 1
    (iii) Kenya: point 6
    (iv) Peru: point 5
    (v)   Taiwan: point 2
    (vi) South Korea: point 3
    (vii) Tanzania: point 7

b. (i)   Brazil: fiscal and monetary austerity (decrease in absorption) plus real appreciation (decrease in P)
    (ii) Chile: monetary and fiscal stimulus plus real appreciation
    (iii) Kenya: austerity plus depreciation
    (iv) Peru: austerity plus depreciation
    (v)   Taiwan: stimulus plus appreciation
    (vi) South Korea: mild austerity plus appreciation
    (vii) Tanzania: austerity plus depreciation

c. Starting at point 7, absorption in Tanzania is less than what is required to achieve internal balance, *but* the exchange-rate adjustment that is needed to restore external balance will alter conditions in the market for nontradables. The initial condition of excess supply will change to a condition of excess demand unless the exchange-rate adjustment is accompanied by fiscal and monetary austerity.